A Soldier's Story

A Soldier's Story

Mike Wood

ROBINSON

ROBINSON

First published in Great Britain in 2020 by Robinson

1 3 5 7 9 10 8 6 4 2

A CIP catalogue record for this book
is available from the British Library.

ISBN: 978-1-47214-459-1 (hardcover)
ISBN: 978-1-47214-458-4 (trade paperback)

Typeset in Dante MT by SX Composing DTP, Rayleigh, Essex
Printed and bound in Great Britain by Clays Ltd, Elcograf S.p.A.

Papers used by Robinson are from well-managed forests
and other responsible sources.

Robinson
An imprint of
Little, Brown Book Group
Carmelite House
50 Victoria Embankment
London EC4Y 0DZ

An Hachette UK Company
www.hachette.co.uk

www.littlebrown.co.uk

In Loving Memory of
Neville Dalby Wood
21 June 1920–20 February 2015
'A good type of man'

Contents

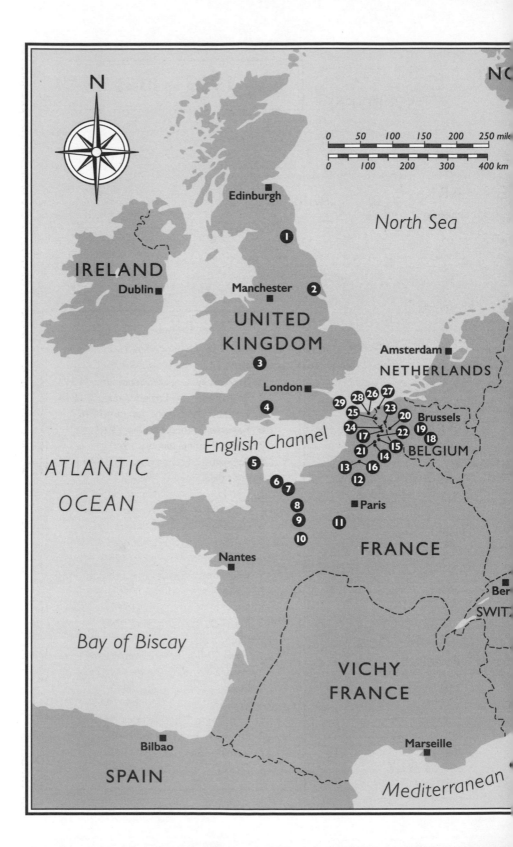

NORWAY

SWEDEN

May 1939 – June 1940

DENMARK

Copenhagen ■

Baltic Sea

Königsberg ■

U.S.S.R.

■ Hamburg

■ Berlin

GREATER
GERMANY

■ Frankfurt

Prague ■

Munich ■

POLAND

■ Milan

■ Venice

Genoa

Adriatic Sea

ITALY

Key

1	**Durham**, England, *May 1939*
2	**Hull**, England, *August 1939*
3	**Broadway**, England, *September 1939*
4	**Southampton**, England, *January 1940*
5	**Cherbourg**, France, *January 1940*
6	**Bayeux**, France, *January 1940*
7	**Caen**, France, *January 1940*
8	**Argenton**, France, *January 1940*
9	**Alençon**, France, *January 1940*
10	**Le Mans**, France, *January 1940*
11	**Chartres**, France, *February 1940*
12	**Beauvais**, France, *February 1940*
13/16	**Amiens**, France, *February 1940*
14	**Arras**, France, *February 1940*
15	**Billy-Montigny**, France, *February 1940*
17	**Loos**, France, *March 1940*
18	**Wavre**, Belgium, *May 1940*
19	**Brussels**, Belgium, *May 1940*
20	**Pecq**, Belgium, *May 1940*
21	**Vimy Ridge**, France, *May 1940*
22	**Pont-à-Vendin**, France, *May 1940*
23	**Menen**, Belgium, *May 1940*
24	**Pérenchies**, France, *May 1940*
25	**Poperinge**, Belgium, *May 1940*
26/28	**Dunkirk**, France, *May 1940*
27	**Veurne**, Belgium, *May 1940*
29	**Dover**, England, *2 June 1940*

Key

1 **Dover**, England, *June 1940*
2 **Hull**, England, *June 1940*
3 **Haslington**, England, *June 1940*
4 **Ilminster**, England, *June 1940*
5 **Glasgow**, Scotland, *May 1941*
6 **Freetown**, Sierra Leone, *June 1941*
7 **Durban**, South Africa, *June 1941*
8 **Port Said**, Egypt, *July 1941*
9 **Famagusta, Limassol, Polemidhia,** Cyprus, *July–August 1941*
10 **Haifa**, Palestine, *November 1941*
11 **Bet She'an**, Palestine, *November 1941*
12 **Al Mafraq**, Jordan, *November 1941*
13 **Ramadi**, Iraq, *December 1941*
14 **Baghdad**, Iraq, *December 1941*
15 **Kirkuk**, Iraq, *December 1941*
16 **Irbil**, Iraq, *January 1942*
17 **Baalbek**, Lebanon, *January 1942*
18 **El Alamein**, Egypt, *February 1942*
19 **Tobruk**, Libya, *February 1942*
20 **Cairo**, Egypt, *April 1942*
21 **Mersa Matruh**, Egypt, *April 1942*
22 **Sidi Barrani**, Egypt, *May 1942*
23 **Fort Maddalena**, Libya, *June 1942*
24 **Ruweisat Ridge**, Egypt, *July 1942*
25 **Alexandria**, Egypt, *July 1942*
26 **Alam Halfa**, Egypt, *August 1942*

27 **Mersa Matruh**, Egypt, *November 1942*
28 **Benghazi**, Libya, *November 1942*
29 **Buerat**, Libya, *January 1943*
30 **Mareth**, Tunisia, *February 1943*
31 **Wadi Akarit**, Tunisia, *April 1943*
32 **Enfidaville**, Tunisia, *April 1943*
33 **Alexandria**, Egypt, *April 1943*
34 **Augusta**, Sicily, *July 1943*
35 **Messina**, Sicily, *August 1943*
36 **Southampton**, England, *December 1943*
37 **Thetford**, England, *December 1943*
38 **Southampton**, England, *June 1944*
39 **La Rivière, Gold Beach,** France, *June 1944*
40 **Falaise**, France, *August 1944*
41 **Vernon**, France, *August 1944*
42 **Crèvecoeur**, France, *August 1944*
43 **Arras**, France, *September 1944*
44 **Brussels**, Belgium, *September 1944*
45 **Eindhoven**, Holland, *September 1944*
46 **Roeselare**, Belgium, *November 1944*
47 **Rees**, Germany, *March 1945*
48 **Bad Oeynhausen**, Germany, *June 1945*
49 **Wilhelmshaven**, Germany, *June 1945*
50 **Bergen Belsen**, Germany, *August 1945*
51 **Berlin**, Germany, *September 1945*
52 **York**, England, *April 1946*

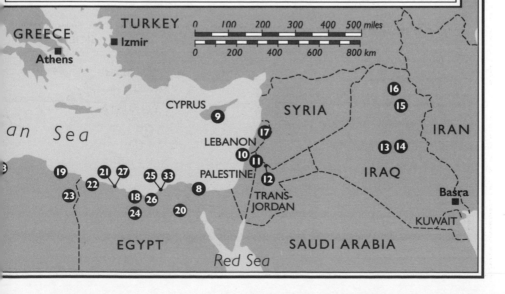

Preface

My dad was rarely lost for words. One such occasion, however, was Father's Day 2006 when I presented him with a full transcription of his war diaries and recollections. So many memories and emotions must have raced through his mind as he held the book, visibly moved.

It was a labour of love turning the diaries into a fascinating chronological history of one man's unique experiences of the Second World War. I am fortunate to have the originals, written with great foresight – albeit against regulations, but then Dad did seem to be a bit of a rebel. It is remarkable that they survived the war and the seventy subsequent years largely intact.

The whole process of transcription, and the discussions we enjoyed, provided a fascinating insight into the many emotions experienced during the years of active service: the fear, frustration, anger, humour, sadness, joy, stoicism, uncertainty and relief. Some of the events described lend credence to my dad's own view that someone must have been watching over him.

It has long been my ambition to weave his unique experiences into a biographical account. I can only try to imagine what those seven long years of war must have been like. Despite wider research I have had to utilise fictional licence to build the story around the actual events. No doubt a discerning military historian could point out some errors and any errors are solely my responsibility. My primary goal has been to capture the war through the eyes and feelings of one man who endured it from the beginning to the end.

All the characters in the book are real. There were a number of instances where all I had was a first name so I have made up some of the surnames. Several of the main characters will be recognisable by respective family and friends and I hope all will agree that I have tried to be careful with what I can't know as much as with what I do know. What is clear is that they all formed incredible bonds of comradeship and often showed great humour during dreadful times.

This story takes place in the middle of the last century and there is no point pretending that they didn't use words that would be considered unacceptable now. The story is totally authentic, as is much of the dialogue, lifted directly from the diaries. For that reason I have retained language that would not be appropriate today. For example, the word 'wog' is used very occasionally to describe a native of the Middle East and North Africa. I apologise if this causes any offence but I hope you will understand my reasoning. Also I have used the spellings of the place names as they appeared in the diaries. Subsequently, some of the names may have changed completely or now have a different spelling.

There are so few of these remarkable men left and soon their memories will be consigned in full to the history books. So here it is, warts and all. A unique insight, a priceless record and one which, while making me feel very humble, also makes me incredibly proud to say that this is the story of my dad's war.

Chapter 1

Meeting my Mates

April 1946 and May 1939

April 1946

Beneath the Victorian grandeur of the curved roof of York Railway Station stood a man with a suitcase and a mind full of memories. Seven years earlier, in May 1939, Neville Wood had waited for another train, one that would take him to Durham and the beginning of a life-changing adventure. The war might have been over, but it would never leave Neville, or the millions of others who had fought for their country.

York Station was both familiar and different all at once: the steam from the trains and the smell of the coal filling the air brought that day back to him as though it was yesterday. All around Neville, people rushed: young couples in the early stages of romance, workers hurrying off to work; people with lives to lead. But dotted along the platform were men like Neville – tall and still as statues, stiff in their pinstripe suits, there and not there at the same time. Veterans. Could these really be the same men who had shown Hitler he couldn't mess with England?

Neville didn't need to speak to these men to know how they were feeling. Bemused. Uncertain. Even a little scared. Like him, they didn't share that sense of euphoria when it was announced that the war was finally over – more a sense of sadness that those they had shared years of hell with were to be left behind. So many of their friends would never return home – some striking out for a new life in a far-flung land, others forever England in some corner of a foreign field.

For those back in Britain, stepping out on Civvy Street felt as daunting as anything they'd faced abroad. Neville watched those other people scurrying by and envied them their lightness, their effortless ability to get on with their daily lives. *Do they understand what we've been through? Do they even want to know, wrapped up cosily in their world of normality? Not even a glance*, he thought. *They don't damned well care.*

'All aboard!'

The sharpness of the shout from the guard pulled Neville back to the here and now. The way the guard had barked, it was almost like an order. *Blimey, it could have been Sergeant Major Thorpe himself.* Neville found himself standing up straight, pulling back his shoulders. He joined the rush of passengers clambering on to the train, making his way down until he found a compartment with a seat free. In the compartment, already settled, were two couples, laughing to each other and oblivious to the rest of the world. Neville lifted his luggage on to the rack and tucked himself into the corner. As he did, another male passenger took the final seat in the compartment. His actions mirrored Neville's: the same placing of the luggage on the rack, the same tucking himself into his seat opposite Neville, the same vacant stare through the grime on the carriage window.

Just after midday, the train pulled out with a whistle and a jolt.

The jolt shook Neville forwards and he caught the eye of the other lone passenger. There was a wariness in the stranger's stare, a reluctance to reach out that Neville recognised.

'You just on your way home?' he asked.

'Aye, I guess you can tell.' Neville watched as the man relaxed in front of him. 'I was thinking exactly the same about you. Bob Morris,' he introduced himself, offering his hand.

'Nev Wood. Good to meet you, Bob.' Neville shook his hand firmly. 'Army?'

'Fiftieth Division before they disbanded it and bloody proud of it. East Yorkshires, then stayed on with Second Army. What about you?'

'Fiftieth Div too, Royal Army Service Corps.'

'Ah.' Bob nodded in recognition. 'You lads did a great job for us on more than one occasion. How long were you in?'

'I was training to be a vet when I joined the Territorials in 'thirty-nine. Dad thought I was crackers! "Don't worry, Dad," I said, "it's only for a maximum of four years."' Neville smiled at the recollection. 'We could see it coming; bloody Germans. Went to Durham for training and damn good thing we did. Twelve weeks or so later I remember me and the lads were in barracks back in Hull crowded round the radio. September third it was and I can still hear those words as if it was yesterday.'

I have to tell you now that no such undertaking has been received, the Prime Minister had informed the nation. *And that consequently this country is at war with Germany.*

Neville broke his eye contact with Bob and stared out through the grime-encrusted window; the streets of York were giving way to the greens and browns of the Yorkshire countryside. He knew the landscape well, the soft sweep of the Wolds ahead of them, his home town of Hull on the other side. But Neville's mind was moving elsewhere now, remembering another journey, and where the shit of the last seven years really began.

May 1939

'Well, if I'm going to spend goodness knows how long with you gentlemen, I'd feel a whole lot happier if I knew who you are. Charles Spandler Esquire at your service.'

It was ten minutes into the transfer in the army wagon from Durham Station before anyone spoke. Neville had disembarked from his train to be greeted by a wall of sergeants and corporals, all shouting and pointing and steering the new batch of recruits into a convoy of wagons. Following the instructions, he found himself squeezed on to an unsympathetic wooden bench lining the inside of one such wagon. Once the wagon was full, the tailgate was raised and slammed shut, and the bright May sunshine was replaced with a haze of semi-darkness.

As the wagon set off Neville counted up that there were eighteen or so men in the back, each bouncing and bumping and clinging to the benches to stop themselves from falling off. As his eyes adjusted to the darkness, the silhouettes became people and he could see their expressions more clearly. Some were leaning back against the stiff canopy, looking pensive. One or two looked almost tearful. A few were hunched forward, staring at the floor, while others just sat bolt upright, staring straight ahead. As the journey continued the silence seemed stifling and hung heavy in the air. Until, that is, Charles Spandler spoke up.

Neville, along with everyone else, turned towards the corner of the truck nearest the driver's cab, where Charles was sitting. He had his trilby in his hand, held aloft above smartly combed, slightly quiffed hair.

'Come on, you lot.' He smiled with mild amusement. 'Loosen up a bit. It's not the end of the world. At least not today, anyway.'

That got a few smiles from those sitting around him and a hand-shake from the man to Charles's left – a heavily built man with short, combed-back hair.

'Alan Such, Charlie. Good to meet you.'

'Good to meet you, Suchy.' Charlie shook his hand back. 'Just call me Span.'

'Freddie Nichols,' chipped in a short, slightly older man.

'Jim Oliver,' added a slim, broad-shouldered man with a piratical gap in his teeth.

'Stan Curlew,' shouted another.

'Nev Wood, Span.' Neville was the next to speak up. 'Just call me Nev!'

'Woody!' Span gave him an impish grin. 'Well, by the look of you I expect you will always be falling over, so we'll call you Timber.'

Span got a chuckle from the rest of the wagon. And Neville got a nickname that was to last the rest of the war.

The first Neville and the others realised they had arrived at Hardwick Camp, Sedgefield, was when the wagon pulled to a halt and the tailgate was dropped with a crash. The next thing he knew, voices were shouting at them to get out and stand in line. Neville blinked in the warm sunshine and took his place alongside his new-found friends. Together they were marched off and lined up in front of someone Neville would come to know well.

'Squad . . . attention!'

Sergeant Major Thorpe had a voice that could wake the dead. Neville and the others jumped to. Shoulders back, head up, feet shuffled into position. Thorpe looked up and down and gave a firm, disappointed shake of his head.

'Squad will turn to the left in file, left turn!' he bellowed. 'By the left, quick . . . march!'

Standing alongside Thorpe was another soldier, Sergeant Moore. As Neville's line meandered forwards with all the precision of the hind legs of a donkey, Thorpe turned to him. 'And we're supposed to get this lot ready to win a bloody war?' He shook his head again. 'Take over, Sergeant.'

Neville's squad were marched in line to the end of a pathway where there were a set of tables draped in the Union Jack. The pathway led on to a large square, half the size of a football pitch, bordered on three sides with Nissen huts, alongside the occasional, more robust-looking, single-storey timber-framed building. The camp looked exactly what it was: one constructed in haste.

One by one the men stood before one of the tables, where they were asked their name. Neville gave his, saw his name found and ticked off a list, then was handed a booklet.

'Dismiss.' The officer pointed to his right. 'Get reading and report to the NAAFI, that way.'

Neville moved off to join the rest of his group, scanning the booklet as he walked. It was the programme for 59 Company, Royal Army Service Corps (Mechanical Transport). With a gulp, he read how he was now recorded as having reported at his 'place of joining' and, having been attested into the Territorial Army, was subject to military law.

'Hey,' said Jim Oliver, who was reading ahead of him, 'look at number three: "Your first duty will be to tear off the ticket in the top right corner of this page and to exchange it at the counter for a cup of tea and cake." Now that's what I call hospitality!'

Neville followed Jim over to the NAAFI counter, where Span and Alan were each receiving an enamel mug of lukewarm tea and a piece of fruit cake.

'Hmm. Maybe the hospitality is not so great after all,' murmured Jim, taking a sip.

'Hey, Span,' Neville looked up from the programme with a smile on his face, '"A welfare officer is available but only to those applying on compassionate grounds for exemption from training." They're bound to be compassionate to a skinny bloke like you.'

Span laughed. 'You wait till we get training, Timber, and then we'll see who needs compassionate grounds.' He danced lightly on his toes and assumed a classic southpaw stance.

'You'll all be begging for bloody compassion when I've finished with you.' The pair looked up to see Sergeant Ron Moore standing in the NAAFI entrance, his six-foot-plus frame filling the doorway. 'Now stop the little party and get yourselves into line over there for medical inspection.'

Neville, Span and the others joined the back of the queue, which snaked across the Barrack Square at the entrance to a long Nissen hut. Neville was ready for a long wait but inside there were four examination rooms in use, two to the left and two to the right, and everything moved with surprising speed. Neville was directed to the second door on the left, where he was met by Dr Munro, a tall, bespectacled man in a white coat, a stethoscope around his neck, with little in the way of niceties.

'Strip to underpants, Wood.'

As Neville undressed, placing his clothes over the back of a wooden chair, Munro made notes in an A4 file.

'Any illnesses, operations or other medical conditions we should know about, Wood?'

'No, Doctor; fit as a fiddle.'

Munro eyed him above his spectacles. 'Any medical history with your immediate family: father, mother, brothers, sisters?'

'Mother died four years ago, Doctor, when I was fourteen. Cancer.'

'Sorry, Wood. Sit down.' The fleeting tone of compassion disappeared as Munro examined both ears. 'We'll keep an eye on those, Wood. May need syringing, but okay at the moment. Right, look at the wall over there and the letters. Cover your left eye first then the right and read the top line down.'

Neville read the letters down to the line second from bottom. Munro nodded to himself as he scribbled. He moved closer and said, 'Open mouth.' Neville's teeth were examined, followed by the stethoscope being placed on his chest and then his back. 'Breathe deeply . . . and out again. And again.'

Munro gestured for Neville to stand up. His abdomen was prodded and poked and then the doctor's hand went to the genitals. 'Cough.' Down the examination went to the knees, legs and feet.

'Up against the door, Wood.' Munro noted the measurement. 'Five feet ten. Now on the scales.' He peered over. 'One hundred and forty-nine pounds.'

Munro moved away, finished making notes and passed Neville a slip of paper. 'I'm pleased to say you are fit for active service,' he said, without sounding remotely pleased. 'Dress and dismiss.'

Back out in the Barrack Square, Neville found Span, Jim and Suchy. 'Flippin' blimey,' he exclaimed. 'I felt like a piece of meat.' He looked around at the group. 'Everybody staying?' They all nodded.

'When you've quite finished,' Sergeant Moore shouted from behind, causing them all to jump. *Is he always here?* Neville wondered. 'Everyone passed fit over there.' *What now?* thought Neville as he followed Moore's directions to another long hut to the left of the Barrack Square. Inside was a row of three desks, with a uniformed clerk behind each. Neville waited his turn, then stepped forwards and stood to attention.

'Number and name?' the clerk asked.

'81874. Private Wood, Neville Dalby, sir.'

'Address and National Insurance number?'

'778 Holderness Road, Hull, East Yorkshire. National Insurance number SK047428B, sir,' Neville added.

'I have next of kin as father, Frederick Wood, at the same address. Is that right?'

'Yes, sir.'

'Okay, Private Wood, please hand in your civilian ration book and railway ticket.' Neville handed the items over and the clerk opened a metal box from which he counted out ten shillings. 'Advance of pay. Sign, please.' Neville put the money in his trouser pocket and signed the form presented by the clerk.

Next, the clerk produced two coloured discs and a three-foot length of thin cord. 'Identity discs,' he explained. 'A green one and a red one, okay? Both are to be worn at all times under your shirt. The red disc goes on this piece of extension cord. That's so it can be removed. This disc will attach to your respirator when you get your equipment. The red disc will be removed before we bury you, but the green one will go with you to the grave.' The clerk gave him a crooked grin.

Some sense of humour, thought Neville, not deigning to smile in return. He looked at the discs. Each had his army number, initials and surname, plus the letters CE denoting his religious denomination. *At least they'll put me in the right cemetery!* he thought.

With medical and identity details sorted, Neville joined a third queue outside one of the more substantial timber buildings on the other side of a concrete roadway. After another wait, he and the other recruits filed in to stand around a group of tables. At one side of the hut was a long counter, with columns of shelving behind. A corporal stepped forward to issue instructions.

'Each of you take a kitbag,' he ordered. 'Open the top and pro- ceed along the counter where your kit will be dropped in. You should all know what items will be issued to you, but since some of you may have memories like a sieve the lists are displayed above the counter. If the issue does not tally with the list, complain at once. No complaint of non-issue will be considered after you leave the issue counter. Your responsibility. Now keep moving.'

Neville moved along the tables, kitbag open. Into the bag was dropped an array of items – two angola and bush shirts, anklets, socks, shorts, cap, woolly pullover, braces, gloves, vest, canvas shoes and hand towel. Next came a pair of stiff, sturdy boots and a great-coat. The khaki serge jacket with its buttoned epaulettes and fastened down the front with five buttons hidden by a fly front was folded neatly on the table. It had two-pointed flap breast pockets, each buttoned, and an integral half belt which fastened on the right hip with a built-in buckle of dull metal. On each side of the jacket just below the epaulettes was the insignia of RASC, underneath which the two bright red letters 'T' interlinked on a black back-ground denoting Tyne Tees and Humber, the area from which the 50th Division was drawn.

Next, a stiff backpack was pushed across the table complete with ground sheet and blanket rolled on the outside. Neville was ordered to check the pack contents on the table, glancing up several times to compare the printed inventory with the items in front of him. He mentally ticked off one water bottle, knife, fork, spoon, two rec-tangular mess tins and white enamel mug, hair-, tooth- and shaving brushes, razor, soap, comb, spare boot laces and anti-gas cape.

On the final table, Neville was provided with an anti-gas respirator; a Mk 1 steel helmet; the .303-inch rifle, No.1 Mk III, Short Magazine Lee-Enfield (SMLE), and a long, sword-type bayonet, which clipped on to a boss below the end of the barrel. The bayonet was eighteen inches in length, almost half as long as the rifle itself.

It was quite a lot to carry. As Neville exited the building, haversack on his back, kitbag over his right shoulder, rifle over the left, helmet looped over the arm and bayonet tucked into his belt, he caught up with Span.

'Didn't know I was training to be a bloody Sherpa,' he grumbled.

But before Neville could reply, Sergeant Moore appeared again.

'Look after that kit, you lot. It doesn't grow on trees. Right, you can now follow me to your barracks rooms, where you will all change into uniform. You may keep your civilian clothes at your own risk or take them for safekeeping to the Company Quartermaster Stores.

'Food,' he continued. 'Tea will be between 1600 and 1800 hours, supper 1900 to 2359 hours, then I want you all up bright-eyed and bushy-tailed for breakfast between 0700 and 0730. You will be on time and dressed smartly for check parade on the Barrack Square at 0800 tomorrow.' Sergeant Moore put a strong emphasis on the words *will be on time* and glared at the group. 'Is that clear?'

'Yes, Sergeant.' Neville joined in the collective response.

Sergeant Moore marched them briskly towards a timber framed hut with a corrugated iron roof. 'Your hotel,' he snarled. 'No rooms allocated so sort it among yourselves. If you need any information there is an information room. Turn right on exiting your block and follow the signs. You'll find a training programme and plan of the camp in your barracks block. You are now free to settle in. Just make sure you're ready for the 0800 check parade tomorrow.'

Still carrying all his kit, Neville entered the hut. Moore wasn't kidding: in front of him were rows of identical bunk beds, with what looked like rudimentary washing facilities at the far end. Neville was still debating which bed to claim when Span dropped his kit on the floor and clambered to an upper bunk.

'Come on, Timber,' he said with a grin, 'I can see you've no head for heights. You take the bottom one.'

Neville put his kit down and sat on the bed. It was every bit as hard as it looked. *Welcome to the British Army,* he thought. *One day down. How many more to go?*

If someone had told him the answer to that question was going to be 2,550 days, he'd never have believed them.

Chapter 2

The Phoney War

May 1939 to January 1940

At 0800, the 120 recruits of 59 Company, Royal Army Service Corps, were standing two lines deep with the rain stinging their skin and soaking their new uniforms. The rain was lashing down, bouncing off the concrete of the Barracks Square. Neville could feel his uniform becoming leaden and chafing.

'Think they'll let us nip in for another cup of tea until it stops?' asked Span mischievously.

'Quiet over there, on parade!' barked Sergeant Major Thorpe, who was standing in front of the recruits, alongside Sergeant Moore. Moments later, Thorpe shouted, 'Atten-*shun!*' He let out a barely audible growl. 'You'll bloody well do better than that.'

From one of the buildings across the square, Neville spied a lean, angular figure of medium height marching over towards them. He had the bearing of authority that caused Neville to stand up that little bit straighter. The officer stood behind Thorpe, scanning the recruits with blue eyes that pierced through the rain. Neville stood up straighter still.

'My name is Captain Bonner,' the officer introduced himself, 'and I am your commanding officer.' Bonner's voice was clipped and clear, easily audible through the hiss of the rain. 'I apologise for not arranging better weather for your first parade, but this is County Durham and you'll get used to it.'

Bonner paused, as if considering his words carefully, creating an air of expectation in the process. 'You are now part of the best army in the world. You will regale your children and grandchildren in years to come with the heritage and achievements of this Company. We are 59 Company, Royal Army Service Corps, a big cog in a big wheel which is 50th Division. We are part of a big and formidable family of north-countrymen. We will be joining up with the East Yorkshires, the Green Howards, Durham Light Infantry, Royal Northumberland Fusiliers and artillery regiments drawn in the main from Tynecastle. We will serve those units with efficiency, pride and distinction. Whatever they may achieve, they will say it could only have been done with the support of RASC.

'You will note that on your shoulders you bear the insignia of the two superimposed Ts.' Neville glanced sideways at the badge, the Ts red on a black background. 'They stand for Tyne Tees,' Bonner continued, 'but if you look at the badge sideways they form an H for Humber. As you know they are the main rivers of Northumbria, the Tyne and Tees to the north and the Humber to the south. The majority of you men come from Hull and you will make your city proud.

'Work hard, become good soldiers, be proud you wear the TT and help make 50th Division the pride of the British Army. Good luck, men. That is all. Carry on, Sergeant Major.'

As Bonner marched back inside, Neville's attention turned to Thorpe, who stood in front of the recruits, impressive, stern and professional. 'You heard the officer. You will work hard, harder than

you've ever worked in your life. We can all read the papers and the
Germans are throwing their weight around again. You may have
heard rumours that they can't possibly have rebuilt their army since
nineteen thirty-three and the tanks on parade are cardboard for
show. To believe rubbish like that is to vastly underestimate a
formidable nation and bloody good soldiers. So, yes, you will work
hard and you'll hate me for it. But remember everything I make you
do here and be grateful when you meet the enemy and beat him.
And look,' Thorpe glanced up to the sky, 'the rain is stopping just in
time for your first bit of exercise. Carry on, Sergeant.'

Moore stood to attention and saluted. 'Okay, you lot. Back here,
thirty minutes. PT kit. Dismiss.'

Six weeks of intensive training began in earnest. The programme
covered parade-ground drill, rifle and pistol shooting, physical
training, gas training, elementary map reading and tactics.

Basic drill entailed hours of 'square bashing': learning to mark
time by marching, without forward movement, in the quick-time
pace of 116 paces to the minute. Neville and the others learned to
turn in file to the left and the right, forward march in quick time
without breaking step and to change step on the march. Within six
weeks the drill was smart and precise, meriting a barely discernible
smile of approval from Thorpe.

Not all the training went as smoothly. Weapons training focused
on the rifle, light machine gun and anti-tank rifle. The new recruits
learned to strip, clean and reassemble the weapons at speed, as well
as target shooting. Practice with bayonets saw the recruits, in
threes, assume the left-foot-forward prepared stance and charge at
straw-filled bags, screaming in simulated aggression. Following a
charge by Alan Such, Neville overheard Freddie Nichols taking the
opportunity to wind him up.

'That won't frighten the bloody Germans, Suchy. You sounded more like me mam when her knickers are too tight!'

The simulated aggression quickly became the genuine article as Such shoved Nichols back, the banter giving way to a more primal form of combat. Only the rapid intervention of a corporal standing close by stopped things from escalating further. Such was the pressure the recruits were under.

The first five weeks of training brought its mix of hardship, anger and tension, but it also created a close-knit camaraderie and a sense of belonging. Neville and the others were drilled rigorously and repeatedly until they were able to unpack and secure their gas respirators within fifteen seconds. They endured forced marches into the Durham countryside, in full battle kit, where combat simulations had them crawling, running and hitting the ground in cold muddy fields.

'Hell, Curly, we've got to clean this lot later,' groaned Neville, as he and Stan Curlew, working in a pair, threw themselves to the ground in thick, clinging mud.

'Come on, Timber, stop moaning. It might be muddy but at least we get a bloody rest!' retorted Stan.

The final week of basic training brought with it the TOET, or Test of Elementary Training. The rifle test included aiming and rapid firing. Recruits had ten seconds to assemble the light machine gun and aim accurately and twenty seconds to fill the anti-tank rifle magazine.

However, what really stoked the good-natured rivalry among the men were the basic physical efficiency tests. On Friday 16 June, Neville, Charlie and the others found themselves loaded on to wagons in their PT kit, and taken to Sedgfield Athletics Club for their physical tests. Marks were to be awarded for each event: an achievement of 84 per cent or better was classified as Special. A score greater than 68 per cent was First Class and above 48 per cent Standard.

'You know what, Span,' said Neville, with a steely glance at Charlie Spandler, who was sitting next to him in the wagon. 'It's my birthday in five days and I could think of no greater present than giving you a good hiding today. Nev Wood: Special; Charlie Spandler: Sub-standard!'

'In yer dreams, Timber.' Span grinned. 'I should've been in Berlin in 'thirty-six, but they didn't want me upsetting Hitler!'

Sedgefield Athletic Club turned out to be a grand title for what was little more than a flat field with faded lap markings. The tests began with the 100 yards: marks were awarded for the time achieved, with ten marks given for twelve seconds, eight marks for thirteen seconds and so on. The high jump was graded in four-inch increments with ten points awarded for a jump of four feet eight inches or better. The running long jump was marked in one-foot increments with the maximum ten points scored for a jump in excess of sixteen feet. Heaving the nine-pound medicine ball involved standing feet astride with the ball in both hands, in front or above the body. You started the throw by bending the trunk downward, swinging the ball between the legs then forward and releasing. The marking was done in four-foot increments, with ten points awarded for a thirty-four-foot throw or better.

The final event of the day was the one-mile run. As Neville and the others lined up, they were told that points were awarded in twenty-second increments, up to a ten-point time of five minutes thirty seconds. Although the day had been long, the element of competitiveness had not diminished. The race began with the recruits bunched together in a large group, with much jostling and jockeying for position. But it didn't take long for the runners to spread out. At the end of the second lap Alan Such accelerated away, with the rest of the group stringing out behind him. Such's kick of speed continued, and by the final lap, he was twenty yards clear, with Neville and Charlie leading the chase group. The two were neck and neck, matching each other pace for pace, until they rounded the final bend and Charlie hit the gas for home. He burst clear, and for a moment it looked like second place was his. Neville, though, was not to be outdone. The first Charlie knew about it was when he gave a flick of the head, and saw Neville on his right shoulder. Then, with a clearly audible grunt, Neville accelerated away to finish in a time of six minutes ten seconds.

'Bastard,' gasped Charlie, hands on knees, chest heaving, as they caught their breath. 'You held me back.'

'You're not turning into a bad loser, are you, Span?' wheezed Neville.

At 1700, back at camp, the recruits gathered around the notice-board, waiting for the test results. As Sergeant Moore pinned them up, everyone crowded round closer, desperate to see what their scores were.

'Look at that! Suchy got 92 per cent. Well, that figures; he thinks he's special anyway. Spends hours polishing his halo.' Freddie Nichols was closest to the board and read the results out to the others. 'Here we go, lads. Span, you score 68 per cent. Timber, 72 per cent . . .'

Charlie punched Neville on the shoulder. 'Guess that makes us both first class.'

'Yes, Span,' agreed Neville with a smile. 'It's just that some are more first class than others!'

Hull, late August. It was two months since Neville and the other RASC recruits had finished their training. Life, in limbo, had carried on; normal lives, as far as they could be, had resumed. The prolifer-ation of men in uniform was the most outward sign that things were different. But there was a sharpness to these individuals, too: callow youths disciplined into shape, poised and ready to step up when the command came. In the meantime, all they could do was bask in the sultry, late-summer heat, and wait.

If Hull was hot in August, it was even hotter in Neville's father's butcher shop. On the last Monday of the month, Neville was at the counter in his greasy, smeared butcher's apron, feeling the heat prickle on his forehead when Fred came running through from the back.

'Get yourself home quick, lad. That was your mum on the telephone. Fritzy has the window cleaner trapped up his ladder.'

Fritzy was a German shepherd, generally as daft as a brush. Except, for whatever reason, he would let people into the garden but he wouldn't let them out again. Neville whipped off his apron and hopped on to his bike to ride the short journey down Holderness Road. It wasn't far, but the cooler air from the cycling was a welcome change from the shop. As he pulled into number 778 and propped his bike against the garage wall, Neville could hear the barks and shouts. Running round to the front of the house, he saw his stepmother, Hilda, attempting to restrain the dog as the terrified window cleaner clung to his ladder halfway up.

'Fritz!' Neville shouted. 'Heel, now! Here!' He pointed to his side. With a growl and a grumble, the dog ceased its barking and walked over to sit by Neville.

'You keep that bloody thing away from me or you can clean your own windows,' snapped the window cleaner. 'The brute let me in, 'appy as Larry, but wouldn't let me out again. Sure you've got him?' he asked, glancing down. He descended the ladder step by step, pausing each time Fritzy looked up at him and growled. But when the window cleaner hit the ground, he was suddenly all speed: the ladder was on his shoulder in one movement as he lunged past Hilda, out of the garden gate, and scurried off down the road.

'Best get back, Mam,' said Neville, ruffling Fritzy's fur.

'Before you go,' Hilda said, 'the post has been. There's one for you. Looks official.'

Neville followed Hilda into the kitchen where she handed over a brown envelope. It did look official. Neville felt both nervous and excited as he ripped it open and quickly scanned the one-page letter and attachment. It was what he had been waiting for: he was being called up for active service in His Majesty's armed forces, effective from Friday 1 September. This was to be his official Date of Embodiment and he was required to sign the attached form agreeing to permanent and overseas service. This was it: there was trepidation at what lay ahead, but the great adventure for which he had trained was now beginning. It was all finally happening.

On the first day of September, Neville reported to the Fairground Barracks, Walton Street, Hull. The barracks were abuzz with noise and people. At first it all felt a little bewildering, until the warmth of familiar faces welcomed him in: Span, Alan Such, Freddie Nichols, Jim Oliver and Stan Curlew. Neville had last seen most of 59 Company at a 50th (Northumbrian) Motor Division Church Parade Service at Holy Trinity Parish Church, Hull, on Sunday 20 August. That day Major General Giffard Le Quesne Martel DSO, MC, AMIME, Commander 50th Motor Division had read the lesson, Proverbs 3, 1–20, something about trusting in the Lord and seeking wisdom. Span reckoned he was already the fount of all wisdom and got an elbow in his ribs for his trouble.

'I was just saying, Timber,' said Jim, welcoming him with a warm handshake, 'trouble brewing if Herr Hitler invades Poland.'

'We've been called up for a reason,' said Stan, 'and I don't suppose it's guard duty for His Majesty at the palace.'

Over the days that followed, life began to settle into a routine. All members of 59 Company reported at 0900 to the Fairground Barracks, went through a morning of drills, paraded at 1200 hours and then wandered into the city for light refreshments at the Regal Café. But on Sunday 3 September, at 1100, drill was interrupted by Captain Bonner.

'Smartly now! I understand that our Prime Minister, Mr Neville Chamberlain, will be making an announcement to the nation at 1115 hours. Get along to the NAAFI, the radio will be on. Carry on, Sergeant.'

That news and the rumours that followed went through the barracks like wildfire. But there was little time to speculate: Neville and the rest of 59 Company crowded into the NAAFI just as Chamberlain began his speech.

'I am speaking to you from the cabinet room at 10 Downing Street. This morning the British Ambassador in Berlin handed the German Government a final note stating that, unless we heard from them by eleven o'clock that they were prepared at once to withdraw their troops from Poland, a state of war would exist between us. I have to tell you now that no such undertaking has been received, and that consequently this country is at war with Germany.'

The absolute silence in the NAAFI was punctuated by a sharp intake of breath. *At war with Germany.* Chamberlain's words echoed around Neville's head.

'You can imagine what a bitter blow it is to me that all my long struggle to win peace has failed.' Chamberlain's tone remained clipped and precise, but even so, his emotions seemed to seep through into every syllable. 'Yet I cannot believe that there is anything more or anything different that I could have done and that would have been more successful.

'Up to the very last it would have been quite possible to have arranged a peaceful and honourable settlement between Germany and Poland, but

Hitler would not have it. He had evidently made up his mind to attack Poland whatever happened, and although he now says he put forward reasonable proposals which were rejected by the Poles, that is not a true statement. The proposals were never shown to the Poles, nor to us, and, although they were announced in a German broadcast on Thursday night, Hitler did not wait to hear comments on them, but ordered his troops to cross the Polish frontier. His action shows convincingly that there is no chance of expecting that this man will ever give up his practice of using force to gain his will. He can only be stopped by force.'

Neville glanced around the room as Chamberlain continued to talk. Everywhere he saw quiet, contemplative, intense expressions.

'We and France are today, in fulfilment of our obligations, going to the aid of Poland, who is so bravely resisting this wicked and unprovoked attack on her people. We have a clear conscience. We have done all that any country could do to establish peace. The situation in which no word given by Germany's ruler could be trusted and no people or country could feel themselves safe has become intolerable. And now that we have resolved to finish it, I know that you will all play your part with calmness and courage.

'At such a moment as this the assurances of support that we have received from the Empire are a source of profound encouragement to us. The Government have made plans under which it will be possible to carry on the work of the nation in the days of stress and strain that may be ahead. But these plans need your help. You may be taking your part in the fighting services or as a volunteer in one of the branches of Civil Defence. If so you will report for duty in accordance with the instructions you have received. You may be engaged in work essential to the prosecution of war for the maintenance of the life of the people – in factories, in transport, in public utility concerns, or in the supply of other necessaries of life. If so, it is of vital importance that you should carry on with your jobs.

'Now may God bless you all. May He defend the right. It is the evil things that we shall be fighting against – brute force, bad faith, injustice,

oppression and persecution – and against them I am certain that the right will prevail.'

The radio was turned off, but the hush that had descended on the soldiers gathered in that room continued. Seconds, minutes slowly ticked by. Neville glanced across at his friends: they all looked at their hands, the ceiling, each other, unseeing, disbelieving.

'Parade at 1200!' Sergeant Moore broke the silence with a shout that made some of the soldiers jump. As he marched out, the hush became first a hubbub of whispers, then suddenly everyone was talking at once.

'So this is it, then. It's about to happen all over again.' Neville breathed out.

'Looks like it, and God help us all, because no one else will,' murmured Suchy.

'We'll sort Herr Hitler out. Be home by Christmas,' said Span confidently.

'Shut up, Span,' Freddie came back. Usually Charlie's humour could be relied on to lighten the mood. But there was little tolerance for his frivolity today. 'That's what we said in nineteen fourteen.'

On Monday 11 September, Neville turned up at 0900 as usual, expecting another week of drill, parade, the Regal Café and returning home by late afternoon. Instead, he found himself immediately instructed to be on parade. Sergeant Major Thorpe stood the Company at ease, then gave them the announcement.

'You have two hours to get your kit together. You will report back directly to Paragon Railway Station no later than 1130 hours. The train leaves at 1200 with or without you. Dismiss.'

Within half an hour Neville had everything he needed together and was hugging his stepmother as he prepared to take his leave.

'I must go, Mam. I want to stop off at the shop and see Dad.'

'God go with you, Neville.' Hilda hugged him one last time. 'Come back safely,' she shouted after him and Neville raced for his father's shop.

When the bell to the butcher's rang, Fred looked up. When he saw Neville there, in full kit, he paused, his meat cleaver in mid-air. Neville didn't need to say anything for his father to know what this meant.

'You're off then, lad?' he said finally, lowering the cleaver on to the counter.

'Train leaves at noon. Not a lot of time for goodbyes, I'm afraid.'

'Sometimes that's best. Where are you going?'

'No idea. You know what it's like, last to find anything out.'

Neville knew that Fred knew that feeling only too well. Back in 1917, he had left England with the West Riding Division, heading for the mud, trenches and slaughter of the Western Front. As he looked across at his father, and his father looked back, Neville wondered whether he was remembering that moment.

'There's nothing much I can say, lad, other than look after yourself. I know you'll do us and the country proud.'

His father stepped out from behind the counter, and after giving it a wipe on his apron, offered Neville his hand. There was a warmth in the handshake, a length to it that at one point Neville wondered if his father was going to let go. When he turned to leave, he felt a pat on his shoulder to send him on his way. Neville left the shop without looking back, not wishing his father to see the anxiety and distress etched on his face. *Come on, Nev*, he admonished himself. *Shoulders back, stiff upper lip and all that!*

By 1120, Neville was at Paragon Station: ten minutes to spare, to catch his breath and watch the other soldiers make it back in the nick of time. Thorpe, as usual, was true to his word: at 1130 sharp,

59 Company marched down platform 3 and boarded the train. At noon, it pulled out. The journey was long, taking them first across Yorkshire to Sheffield, then further south and west. Neville and the others watched the countryside as the train pushed on until, after six hours, it shunted to a stop at Evesham and a shout of 'Everyone Out' rang down the carriages.

'Where the hell are we?' asked Stan Curlew.

'Did they not teach you geography at school, Curly?' chided Jim Oliver, grabbing his kit. 'Evesham is in Worcestershire – you know, where they get the sauce from. We're in the Cotswolds. Wonder if we're staying. It's supposed to be quite pretty around here.'

Neville and the others were escorted on to a convoy of waiting trucks, and were taken to camp eight miles away at Broadway, a picture-postcard village at the base of the Worcestershire hills. Once in camp they were grateful to be given an evening meal after the journey. Afterwards, they were called together for a briefing, Captain Bonner marching on to a raised dais to address the assembled and intrigued Company.

'Welcome to the Cotswolds, men. Sorry about the lack of notice of deployment but we are now at war and rapid deployment is what we are about. We will be here for a few weeks,' he explained, 'forming part of 522 Ammunition Company. Our objective is to train you all further in the art of mobilisation and the techniques for acting and moving in close cooperation with armoured forces. We will become a highly effective mechanised strike force, driving deep into enemy territory, disrupting his communications and supplies and creating havoc. I apologise in advance for the antiquated equipment you will be using for your training pending resupply, but as typically good north-countrymen I know you will make the best of it.'

★ ★ ★

'Step forward any of you who can drive.'

The following day 522 Company was paraded before Sergeant Major Thorpe. At first, no one moved at Thorpe's request. He waited. Finally, Neville stepped forward.

'I have a provisional driving licence, Sergeant Major.'

'Amply qualified, Wood. Fall out with Sergeant Moore. The rest of you have a lot to learn!'

Moore took Wood over to a group of vehicles, all 1914–18 legacies called Thornycrofts. A group of drivers had gathered there and each was assigned a particular vehicle. Neville stood beside his, alongside Span who had been allocated as his co-driver.

'I can't believe what I'm looking at,' Neville said with incredulity. 'Is this it?' They examined the solid rubber tyres and canvas front canopy.

'Let's hope the weather's bloomin' good, or we'll get soaked in this heap of junk,' muttered Span.

'Thornycroft J Type, Wood, Spandler. State of the art, top of its class in luxury,' said Moore with a grin.

Neville and Span familiarised themselves with the basic mechanics. Then the cranking handle was inserted and the engine fired up with a judder, shaking the whole vehicle. Infantry troops from the East Yorkshires piled into the back, causing the wagon to lurch from side to side.

The drivers were issued with their orders. They were to take the infantry up Fish Hill and disembark them at Broadway Tower, the highest point of the Cotswolds. The infantry would complete their manoeuvres and 522 Company would bring them back to camp.

The vehicles, fully laden, left camp and drove through the wide, grass-fringed main street of Broadway to begin the ascent of Fish Hill. As they climbed so the vehicles slowed. Less than a third of the way up the long incline, Neville's vehicle ground to a halt. Despite revving and gear crunching, it refused to move an inch further. Neville was just debating what he should do next when a commanding voice came from the back of the wagon.

'Right, you lot, out and push.' The East Yorkshires leapt off the tailgate and started pushing. The exercise in unit cooperation started in good spirits but became more fractious as the road seemed to stretch ahead around interminable bends.

'I thought they were supposed to be delivering us, not us them!' complained an infantry corporal. 'As much bloody good as a fish and tatties van.' From that point on, 522 Company were known as the Fish and Tatties Brigade.

The spirits of the men of 50th Division continued to build steadily as training continued. By the end of the year they were ready for war, although the dearth of up-to-date equipment remained a cause for concern.

Early in January 1940, Neville, Span, Ollie and Stan went down to the local pub, the Lygon Arms, for a pint of weak beer. George, the landlord, was behind the bar as usual, busily polishing glasses.

'Evening, lads, pints all round?' He began pulling the beer and smiled. 'Great news about the King.'

The soldiers looked at each other, nonplussed. George glanced from face to puzzled face. 'Not told you yet? Three days hence the King and Queen are coming here to Broadway. Never been a King of England here since Charles I. Mind, look what happened to him.' He grimaced and rolled his neck to illustrate.

So it was on 17 January 1940 that the villagers and those khaki-clad soldiers not involved in the formal review crowded the broad village street as King George VI and Queen Elizabeth walked down between them. The crowd cheered with gusto as the royal couple walked down the centre of the main street waving and stopping occasionally to exchange a few words with the soldiers and the locals. Neville watched on, fascinated.

'Tell you what,' said Stan Curlew as the King and Queen passed by, 'just look around you. Here we are, the English people, in a beautiful English setting, with our very own King and Queen. Helps you realise what we've been trained for: to defend a whole way of life.' Stan looked thoughtful; the others looked astounded.

'Bloody hell, Stan, that's profound.' But they could all sense the truth of what he was saying.

Later that day the Company were ordered to prepare to move out. On 18 January they journeyed to Glastonbury. The following day they travelled to Southampton where they received orders to be ready to board a troop ship late on 21 January.

'Time to go, lads.' Span clapped his hands together. 'Charlie Spandler's on his way, Mr Hitler, so just watch out.'

Early on the morning of Wednesday 22 January 1940, the TSS *Fenella* sailed from Southampton packed with troops for the five-hour crossing to Cherbourg. The morning was bright, crisp and dry as the ship slipped its moorings and the soldiers of the British Expeditionary Force crowded the railings, waving to the sparse crowd gathered to see them leave. Neville watched the people on the dockside become dots in the distance as the ship, with its destroyer escorts, pulled away from the harbour into the open sea.

Neville, Span and many other troops continued to stand by the stern rail, smoking in companionable silence. The chill sea wind whipped through them, as they gazed back at the receding coastline of England at the end of the tapering wake.

'Penny for them, Nev?' asked Span.

Neville drew steadily on his cigarette. 'I was just thinking, Charlie . . .' He paused then said quietly, 'I wish I was going back.'

'Me too, old son, me too.'

Chapter 3

The Long Walk to Dunkirk

January 1940 to June 1940

———————

'Welcome to France, my little beauty!' Neville said while leaning against his Thornycroft, smoking a cigarette.

'It's a bloody lorry, Wood,' Sergeant Moore laughed, 'not a woman. Now get it started and move out to the assembly park.'

Neville had been on the docks in Hull many times over the years, but he had never seen a sight like Cherbourg. Military ships of all types and sizes were manoeuvring in and out of the harbour: some sliding in to moor, others heading back out to sea. Tanks and armoured cars, artillery and munition stores were being unloaded by a myriad of cranes and vehicles; such was the speed and the constancy, it was as though they were dancing to a mechanical rhythm. All the while, men were marching onshore; the sound of their boots on the cobbles rang in time, underneath the noise of orders being shouted and equipment rattling. As Neville stood there, taking in the smell of the sea intermingled with fuel, fumes and food, he felt full of confidence for what lay ahead. It was time to put Jerry firmly in his place. With this lot unleashed, how could he possibly withstand?

Then a horn sounded, making Neville jump and drop his cigarette.

'Come on, Timber, show me the sights of Cherbourg.' Jim Oliver had pulled up behind Neville on the dockside, and popped his head out of the cab window. 'Charlie's just bringing the captain in the staff car. Time to go.'

Neville took one last look at the *Fenella* and climbed into the cab of his Thornycroft. The engine fired with a cough and a stutter, smoke belching out from the exhaust. Then he pulled out to join the rest of 522 Ammunition Company, Royal Army Service Corps, gliding away from the quayside to the assembly point on the outskirts of Cherbourg. When they got there, waiting for further instructions, what Neville noticed most was the cold. The winter of 1940 was bitter, one of the coldest for fifty years. 522 Company were gathered in a group. They huddled together for warmth, resembling a flock of birds about to take flight as they flapped their arms and stamped their feet.

'How much longer?' groaned Jim Oliver.

'Bloody officers will be warm somewhere, having a cup of tea while they decide what to do next,' shivered Stan Curlew.

After what seemed like an age, Thorpe and Moore appeared, bellowing for the men to gather round. As he gave out the instructions, Neville could see Thorpe's breath in the cold air. 'I know it's chilly but stop fidgeting and listen carefully. The Company will leave immediately for Le Mans, where we will remain temporarily pending a move to Lens in Belgium.'

'Wow, Le Mans!' Span nudged Neville. 'Racing Thornycrofts at twenty-five miles per hour! Assuming they go at all.'

'Spandler!' barked Moore.

'It's a bit of a beggar's muddle at the moment,' Thorpe continued, 'but this is the British Army and we are at our best when we muddle through. We leave at midday.' He glanced at his watch. 'It's 1130 hours now, so you've got thirty minutes. Sergeant Moore has your journey details.'

Moore passed round small slips of paper, each about an inch in depth and six inches long. Neville took his and read the simple directions written out: *Cherbourg – Bayeux – Caen – Argenton – Alençon – Le Mans – 176 miles.*

'We are short of maps currently,' Moore said, 'so I will lead. The sergeant major will travel with Oliver.' In the background, Jim could be heard to groan. 'Nichols, you will bring up the rear with the sick wagon.'

The journey to Le Mans was not exactly taken at racing pace. It took the convoy eight hours to weave its way through the fields and hedgerows of the French countryside. It was a winter wonderland, with the frost and a dusting of snow glistening in the weak winter sunshine. Most of the journey was quiet: it was only when passing through or close to the towns that Neville saw anyone. Here the convoy was greeted with an occasional wave, sometimes a salute perhaps from a First World War veteran, but mainly a sullen watchfulness, as if the British and the Germans were to fight a war that France wanted no part of. *A welcome as cold as the weather*, thought Neville.

By the time 522 Company arrived just outside Le Mans, Neville was more than ready for the hot food they'd been promised. But the cold weather meant that the meat they were supposed to eat was now frozen solid. With their butcher skills, Neville and Jim attempted to resolve the situation by taking a hacksaw to the beef.

'Come on, Jim, put your back into it.' Neville grinned as he watched Jim sweating and grunting, attempting to hacksaw the joint into manageable chunks of edible meat.

It was a late, but warm and welcome supper.

The next two days were spent on vehicle maintenance, checking equipment and stores and waiting around for further instructions. On 27 January the Company were told that the move to Lens would take place the following day, but when they gathered for departure at 0700 the next morning they were stood down.

'The move has been postponed,' explained Thorpe. 'The roads en route have been closed due to the frost and thaw conditions. In addition, there are some difficulties arranging billeting for the Division in the area around Arras, which is where we expect to be based. In the meantime, check your vehicles and complete your vehicle maintenance records in Army Book 412.'

'I did that yesterday, Sergeant Major,' braved Jim.

'Well, bloody well do it again, Oliver, and do it properly this time. Vehicle inspection will be at 1100 to make sure you have.'

All eyes swivelled to Jim. 'Marvellous, Ollie, you managed to earn us an inspection. In future, please keep your moans and groans to yourself,' chided Stan. Jim grunted and headed for his wagon to complete the sixteen checks, ranging from the engine, fuel supply, ignition and steering to starter motor, clutch, brakes, tyres and tools.

On Saturday 3 February, 50th Division received orders to move from Le Mans to Billy-Montigny, Pas-de-Calais, three miles south-east of Lens. The journey was a distance of 313 miles and went via Chartres, avoiding Paris by taking the north-west route through Beauvais, Amiens and Arras. They left at 0800 on Sunday and arrived at Billy-Montigny at 2040 hours that night. Neville was exhausted by the time they got there, dismounting from his vehicle stiff, aching and with red-rimmed eyes.

The Division was there to work in the II Corps reserve line known as the 'Fromelles Switch', but because of the bad weather and poor travel conditions, the troops were arriving piecemeal. It wasn't until 14 February that everyone had finally arrived – at which point they received orders to move to a training area at Amiens, seventy-nine miles back the way they had come.

'Headless chicken syndrome!' grumbled Jim, out of earshot of Thorpe.

The Division was stationed at Amiens for just over a month, undertaking further intensive training focusing on weapons drill, use of gas masks and physical fitness. Little was done in the way of coordinated inter-unit, cross-service battle cooperation, combatting a new type of warfare shortly to be unleashed by the enemy – 'blitzkrieg' or 'lightning war'. So when Moore announced they'd be on the move to Loos on 28 March – 'No damn jokes about the name' – Neville went through his final vehicle checks with a mixture of excitement and trepidation.

'Think this is it?' asked Stan. 'Think we'll get to meet some real live Germans?'

'I hope not, Curly.' Neville dropped a hand on his shoulder. 'The only good German is a dead one. So if you do meet one make sure you pop him off before he pops you. You can introduce yourself afterwards.'

Arriving at Loos to form part of II Corps, the Division set about digging a defensive line covering eight miles from Seclin to Wavrin, just south-east of Lille. It was back-breaking work. The earth was still hard from the cold, plus they had to excavate wide, deep anti-tank obstacles and construct concrete pillboxes.

'Look at my poor hands,' groaned Jim at the end of another hard shift of digging. He held up his hands, which were red-raw, blistered and bleeding. 'I'm not cut out for this kind of stuff. It's okay for all those ex-miners in the Durham Light Infantry. *We don't need an excavator. We can dig it quicker.* Well, they never asked me if I'd sooner have the excavator. I'd have learned to drive the damn thing if necessary.'

Late one afternoon, after they had been dismissed, Neville took Stan and Charlie into Loos in his Thornycroft. There was a house near the Town Hall that bore the Crusader Shield: it had been commandeered by 50th Division's Senior Chaplain, Reverend Newcombe, to create a haven of peace and quiet. The troops could pray in the chapel created in the room at the top of the house or write letters home in one of the other rooms.

On the drive in, Neville announced to the others that he was going to take a short detour. Ignoring their puzzled faces, he turned off north-west and drove on a quiet road for about four miles, finally pulling up outside a pair of open iron gates in the middle of an extensive high, white, stone wall.

'Humour me.' Neville switched the engine off and clambered down. 'Come on,' he shouted, waving for Charlie and Stan to follow him. As they stepped down and walked through the iron gates, they understood what Neville had been looking for. Row upon row of crosses stretched out in straight lines into the distance. No one spoke, first standing rooted to the spot, then walking between the rows lost in thought, quietly noting the names, regiments and ages of the countless young men buried there.

'I wanted to come here,' Neville finally broke the silence, 'because I know that in the First World War there was one hell of a battle here. It may sound odd, but I just wanted to pay my respects and let all these brave lads know that we won't let them down.' As his voice cracked, he felt Charlie put an arm round his shoulder.

'Thanks, Timber,' he said quietly. 'I'm pleased we came.'

The following morning, at 0900, the Company were called to the Village Hall for a briefing by Captain Bonner. It was a tight squeeze to fit in all 120 men, standing to attention as one when Bonner arrived, alongside Thorpe.

'At ease, gentlemen. As you were.' Bonner smiled. Standing in front of a large map pinned up on the wall, his piercing blue eyes took in the room, full of expectant faces like Neville's, keen for information. 'First of all, men, the bad news and the good news. The bad news is that, as yet, there is no sign of the Germans attacking. The good news is that we know why. It is clear from decoded intercepts that whilst Company Sergeant Major Thorpe is anywhere in the vicinity of France or Belgium, Jerry is staying behind the Siegfried Line as the contest is too uneven. So to encourage the enemy from his lair we are sending the sergeant major back to England where he will ensure the production of high-calibre soldiers just like you men. I am certain we all wish him well.' Bonner paused at the outbreak of spontaneous applause and the odd cheer. He held up his hands to quieten the men. 'Our new CSM Vyse will be with us in forty-eight hours and I am sure you will make him very welcome.'

'Oh, we will, sir, believe me we will.' Charlie grinned and Thorpe gave him his last stern stare.

'Now pay close attention,' Bonner continued. 'Our orders are to hold the sector in front of Lille. However, in the event of a German advance Plan D will be adopted.'

'Any idea what plans A, B or C are?' murmured Neville to himself.

'We expect Jerry to come through Belgium and avoid the French Maginot Line. Should that occur we must move swiftly sixty miles into Belgium and hold the line at the River Dyle.' Bonner pointed at the large map behind him to the area around Brussels. 'The Belgians have prepared defences there and will defend the north of the line, which could, if necessary, be flooded to impede any enemy advance. We will hold the centre near to Brussels and the French 1st Army will hold the south . . .'

'We're in trouble in the south then,' Charlie whispered to Neville.

'. . . The code word for Plan D is "Birch", which will give us six hours' notice to action the plan. That means, gentlemen, a high state of readiness to move into action rapidly. The 4th Royal Northumberland Fusiliers will assume traffic control responsibilities and the 9th Durham Light Infantry will control any issues with refugees to ensure we get to where we need to be. Thank you, gentlemen, that is all.'

Bonner left the building to a buzz of conversation. But the excitement and anticipation soon subsided as the days rolled over into repetitive monotony. This was interrupted briefly on Thursday 11 April, when the code word was received. Neville could feel his heart thumping as 522 Ammunition Company loaded their wagons with twelve-pounder shells and high explosives and were on the road within the hour. But fifteen miles in, the call came to turn around. False alarm. On Saturday 27 April, similarly, the air raid sirens sounded over Lille. But again, the skies remained empty, quiet.

The 50th Division tried to ease the wait and release the frustration by setting up a Boxing Championship, which took place on Thursday 9 May. Both Charlie Spandler and Alan Such were included in the RASC team of six, with Neville and Freddie Nichols the corner men.

'Keep your guard up, feint right and come up with an upper cut,' Neville advised Charlie before his fight. 'He'll never see it coming.'

Charlie nodded, the hand bell rang and he bounded confidently into the centre of the makeshift ring. He feinted right as Neville instructed, only to catch a jab to the forehead and a right over the top, hitting the earth like a sack of potatoes. Neville could feel the force of that from where he was watching and winced. The referee counted Charlie out and Freddie came into the ring to help him up.

'Bloody hell, Timber, thanks a lot,' said a dazed-looking Charlie. 'Have you boxed before?'

'No,' said Neville flatly.

Alan Such did better, winning his bout, but the day was carried by the Signals. The team trophy was presented to them by the General Officer Commanding, Major General Martel, whose booming voice offered a few words of advice as he made the presentation.

'Boxing is one of the great traditions of the British Army,' he told the assembled soldiers. 'Boxing prepares us for war. It teaches you to react, keep your wits about you, keep your head, keep your cool as dreadful things are happening around you.'

Twelve hours later, at 0630 on Friday 10 May, the code word *Birch* was given. This time, it was no false alarm. The Germans were invading Holland and Belgium and dreadful things were about to happen.

'Sounds like the French are copping it,' said Alan Such.

'Not sure,' replied Jim. 'Sounds more like an easterly direction, which will be the Belgians.'

Neville, Charlie, Alan, Freddie, Jim and Stan were standing in a group beside their wagons, which were full of artillery shells, bullets, grenades and other high explosives. They were listening to the distant crump of artillery and could make out the distinctive shriek of the German Stuka dive-bombers. 522 Company were positioned two miles behind the defensive line of the River Dyle, close to Wavre, where the Durham Light Infantry were digging in. As required by Plan D, II Corps were now occupying the sixteen-mile defensive line between Louvain in the north and Wavre in the south. Earlier, when they had arrived in Belgium, they had been overwhelmed by the warm and friendly welcome they had received. Unlike that first journey through France, crowds of people had lined the roadsides, waving and cheering them on, bright and full of hope.

'Seems to be all around us,' said Alan.

'Yes, and I'll be damn well glad to get rid of this lot before it comes any closer,' grunted Neville.

'Let's go, smartly there.' Sergeant Moore strode up, sounding even more serious than usual. 'Word is Jerry has crossed the Albert Canal in strength and is pushing the Belgians back rapidly. The artillery will need this lot damn quickly, about one mile that way.' He pointed towards Wavre. 'You'll be directed when you get there.'

Neville and the others ran to their vehicles, adrenalin pumping through their bodies. This was it: what they were trained for.

On the afternoon of Tuesday 14 May, the guns opened up. 522 Company shuttled between the Dyle and the supply dump eight miles behind the line. The distant crump of gunfire was now the din of battle, screaming Stukas, the thunder of artillery, the crackle of rifle and machine-gun fire. The following day, the Germans made a small penetration across the Dyle but were forced back by a determined counter-attack. Chaos and carnage was all around. 522 ferried and returned, keeping distance between their vehicles to make the target more difficult for enemy aircraft. Stukas came overhead like menacing birds of prey. Neville crouched over his steering wheel, gripping hard, trying to extract every yard of speed he could muster from his old vehicle. It was a relief to hear and see the arrival of Hurricanes. Dogfights began above them, planes screamed towards the earth trailing smoke, incessant, exciting and appalling.

The British held the line, but elsewhere the situation was grave. The new British Prime Minister, Winston Churchill, had flown to Paris to discover the French were already burning their archives and preparing for what they believed was the inevitable – the surrender of the capital and the capitulation of France. Meanwhile, the Dutch had surrendered, Holland having been conquered in less than five days. The French 1st Army on the British right had taken heavy punishment and the Germans had made inroads of nearly four miles. Late on the evening of 16 May, the French made the decision to withdraw from their defensive line. The British had to pull back from Wavre to maintain a line of contact with the French. 522 Company made their last delivery for the artillery to cover the withdrawal with withering fire.

'Retiring! What the hell are we retiring for? We're holding the buggers!' Neville was incandescent with rage.

'Bloody top brass,' agreed Jim Oliver. 'If they got their backsides out of their fancy headquarters and came to see what was happening—'

'Quiet, all of you!' barked Moore. 'We have no idea what's happening elsewhere. We just have our orders and they say we head back to the Dendre. Quit moaning, get in your vehicles and get your arses away from here.'

With barely audible muttering, the men of 522 Company mounted their vehicles and rejoined the main force of 50th Division by the River Dendre, west of Brussels with Ath on the right and Ninove on the left. But the withdrawal did not stop there. During 17 and 18 May the British Expeditionary Force (the BEF) withdrew to the line of the River Escaut. 522 Company found themselves heading towards Pecq, close to the French border, negotiating roads choked with refugees. There were old men, shuffling with walking sticks, and young families with scant possessions hurriedly thrown into a pram or a battered, dusty suitcase. Men, women with heads bowed, children crying or staring, unable to comprehend the disaster that was war. In the warm May sunshine the stench of unwashed people was overpowering.

'My God, look at these poor people.' Stan echoed the thoughts of Neville, Jim and Alan as they stood by their wagons, lighting cigarettes, and awaiting further orders.

'Just think,' said Alan, 'it was only a few days ago that these people were by the roadside, waving and cheering, believing in us. And now look at them. People without hope and we can't give them any. Where are they all heading, for goodness' sake?'

'C'mon, lads.' Neville went inside his cab, emerging moments later with a few packs of cigarettes and bars of chocolate. He walked out into the road. 'If we can't protect them we can at least help the poor buggers in some small way.' He and the others handed out what they could spare. Some of the refugees just took what was offered with a tired, bleary-eyed look. Others murmured '*Dank u*' and managed a weak smile of gratitude. An elderly woman, dressed in black, doubled under the weight of her bag, took a chocolate bar from Neville. She looked up at him with rheumy eyes and gripped his hand tightly.

'God go with you,' she croaked in halting English through parched, cracked lips. She held his hand a moment more, then with a weary smile resumed her tired trudge to wherever it was she was heading.

The position at Pecq was temporary. On the night of 19 May, 50th Division was ordered to concentrate on the Vimy Ridge, north of Arras, and to prepare to go on the attack. 522 Company reached Vimy Ridge the following morning. The briefing at midday was scant but it was clear that the situation was serious. The French were in disarray, only reacting long after the Germans had outmanoeuvred them. There was now a great danger of the BEF being encircled as the Germans drove towards the coast. 50th Division was to come under the overall command of Major General Franklyn, General

Officer Commanding the 5th Division, hence the sobriquet 'Frankforce'. The Germans had taken Albert, Doullens, Amiens and Abbeville and were in force to the south of Arras. Arras itself was a vital road junction: the planned thrust south by Frankforce was intended to disrupt German lines of communication from the east.

The action was to begin on Tuesday 21 May and in the meantime the troops were ordered to rest.

From 0800 hours on 21 May, the build-up began. The infantry set off on an eight-mile march to the start line. Ahead rumbled the tanks, the Matildas, with their thick armour and two-pounders, and the Mark 1s equipped only with machine guns. They clanked, screeched and squealed on worn tank tracks. Two broke down within a quarter of a mile.

'Well, I'm not pushing the bloody thing,' said Charlie as 522 Company prepared to move out to supply the 368th Battery 92nd Field Regiment of the Royal Artillery.

The objective set was to clear the countryside south of Arras as far as the River Cojeul. The attack would be made by two mobile columns supported by infantry and a platoon of motorcycles. At 1430 hours that afternoon, the attack began. The right column advanced to Warlus before encountering two German Panzer Divisions and an SS Division. The left column reached Beaurains, with some units reaching Wancourt on the Cojeul, but they were too weak to hold it for long.

The Royal Artillery moved their guns in support. Neville and 522 Company moved supplies with them. The noise of battle was all around them as the Germans counter-attacked. At 1850 hours, the Luftwaffe appeared overhead like a swarm of angry bees. Over one hundred planes rained bombs, supported on the ground by tanks pummelling the British with savage intensity. The British withdrew to Achicourt and Duisans in response.

The fighting continued through the next day as the British were pushed back to their start line. The troops were stubborn, tenacious, making the Germans fight for every yard of country. Crucially the German encircling movement had been delayed for two days. Such was the ferocity of the fighting, the Germans believed they had been attacked by five infantry divisions of 15,000 men when in fact they had been engaged by two battalions of just 2,000.

As the Germans were ordered to hold their position around Arras, the British were ordered to withdraw northwards and rejoin the main body of the BEF. The one remaining road was congested with wagons, tailboard to radiator, three abreast. 522 Company had what remained of the supplies plus weary infantrymen sleeping on the boxes or hanging on to the sides. Neville found himself rubbing his hooded eyes, shaking his head, pinching himself, anything to stay awake as they crawled the twenty miles to a stop at Pont-à-Vendin. As the infantry disembarked and trudged away wearily, he slumped over in his seat and slept.

On the evening of 25 May, Neville, Alan, Charlie and the others had a much-needed evening off. The following day, 50th Division were assigned to go on the offensive with the French. But before lights out at 2200 hours, they had a precious evening to themselves. Which is how they found themselves in a small café on the south side of the bridge at Pont-à-Vendin. After army rations, a supper of egg and chips had tasted like heaven. Someone suggested a tipple to round off the evening, but no one recognised any of the numerous bottles behind the bar, in every shape, size and colour imaginable.

'Well, what are they?' asked Alan.

'How on earth should I know? They're all foreign,' replied Freddie.

'I know, we'll try something from each of them,' suggested Charlie.

Neville's eyes, meanwhile, were following the petite barmaid as she moved up and down the bar. She was like something out of a dream: blonde, red pouting lips, her full figure emphasised by the low-cut white blouse and black pencil skirt.

'Oi, Timber.' Charlie nudged Neville hard in the ribs. 'Take your eyes off that little mademoiselle. It would be classified as looting!'

'Pretty little thing,' Neville said, lost in thought.

'So what are we going to drink, then?' Stan asked.

'Listen, I speak a bit of the language,' boasted Charlie as he waved to the barmaid. 'Excusez moi, mademoiselle.' He grinned, proud of his linguistic prowess. 'Mon ami, Timber, il,' he grappled for the right words, 'fancies vous a bit et would like to invitez vous for afternoon tea at camp. Bon. Et in the meantime, je suis Charlie et un of those, s'il vous plait.' He pointed at the first bottle.

Over the next two hours bottles came down from the shelf, glasses were filled and emptied with great regularity. For a few precious moments, the war was forgotten, and laughter filled the air. Then Jim, who had abstained from a few refills, glanced at his watch.

'Aw, hell, it's nearly ten,' he exclaimed, standing up. 'We need to go. Alan, you're supposed to be doing lights-out in less than ten minutes.' Alan was the Company bugler but at that moment it looked as if his capacity to blow a note was zero. They staggered to the door, into the warm night air, and were heading back to the village when they heard a splash.

'Ahh, bloody hell,' yelled Stan. 'Suchy's fallen into the soddin' river.' They all turned and held out a helpful hand unsteadily as Alan floundered in the water.

'The bugger'll drown at this rate.' Charlie waded in, grabbed Alan's belt and hauled him out. Alan responded by retching and throwing up over Charlie's boots. 'Thanks a bunch,' he grunted, as he turned back into the river to wash them.

It was half past ten by the time they got back to the village. The quietness of the streets emphasised the lateness of the hour. All the troops had been billeted in the houses, deserted as the villagers became refugees heading westwards. Walking down the street, care had to be taken as each house would hold forty or fifty troops all sharing one urinal overnight. In the event of a queue the most convenient way to satisfy 'needs must' was to wee out of the nearest window into the street below. Keeping an eye on any open windows, Neville and the others crept to their billets and their beds. But just as Neville was nodding off, an awful din cut through the air. He looked out to see Alan standing in the middle of the street, swaying from side to side, bedraggled, bugle to his lips blowing a range of discordant notes that did not remotely resemble lights-out. Neville ran down to stop him, but it was too late. By the time he got there, Sergeant Major Vyse had appeared.

'What the hell is the meaning of this? Stop that bloody racket now.'

Alan swayed, trying to focus on the sergeant major. Then his legs crumpled and he sat back heavily on the ground.

'Get up, Such,' growled Vyse. 'You men, help him,' he ordered Neville and Charlie, who had also run down to help their friend. Each took an arm and helped Alan to his feet. Vyse eyed him up and down. 'Such, I'm putting you on a charge for dereliction of duty. Now all of you get back to sleep.' Alan tried to salute and clattered the side of his head with the bugle. Vyse looked at Charlie and Neville. Neville thought they might be in for what-for as well, but instead he saw the sergeant was trying hard to suppress a smile.

'You two had better look after your mate,' he said, turning on his heel and marching away.

Five hours later, at 0330, the bugle sounded again, this time in tune. Neville and the others were awake instantly, grabbing clothes and weapons. They gathered together quickly on the village street where Vyse waved them close to him. 'Change of plan, men. The attack today is off. The Belgians are having serious problems on our left and we have been ordered to plug the gap. Get yourselves ready, we move out in thirty minutes.'

At that moment, just as the morning was turning to a light grey, the Stukas swarmed over. The scream of the dive-bombers pierced the early morning as bombs rained down on Pont-à-Vendin. The objective appeared to be the bridge – destroying that to prevent 50th Division moving east to fill the gap between the British left and the Belgians. It was a race against time: 522 Company moved out just after 0400 and headed for the bridge. Despite the attacks, it was still intact, allowing them to head over and drive the forty-three miles to the area between Ypres and Menen.

But not everything had been as fortunate. As they approached the bridge Neville slowed down. The café, which had provided such a memorable evening the night before, was now a heap of smoking rubble. As he passed, two soldiers carried out a stretcher covered by a bloody sheet. An arm was dangling loosely from the stretcher, the hand trailing on the ground, limp, lifeless. Just above the top of the sheet a head of blonde hair was just visible, encrusted with blood. Neville closed his eyes: last night suddenly seemed a lifetime ago. He was startled back to reality by a bang on the cab door.

'Come on, get a move on there,' bellowed a sergeant. Neville shook himself, focused on the road and accelerated away.

They were shadowed all the way to Tournai by a German plane. As they neared Menen, German dive-bombers swooped to attack the British convoy. Bombs exploded all around, spattering the windscreen with mud and stones, like vicious hailstones. There was nowhere to hide or divert – you just had to stay in line and hope that it was someone else rather than you who got hit. Somehow,

Neville passed through unscathed and managed to reach his destination: a wood in line with Brussels between Menen and Ypres. He parked his wagon alongside the others, under the cover of trees near to a barn. As he climbed down from the cab, he saw Vyse moving from wagon to wagon, speaking quietly.

'Get some food inside you and settle down in the barn,' he said when he reached Neville and Alan. 'Get some rest but sleep with your rifles loaded and ready.'

'That makes a change,' grunted Alan as Vyse moved on to talk to the next driver. 'He's usually yelling at the top of his voice!'

Neville's thoughts, though, were still full of the image of the pretty barmaid, dead on a stretcher. Rather than laugh at Alan's joshing, he remained serious.

'What?' Alan asked.

'I'm beginning to realise how fickle life can be,' Neville said, heading over to the barn. He tried to get some rest but he slipped in and out of sleep, still seeing the body on that stretcher. At 3 a.m., he was woken up more fully: where once there had been silence, now the barn was full of shouting and commotion.

'Everyone up, sharp!' Sergeant Moore was yelling. 'We're in front of our own infantry. On the road, ten minutes, back towards Lille.'

Neville grabbed his rifle and ran. In less than ten minutes all the wagons were on the move, and only just in time. In a matter of seconds, the air was rent with the scream and whine of shells. High explosives pummelled the barn and woodland where they had been moments before, totally obliterating it. In his mirrors, Neville could see bursts of white and orange, and pushed his foot down on the accelerator hard. He found himself being waved over rivers and canals by Royal Engineers, frantically setting explosive charges to blow the bridges up to slow the German onslaught, once they had passed through. Once again, the convoy found itself picking its way through an endless crowd of refugees fleeing Belgium. Somehow, Neville wasn't sure how, they made it back to Lille by midday, before being sent on again, this time back towards the French–Belgian border to Pérenchies. All the while, the Luftwaffe was their constant companion and menace.

'Where's the bloody Royal Air Force?' demanded Neville as he, Alan and Charlie parked up under another canopy of trees. The sky remained full of German planes, bombs spilling from their undercarriages, flying unhindered, it seemed, by the smoke of anti-aircraft fire.

'Can't remember when I last saw a Spit or Hurricane,' replied Alan.

'Well, *we're* damn well doing our best,' said Neville. 'I hope everyone else is.'

Once again, he and the others tried to snatch rest when they could. They slept away from their wagons, under the cover of trees. The evenings might have been warm, but the din of the planes, bombs and anti-aircraft fire was incessant. Something had to give, and in the end it was Neville's Thornycroft.

'Wood, how much ammo have you left in your wagon?' Sergeant Moore asked the following morning.

'Half a dozen boxes of twelve-pounder shells, Sergeant,' Neville replied.

'Get that off and loaded on to Oliver's wagon, sharpish. Blow your wagon and go with Such.'

'Blow the wagon, Sergeant?' Neville was incredulous.

'You heard, Wood.' The tone of Moore's voice made clear this wasn't for discussion. 'The news is pretty bad; the Belgians have surrendered so we're almost knackered. We're pulling back towards the coast. Such!' He gestured for Alan to come over. 'Wood is now with you on the stores wagon. Head to La Bassée. We're to see what we can do to get the infantry away from the Arras area. Then we'll head north to Poperinge.'

Working quickly, Neville and Alan ferried the little ammunition remaining to another wagon. Then, with a heavy heart, Neville lifted the bonnet of his Thornycroft, took off the handbrake and together they pushed it into the ditch. It settled at an angle of forty-five degrees almost as though it was in repose, resting after having served in two world wars.

'Clear!' Neville shouted. He unpinned a grenade, tossing it under the bonnet into the engine compartment. Then they all dived for cover. As the grenade exploded, metal shot in all directions, puncturing the canopies of other vehicles, shards embedding themselves in nearby trees, but thankfully not causing any casualties. They all got up, dusted themselves down and looked over at the smoking wreckage.

'Bloody hell,' breathed Moore. 'I think we'll have a rethink on that method.'

The road to La Bassée was slow to navigate, choked again with the familiar sight of refugees. It was heartbreaking to see them, those that were strong enough pushing barrows and handcarts with all they could carry of their homes. As they progressed slowly, Alan stood near the tailgate of the stores wagon and threw out the supplies of biscuits and herrings to the lucky few. They reached La Bassée and crossed the canal bridge, which was mined and defended with a twelve-pounder anti-tank gun. By this time, it was getting dark and they passed down the canal side, parking on a narrow lane very near to a 'sub park' – effectively an ammunition dump with enough high explosives to blow La Bassée and its surrounding villages to atoms. A captain from the Royal Engineers spoke hurriedly to Sergeant Major Vyse who in turn gathered the men of 522 together to pass on the information.

'I've just been told Jerry is only three or four miles away. Stay in your wagons, ready to move at a moment's notice.'

That move north started at 0400 the following morning, 29 May, having loaded what ammunition they could from the dump. Almost immediately the familiar sound of the Luftwaffe screeched overhead, swooping down on the column, the rat-a-tat of machine guns blazing. Neville ducked instinctively as bullets tore into the canopies. He could only hope the red-hot metal had hit the stores rather than the ammunition. Alan looked across at him from the passenger seat white as a sheet.

'There but for the grace of God go I.' He tried to force a smile.

'Well,' Neville replied through gritted teeth, 'let's hope someone's looking down on us other than the damn Luftwaffe.'

Before long the sky darkened, the heavens opened and rain began to lash down. The feeble windscreen wiper struggled to maintain any modicum of visibility as they pushed on for Poperinge.

'Least the weather might keep the Jerry planes away,' Neville grunted. Maybe someone was looking down on them after all.

But as they moved closer to Poperinge, Neville's heart began to sink again. Ditches, fields and side roads presented the apocalyptic picture of a smoking graveyard of abandoned stores, guns, vehicles and other equipment. Near Boeschepe, they were waved down by an officer. Captain Bonner climbed from the lead wagon, saluted and the two men moved away deep in conversation. Captain Bonner returned five minutes later and waved the men of 522 Company over to him. He took them into a clearing just off the road. From the look on his face it was clear the news wasn't good.

'That officer is from Divisional HQ at Adinkerke.' Bonner looked away for a moment, and then back at his men. 'I regret to say that the decision of the Commanding Officer of the BEF in consultation with His Majesty's Government is that the army is to be withdrawn from France.' He held a hand up to silence the murmur that went round. 'That evacuation has already begun and the Royal Navy is here for that purpose. Jerry is close behind us and the rearguard will hold the pocket along the Canal de Bergues. The absolute priority is to evacuate troops so nothing can go beyond Poperinge. Our orders are to drive all our vehicles into the ditches and disable them. You will then head to Dunkirk on foot with your rifle only. I'm told the distance is only twenty-seven miles.' He smiled, but his smile was thin. 'Let's be about it and good luck to you all.'

'Jesus, twenty-seven miles,' breathed out Charlie. 'He can't be serious.'

'Very serious, I suspect.' Neville's mood was grim as they moved to the wagons. Following his experience of blowing up the Thornycroft with a grenade, this time he used a pickaxe to hammer through the sump. Once the wrecking job was complete, everyone crammed what stores they could in their pockets. *Twenty-seven miles!* Neville thought. With one last look at the discarded vehicles, he slung his rifle over his shoulder and joined the others to begin the long march to the beaches of Dunkirk.

All that we've been through, and for what? Neville, like the others, was deep in thought as they trudged along in silence. Overhead, they watched the planes circling and diving, listened to the sound of gunfire all around. The route was relatively flat, a combination of fields and hedgerows providing good cover. The villages they passed through were deserted, like ghost dwellings. The houses that were still standing were mostly flickering in flames or already reduced to burnt-out shells.

As night began to fall they reached Rexpoëde: another deserted street, this one looking more eerie in the half-light. Passing the church in the village centre, Neville was just beginning to let his weariness take over, wondering if there might be somewhere to get his head down, when the silence was broken by a familiar 'click'. It was a noise that snapped him to attention, just in time to hear a shout of, '*Schnell!*' Neville dived for the floor, hitting the wet earth with a slap as a spray of bullets zipped and whined above. The church wall behind him took the brunt, showering him in stone chippings that stung and punctured the skin.

Neville loaded quickly, returning fire in the direction of the Germans. That gave him enough breathing space to crawl on all fours under cover of the wall to the corner, where the others had also gathered. Cautiously, he peered round the corner of the stonework. No soldiers were visible, though he could still hear the snap of firing across the churchyard. Neville knew they needed to move: in turn, each man dashed across a small road junction into a minor road where hedgerows and a ditch provided cover. They paused, catching their breath, ears straining for any threat. But none materialised, only a silent cloak of darkness.

They stuck to fields and hedgerows now, stumbling, disorientated, into the night. The Company was completely fragmented: it was down to Neville, Charlie, Alan, Freddie, Jim and Stan to stick together and look out for each other. They crashed out for a short while under a hedgerow, taking turns to watch and listen. When it was Neville's turn, he could feel how taut his nerves were, and how twitchy his trigger finger. He stood, staring out in the blackness: all the while the guns rumbled in the background like rolling thunder.

Just before dawn, they moved out again, sixteen miles still to cover. By noon, they were on the outskirts of Dunkirk, falling in with a steady stream of British troops, and some French, gravitating towards the town – what was left of it, that is. Everywhere smoke drifted skywards, houses and factories burned on all sides, rubble filled the streets. Neville watched locals picking through the carnage to see what they could salvage, while others just stood and wept. The less fortunate were buried; in places, he could see hands and feet sticking out from under the piles of rubble.

They carried on towards the beaches. The way was obvious from the tide of humanity heading in one direction and from the air activity over the dunes and the sea. The street opened out into what looked like a giant car park. Troops were everywhere, along with lines of vehicles.

'You men! What unit?' A sergeant of the Military Police stalked over as Neville and the others were taking in the surroundings.

'RASC, sir, 50 Div,' replied Neville.

'Good, you're needed. Follow me.' Neville and the others exchanged glances as the MP swivelled on his heel and marched away to a large gathering of troops, saluting a captain of the Coldstream Guards. The two fell into conversation, the MP pointing over to Neville and his friends. The captain came over.

'Where have you come from, men?'

'Sir, we've been marching since yesterday from Poperinge,' said Neville.

'You must all be tired and hungry.' Neville relaxed; here, at last was a sympathetic ear. It wasn't, though, to last. 'But, I'm afraid, duty calls once more. I need you to find any of those wagons which will still run,' he nodded over to the line of vehicles, 'and get my men in sharpish.'

'But, sir—' began Jim.

'No buts, I'm afraid. If we don't move now then Jerry will be among us and we won't be going anywhere, other than prisoner-of-war camps.' The captain's tone was even, reasonable, but his eyes were steely, determined and brooked no further protest.

With a heavy heart, they saluted and went and found six wagons, joining others that had been commandeered. The Guards piled into the back and they set off in convoy, not even sure where they were going. Their destination turned out to be towards the Belgian border and a place called Veurne, a distance of just under fifteen miles. Thirty minutes later they were being waved down.

'Guards,' a powerful voice ordered, 'form up on the double!'

'Who's that?' Neville asked the corporal who had travelled with him in the cab.

'Oh, that's Regimental Sergeant Major Bell.' The corporal leapt down. 'Ding Dong, as we lovingly call him. Teddy bear, really. Thanks, mate, and good luck.'

'You too,' answered Neville. As the corporal went to join the other Guards, Bell came along the line of trucks.

'Get this lot off the road and disabled,' he shouted. 'Then make your way back to the beaches. My lads will hold 'em here.'

Neville's heart sank still further. He knew that transporting the Guards here was crucial in keeping the Germans at bay and allowing those at Dunkirk the time to escape. But he thought that, at the very least, he could have driven back. Now they were faced with another fifteen-mile hike across waterlogged countryside under fire.

Orders were orders. As Neville helped to ditch and immobilise the vehicles, he could hear the crackle of gunfire and the distinctive rat-a-tat of the Lewis guns increase in intensity. The Guards were engaging the enemy. It was time to go.

'Buggered or not, I'm out of here,' said Charlie.

The journey back was slow. Everyone was exhausted now, the hunger and thirst eating into Neville, increasingly desperate for something to eat and drink. About halfway back, near Zuydcoote, they saw a deserted farmhouse a hundred yards back from the road. *Might there be . . . ?* Neville thought.

'Let's check it out for food and water,' suggested Jim. After the ambush in the village on the first walk to Dunkirk, they made for the farmhouse with caution. Entering, they covered each other as they searched from room to room. There was no one there, but no food either. The kitchen was a pile of rubble.

'Nothing cooking today,' moaned Alan.

'Here, fellas!' came a call from Stan.

'Where are you, Curly?' shouted Neville.

'Down here. In the cellar.'

Following his shouts, they found the open door and stone steps down into a dingy and dusty basement. Along one wall was an extensive wine rack. Many bottles were broken but a few remained.

'Anyone got a bottle opener?' asked Alan, tongue in cheek.

'Not standard army issue,' replied Charlie. 'Try this.' He tapped the neck of the bottle on the wall edge and it shattered open. 'Watch out for glass fragments.' He took a swig.

Neville followed suit. He had a big gulp of wine, then filled up his water bottle with the rest. 'Oh, boy!' he said as he wiped his mouth. 'I think I'm even thirstier than I was before.' The wine, although wet and welcome, did leave a thirst.

'Not too much,' chided Alan. 'We need to get back. Don't want Jerry finding us pissed in a cellar.'

Buoyed, they set off again, eventually reaching the beach of La Panne late in the evening of 30 May. The numbers seemed to have swelled since they'd arrived before. As far as the eye could see, there were thousands of men from numerous units, queues snaking into the sea. In the distance Neville could just make out the tops of the heads of those at the front of the queue, being hauled into small boats to be ferried to the bigger ships.

A Royal Navy officer was walking among the queues, explaining what was going on. 'We're getting you all off as fast as we can,' he said when he reached Neville, 'but it will take some time. I suggest you dig yourself into the dunes, which will give you some protection. We will direct you to the sea at the appropriate time and in an orderly fashion.' He moved on, conveying his message of hope among the carnage. Neville looked at the others and shrugged: there was nothing to do but hunker down and wait.

As light broke the following morning, the battle of the beaches intensified. Out in the water, ships large and small zig-zagged back and forth. The bigger ships, mainly destroyers, were stationary. Guns were blazing, shells exploding in the clear blue sky like a fireworks display from hell. Stukas screamed as they dived at the dunes and the ships. Sand mushroomed in the air, absorbing some of the force of the explosion. Where it didn't, limbs torn from flesh flailed in all directions, spraying the beach red. After what seemed like an eternal wait, the RAF appeared. Now Spitfires and Hurricanes swarmed through the air, harrying and destroying the German bombers. Those on the beach watched the dogfights criss-cross the sky as the German fighters joined the melee. Planes exploded or plummeted on to the beaches or into the sea, trailing smoke or fire and exploding on impact.

Charlie and Neville had been away from the dunes for an hour. They returned carrying sheets of metal.

'Get under these,' said Charlie to the others. 'Can't imagine Jerry having much use for wagon bonnets but we can sure as hell use them.' They placed them over their foxholes, providing at least a measure of protection from the hot metal flying around. In the mid-afternoon it was their turn to be ordered to head for the sea. Neville felt hope flare as he moved away from the dunes. But that hope diminished when he saw the length of the queue meandering for hundreds of yards into the water. He watched the ships come again, moved into the sea to wait his turn, only to head back to the cover of the dunes. The bitter-tasting red wine taken from the farmhouse was the only thing to drink. Neville's head throbbed with dehydration.

The following day, Saturday 1 June, followed the same pattern. Neville stood in the water, rifle held high, and shuffled and waited and prayed as they were machine-gunned and bombed. As he stood in line, bodies floated by, bloated by the water, of those who hadn't been so lucky. So near and yet so far.

They were sent back to the beaches. There were fewer of them now but still many men waiting to be rescued.

'Do you think we'll make it?' Stan asked forlornly.

'You've got to keep hoping, Curly,' said Neville, patting him on the back. 'The Navy are getting us away all the time. Our turn will come.'

But after two full days on the beaches, two full days of horror and terror, Neville was beginning to doubt. When he saw the Coldstream Guards begin to appear, he knew the perimeter rear-guard was falling back and that Jerry couldn't be far behind. It was a desperate race against time.

Sunday 2 June dawned warm and sunny. Was that a sign? But the bombs continued to rain down, the guns still firing defiantly. The Royal Navy officer moved through the men again, offering the latest information.

'We have about fifteen thousand of you left,' he said. Neville tried to hide his expression of dismay. 'But we *will* get you all away by tonight,' the officer continued. There was something in the determination in his voice that gave Neville hope.

They were directed to the water again. Minutes turned to hours as they shuffled forward, deeper and deeper, lulled by the lapping tide. Water sprayed and choked them as bombs exploded nearby. Such was the wait, it felt as though time had no meaning. There was just the cold, the numbing despair. Then hands grabbed

Neville. He started, hadn't even realised that he was now at the head of the queue beside a Jolly boat. A Royal Navy rating, with HMS *Basilisk* on his cap, grabbed Neville's rifle.

'You won't be needing this for a while,' he said as he reached down, pulled Neville by the pants and hauled him on to the boat and under the seats. He didn't move as more exhausted soldiers fell around him. *He was on!*

'That's it for now, another boat coming!' someone shouted as oars splashed into the water and they left the head of the queue behind. Before long, they were beside a wall of grey steel, pulled and pushed on board the destroyer HMS *Basilisk*. Neville found a blanket thrown around him and was then ushered away to create space. A mug of hot tea – tea! – was placed in his hands and he found a spot on the catwalk of the destroyer over the engines. The pistons slowly came to life, gathering speed. Neville sat, feeling the warmth of the tea in his hands, mesmerised by the machinery pumping, hissing, marching like a mechanical monster. But it was their monster, taking him back to England, to Dover, away from Dunkirk: the graveyard of so much and so many but not his, and *not*, despite the odds, that of the British Army.

Chapter 4

Regroup, Re-arm and Romance

June 1940 to May 1941

It was the oddest noise. Neville was leaning on the ship's rail of the *Basilisk* as it docked in Dover, watching as Regimental Sergeant Major Bell formed his Coldstream Guards into order and marched them off in quick succession. As they made their way on to dry land, there was a noise from the throng of people waiting there on the quayside. It took Neville a second or two to work out what it was: it was cheering. It rippled through the crowd and echoed up to those standing on deck. Some of the crowd had flags, others were clapping and waving. Neville glanced round at the soldiers he was standing alongside. Some, sheepishly, were waving back, caught by the mood. Others, like him, just looked grim-faced, fatigued, shocked.

The order came for everyone to disembark. Unlike the coherence of the Coldstream Guards, Neville found himself in a ragtag assortment of units: the survivors. At the bottom of the gangway, the way was blocked by a phalanx of press photographers, shouting at the troops, their flash bulbs bursting into life.

I'm not in the mood for that, Neville thought, and he tried to remain inconspicuous at the back.

The soldiers were directed away from the ship to customs sheds where ladies of the Red Shield Club were handing out tea, biscuits and cigarettes. They were also generous with their smiles, which warmed Neville and helped lighten his mood.

'Can I have your attention, please?' An army officer jumped up on to a crate, shouting at everyone to listen to him. 'After you've enjoyed your refreshments you can follow the signs to the trains. From there you will be taken to Waterloo Station. A Rail Transportation Officer will provide you with a ticket for home and advise you of where your units will be reassembling and when you need to be there.'

Refreshed after a cup of tea and a cigarette, Neville followed the crowd of soldiers and shuffled along to the station, and down the platform to board a train. If anything, there were more crowds here than at the dock. Many of the troops were hanging out of the train windows as those on the platform were handing out more cigarettes, biscuits, cakes, hugs and kisses. Neville found a carriage and slumped in his seat.

'You're like a bad penny, Timber, always turning up.'

Neville looked up and found a familiar figure standing in the carriage doorway.

'Charlie! Boy, am I glad to see you.' Neville leapt up, his face beaming as he gave his friend's hand a firm shake.

'Just saw you getting on the train ahead of me,' Charlie replied, collapsing down into the seat next to Neville.

'Seen the others?' Neville had been wondering what had happened to everyone ever since he first got on the boat, hoping upon hope that they had made it back as well.

'Not yet,' Charlie said, 'but they weren't far behind when we were picked up. Hopefully they'll be back on terra firma in Blighty somewhere.'

'What do you think of all this?' Neville gesticulated towards the crowds on the platform with a sweep of his arm.

'Way I see it, Nev, is that people over here haven't had much to cheer about. The fact that so many of us got home must be a success of some sort. At least we still have an army, should Adolf get ambitious and decide to pop over for a holiday. Well, an army of sorts, anyway!' Charlie grinned.

Neville, still not convinced, grunted as the train shunted off. The motion of the train had a soporific effect, almost immediately, as the exertions of the last few days caught up with him. The next time he opened his eyes, the train was pulling in to Waterloo.

'Down the platform, please; orderly queue.'

Neville and Charlie were ushered off the train along with the rest of the troops. Bleary-eyed and groggy, they stood in line, waiting for their turn with the Rail Transportation Officers sat behind the tables at the end of the platform.

'And where is home for you?' A bespectacled, balding, middle-aged man with a kindly face smiled at Neville, when he finally got to the front.

'Hull, East Yorkshire,' replied Neville.

'And what unit do you belong to?'

'RASC, 50th Div. Or what's left of it.'

'Oh, plenty left, young man.' The transportation officer ran a podgy finger down a sheet of paper, until he found the details he was looking for. He handed Neville a ticket. 'Here is your ticket to Hull and home. Your unit will reassemble on Thursday 6 June at Haslington, Cheshire.' He gave Neville another paper. 'And here is your pass. You are required to report to your unit no later than 1400 hours on that date. Enjoy your short period of leave. Next.'

*   *   *

'I told you all along, Fred, that if any bugger survived it'd be that one.' Retired Police Constable George Castle grinned over his pint of beer in the Four In Hand. 'I could tell when I clipped him round the ear in that orchard for filching apples that he had an aura. You mark my words, Jerry better watch his Ps and Qs.' He raised his glass in salute to Fred and Neville, father and son. 'Good to see yer back, lad.'

Fred smiled and Neville raised his glass in return. He felt an echo of that ear sting as he remembered that clip, as George called it. Neville would have called it something different: a good walloping followed by another good walloping from his father for getting into trouble in the first place. He turned back to his father.

'It just wasn't right, Dad. There were flags, people cheering, almost a celebration. Anybody would think we'd come home having won the bloody war. We got our backsides well and truly kicked. They were better armed, better trained, better led . . .'

'Better spirited?' asked Fred.

'I wouldn't say that,' he said after a pause. 'They'll know they've been in a scrap. And they won't relish fighting us again if we can get reorganised.'

'We're still here, lad.' Fred took another sip of his pint. 'We lost a battle but we can still win a war.'

We're only just here, Neville thought, as the door of the Four In Hand opened and two Royal Air Force servicemen walked in. *And no thanks to you*, Neville scowled.

'What's that all about?' his father asked. Neville said nothing, but watched as the airmen came to the bar and ordered two pints of bitter.

'Where were you when we needed you?' Neville's look was intense, his voice challenging, his body tensing.

'I'm sorry, old boy, did you say something?' responded one of the airmen.

'Yes, where the hell were you when the bloody Germans were raining bombs on us at Dunkirk?' growled Neville.

'Doing our bit, I can assure you.'

'Well, you didn't do enough, skulking back in England and leaving us to it.'

'Are you calling us cowards?' The other airman spoke quietly, but such was the hush in the pub now that everyone could hear his words.

Neville felt his father's hand on his arm. 'Misunderstanding, gentlemen,' he said, giving his son a squeeze. 'Come on, lad, drink up.'

Without dropping eye contact, Neville drained his glass, his eyes blazing. As the airmen turned their backs, Neville could feel his father hauling him up and guiding him towards the door.

'Out!' his father snapped, pushing him out into the street. 'It's bad enough fighting the Germans, without you lot fighting each other.'

The first time Neville saw Edna Johnson was early one sunny June morning. He'd been at the camp at Haslington for a week and a half: a small, picturesque Cheshire village not far from Crewe. His nights had been punctuated by memories of Dunkirk, the sounds and images reverberating around his mind. So he was grateful for the start of each day, and the chance to take a walk around the village before breakfast to clear his thoughts. It was a short but scenic stroll, past the ivy-clad Crewe Cottage, the impressive Tudor Haslington Hall and into the main road just by the post office.

'Morning!' A cheerful female voice broke through his reverie. Neville turned to see a young lady pushing a handcart laden with bottles of milk. She was short and slim, with blonde hair pulled back into a ponytail. As she smiled at him, her blue eyes twinkled and her mouth revealed white, even teeth. Neville's heart lurched and his mouth went dry.

'Taking a walk from the camp?' asked the girl.

'Yes, yes, I, er . . .' Neville's pulse and mind raced. 'Can I help you with that cart? Delivering milk?' Neville groaned inwardly. *Of course she's delivering milk, you idiot!*

'If you don't mind, that would be kind of you.' There was that smile again. 'My name is Edna Johnson.'

'Neville, Nev Wood. Very pleased to meet you, Edna.' Neville stepped behind the cart and grunted as he realised how heavy it was. 'Goodness, how do you manage with this?'

'Oh, it's not too bad. Could be worse if we go back to milk churns and tin cans. Is it a bit heavy for you?'

'No, no. Light as a feather.' Neville suppressed a grimace and tried to walk without staggering.

'So where are you from?' Edna asked as she walked alongside the cart.

'Hull, East Yorkshire.'

'Are you likely to be here for long?' Neville's heart skipped a beat. Was he reading too much into the question?

'I'm hoping so. It's very nice around here.' He glanced across in Edna's direction. Together, they made their way down Main Street, past Fox's Sweet Shop, the Crewe Co-operative Friendly Society, Hilditch Garage and the Fox Inn. Edna scurried back and forth delivering the milk as Neville pushed the cart, which to his relief became lighter by the minute. By the time they reached the Old Vicarage, the milk had all gone.

'Well, I must be off,' said Edna. 'Let me take the cart back off you. Maybe I'll see you again one day?'

'Yes, I'm sure you will,' smiled Neville. *Bank on it*, he thought.

Back at camp he had missed breakfast. Not that it mattered in the circumstances.

'Where've you been, Timber?' asked Stan.

'Oh, just had a walk around the village.' Knowing looks and smiles passed between his friends.

'It must have been a nice walk. You look a bit star-struck. Maybe there's something in the milk!' Charlie said with a grin.

The whole routine of the camp was generally relaxed. On the one hand, perhaps, this was recognition of what the majority of men had been through and provided time for further recuperation. On the other, decisions needed to be taken up the chain of command on what next after the debacle of France. Added to which, they had little in the way of equipment, most of it abandoned, wrecked, around Dunkirk. Not that much of it had been worth saving.

Instead, the days back in camp were principally a series of debriefs, looking back on the Battle of France from beginning to end and extracting lessons to be learned. The RASC had been commended for their actions, successfully delivering shells to the guns until the last possible moment. As Neville chatted to Charlie, Stan, Alan, Jim and Freddie following his meeting with Edna, Corporal Clarke, who was new to the Company, walked by.

'More debriefs today, Corp?' asked Charlie. 'Picking over the wreckage that was the British Army?'

'No talk like that, Spandler. Today we will be doing some field work. You will be instructed on how to take cover under fire.'

They all looked at each other incredulously.

'Bugger off, Corp,' they all seemed to speak as one. 'We know a bloody sight more about taking cover under fire than you do.'

Clarke decided it wasn't the time to argue and moved away hastily.

Two days after Neville's meeting with Edna, there was a garden fete in the village with an open invitation to the soldiers. Maybe he might see her again? As he looked around the guests congregating on the lawn, Alan Such waved him over.

'Hey, Nev, come over and meet Madge,' he said. 'This is Edna's sister. We think you may already be acquainted with Edna?' He winked at Madge, who smiled. Neville coloured but maintained his poise.

'Pleased to meet you, Madge. Is, er, Edna here today?'

Madge shook her head. 'Sorry, she's working. But she has more milk to deliver later . . .'

That afternoon Neville joined Edna and once more took charge of the milk cart. They chatted happily, the time feeling as though it was passing too quickly. Although he'd only met her twice, Neville realised he was growing very fond of this pretty young girl. He was unsure if his feelings were reciprocated but plucked up the courage to ask her out.

'That would be very nice.' Edna smiled. 'I'll be finished work by six tomorrow. Shall we meet at seven by the Hall?'

The following evening was of the glorious midsummer sort. Edna suggested they went for a walk, slipping her petite hand inside Neville's and leading him towards a bridle path. They strolled across a number of fields in the warm evening sunshine, pausing by a small stream. To Neville, it all seemed so idyllic: the green fields and hedgerows, blue sky and sunshine, birds seeming to sing along to the music of the rippling water. It was such a far cry from the din and carnage of war. He turned to face Edna, a little uncertainly, before all reserve dissipated and they fell into each other's arms, kissing each other passionately.

Dusk was beginning to fall as they headed back to the village. Just before reaching the Hall, they lay down together on a grassy bank.

Neither spoke for a few moments, each just enjoyed the shared silence and the tranquillity of the warm evening. The quiet was only broken when Neville turned his head and said, 'I love you, Edna.'

Edna looked across at him in surprise, then she giggled.

'Oh, Nev, we hardly know each other.'

Neville persisted. 'I know I love you,' he said.

As Edna looked at him, her blue eyes seemed unfathomable. 'Come on,' she said, 'it's starting to get dark and I need to be home.' They walked through the village until they reached the terraced cottage.

'Maybe see you tomorrow?' asked Edna.

'You can be sure of it,' said Neville as they hugged and kissed each other goodnight.

As Neville turned to leave, Edna said, 'I am very fond of you, you know. And I really want to see you tomorrow.'

Neville smiled back. 'That'll do me just fine.'

He walked back to the camp unaware of his surroundings. He felt like he was walking on air. After everything he'd gone through, it felt as though life could be good after all. The future looked so bright and full of promise. But all his new-found happiness and optimism disappeared the moment he arrived back at camp to find Corporal Clarke waiting for him.

'And where the hell have you been?' asked Clarke. Without waiting for a reply he continued. 'We move out in the morning, 0700. You need to get your stuff ready.'

Neville was rooted to the spot, the enormity of those simple words echoing across the evening air. His feet no longer felt like they were walking on air but rather were set in concrete.

'Got to go.' Neville turned and ran from the camp.

'Wood!' Clarke shouted after him, but Neville didn't look back, dashing through the gathering gloom back to the village. When he got there, lungs bursting, he went straight back to the terraced cottage. Edna was still outside preparing the milk cart for the morning. She looked startled as Neville leaned on the gate gasping, clearly in distress.

'Neville? What on earth is the matter?' She placed her hand on his arm.

'We're leaving,' he blurted out. 'First thing tomorrow morning.'

Edna looked at him, her mouth open. Neville was unsure what to say next.

'Write to me,' pleaded Neville. 'I will come back to see you.'

'Of course I will,' said Edna. 'Do you know where you're going?'

Neville shook his head. 'No idea. But I'll get some leave and come back and see you.'

'Bless you, Neville.' She smiled. 'Now you must go back. Write to me when you know where you're going.' As they kissed each other, Neville couldn't drag himself away. But he knew he had to get back to camp, back to his duty.

The following day, Friday 21 June, was Neville's birthday. He was turning twenty, but didn't feel like celebrating. Instead, as the division pulled out at 0700 as planned, he peered through the grey drizzle of the early morning in the hope of a final, farewell glance of Edna. But the village streets were deserted.

'C'mon, Nev, it's your birthday.' Charlie patted his shoulder as the convoy headed for Crewe station. 'Why don't we come back on our next leave?' At that suggestion, Neville brightened a little.

'Yes. I'll write to her tonight and tell her.' Maybe the promise of seeing her again would help him through whatever the war was about to throw at him next.

'Welcome back to familiar territory, men.'

When the Division arrived at their next camp at Ilminster,

Captain Bonner was there to brief them. The camp was close to the area they'd occupied before embarking for France, though France wasn't their immediate destination this time round. 'The fightback starts here, but first we need to be sure that if Jerry pops over the Channel, we have a very enthusiastic reception awaiting him.' Bonner chuckled, but no one else did. Clearing his throat he continued. 'Divisional HQ will be based at Blandford and the 50th is now responsible for the coastline between Lyme Regis and Christchurch, a stretch of approximately seventy miles. We will be re-equipped, will work on our fitness and tactics, but above all we will stop the Germans in the sea should they decide to invade. They will not pass the 50th.' He said the words slowly for emphasis. 'That means building concrete, shell-proof machine-gun posts, gun emplacements and the laying of petrol pipes under the sea to provide a fiery welcome. We will accomplish this with great rapidity, as Jerry is unlikely to be gracious enough to wait until we are finished and issue an invitation.' He paused, looking around the room as he considered his next words. 'You all performed magnificently in France. But it doesn't change the fact that we were second best to a highly effective German war machine. However, should that machine choose to come across the water we will destroy it. No one has successfully invaded these islands since 1066 and that is damn well not about to change now.'

After the briefing had finished, Alan asked Neville what he thought about their next assignment. Neville looked at him blankly.

'Weren't you listening?' asked Alan.

'Some of it.'

'Come on, Timber,' Charlie chipped in. 'You can't keep moping about.'

'I can't get her out of my mind,' replied Neville. Edna back in Haslington seemed a long way away.

'Bearing in mind you've only known her a few days, would you get engaged?' asked Charlie.

'Oh, definitely, yes,' Neville replied without hesitating.

'At least there are still some signs of life,' smiled Charlie to the others.

The days settled into a new routine, beginning with the morning five-mile cross-country run. They could walk, run, creep, hop or skip, it didn't matter, but everyone had to finish. Alan showed he was still the fittest by giving Freddie Nichols a piggyback for half a mile.

'When we need that sick wagon, Freddie, you make damn sure you pick me up first,' gasped Alan as he set Freddie down with half a mile to go.

Neville was given charge of the Quartermaster's stores. Gradually the Division began to be resupplied and re-equipped. Six days after arriving at Ilminster, he received a letter from Edna. He ripped it open and his eyes scanned it feverishly. The letter was endearing and lifted his mood. But this mood change turned out to be temporary: later, as he stood at the bar of the local pub, the Stonemasons, he had some news for Alan, Charlie and Jim.

'I'm thinking of leaving the Company,' he announced. The others looked at him in surprise.

'I didn't realise we had a choice in the matter,' commented Jim.

'I'm thinking of volunteering for one of the suicide companies,' Neville explained. The others looked at each other in astonishment.

'Don't be so bloody daft!' exclaimed Alan.

'What on earth are you talking about?' asked Jim.

'I've heard they undertake missions like being dropped behind enemy lines and sabotaging things.'

'What things?' asked Jim.

'Fuel dumps, bumping off officers, stuff like that.'

'Okay,' said Alan. 'And what makes a driver in the RASC qualified to do that?'

'He hates bloody Germans,' answered Charlie.

'Pining after Edna, more like,' said Alan. 'You're no good to her dead, you know.' Neville said nothing further after that.

Wednesday 10 July was not a good day for the Company. Freddie came over and joined Jim and Alan. 'Have you heard?' he asked. 'Four of our lads have been in a car crash. Had to go and collect them, and two are being kept in hospital. On top of that the barber has shot himself.'

'Must have just cut Timber's hair,' murmured Jim drily.

Later in the month, the Division was resupplied with wagons. This time, rather than the Thornycrofts, they were kitted out with British-manufactured Bedford Commer 4x4s. Neville immediately took his out for a spin and his mood lightened.

'Pretty good,' he said when he returned and dismounted from the cab. 'I was sorry to see old Thorny go, but this is much better.' He grinned for what felt like the first time in weeks.

But a few days later he sought out Charlie, brandishing the letter he'd just been sent.

'You look like Neville Chamberlain waving that around like a fairy, Timber,' said Charlie. 'Although I suspect from the look on your face it isn't peace in our time?'

'She's finishing with me,' Neville spluttered with indignation. 'Thinks the distance is too much and we should move on.'

'I'm sorry,' Charlie said. 'Though ultimately, what did you really expect?'

'I thought she might wait.'

'For what?' Charlie snapped the question. Neville paused and considered.

'Well, I'm writing a nasty letter back telling her it's over between us.'

'Good idea, old son, you do that,' encouraged Charlie, adding, 'And maybe then we'll have the old Timber back.'

During August the Company moved twenty-three miles to Glastonbury. Camp life became more rigid and formal as the Division, as a whole, transitioned from coastal defence to preparation for offensive operational capability. All of which meant that soldiers sometimes had to be more creative to enjoy a bit of downtime.

'Great film on at The Street,' announced Charlie one afternoon at the NAAFI. '*The Great Dictator*, Charlie Chaplin. Anyone fancy it?' Alan, Freddie, Jim and Stan shook their heads.

'I'll go,' volunteered Neville. He was beginning to feel cooped up inside the camp and any chance to escape he'd take.

'But you'll need a pass to leave camp,' said Alan, 'and The Street is six miles away. Long walk.'

'Thought of that.' Charlie clicked his fingers. 'Come on, Timber, no time to waste.'

They left the NAAFI and walked across the square. 'So how are we getting out and getting there?' Neville was curious.

'Bonner is tied up for some time, so, as the captain's driver, I've been stood down until further notice,' Charlie explained. 'But if I drive out in the staff car, the guards won't blink twice. I need you in the back, pull yer cap down and salute smartly.'

'You've got to be kidding me,' gasped Neville. Impersonating Bonner?

'Oh, come on, let's live a little dangerously.' Charlie punched his arm. 'I know how tight you are so I'll pay for your cinema ticket, but no kissing me in gratitude in the back row.'

Trying to act calm, they strolled towards where Bonner's Humber Super Snipe was parked. Satisfied they were unobserved, Charlie got in the driver's seat and Neville slipped into the back.

'Nice,' he said, relaxing into the seat. 'Maybe I should become a captain.'

They drove slowly towards the camp gates. Charlie opened his window and waved at the guards as though everything was normal. In the back Neville pulled down his cap and saluted. The guards snapped to attention as they passed through the gate on to the open road.

'Told you,' grinned Charlie, putting his foot down on the accelerator. 'Piece of cake!'

The film was every bit as good as Charlie had promised. Neville was enjoying himself – after everything with Edna, it was good to be able to kick back with an old friend. There was something, too, about not being meant to be there – that bunking-off-school feeling – that added an extra frisson to proceedings.

'Now, remember, Timber,' said Charlie as they made their way back to camp, 'same routine on the way in as on the way out.'

They turned off the road between the camp gates. Charlie waved at the guards again, but as Neville saluted, he murmured, 'Uh-oh!' As he pulled the car to a halt a familiar figure with piercing blue eyes popped his head through the window, giving Neville a firm stare.

'Ah, Captain Wood, welcome back,' the real Captain – Captain Bonner – said with withering sarcasm. 'Would you care to get out of the car, please, gentlemen.'

'Yes, sir.' Neville and Charlie clambered out of the car. Neville felt sick as he stood before Bonner.

'A rapid promotion, Private Wood,' he fixed his eyes on Neville, 'but not one of which I have been made aware. I believe I am still in command of this Company. What have you to say for yourselves?'

Charlie and Neville stood to attention, looking directly ahead.

'Nothing, sir. Very sorry, sir,' Neville and Charlie mumbled.

'So you will be,' said Bonner. 'Taking a vehicle without consent is a serious business, particularly *my* vehicle.' He let the silence linger, prolonging the agony. 'You will both spend the night in the guard room on a charge of taking a vehicle without consent. You will be docked one week's pay and be confined to barracks for two weeks. That is, Spandler, with the exception of when a fully commissioned officer – me – wishes to use the car and its driver for official purposes. Now get out of my sight.'

As they trudged over to the guard room, Charlie turned to Neville and grinned. 'Great film, though,' he said.

As late summer turned to autumn, and autumn into winter, such opportunities for fun became fewer and further between. The winter of 1941 was almost as bitterly cold as 1940 and Neville spent much of it on Exmoor – the bleak, wintry theatre for progressively more intensive training for the 50th Division. By now the focus had completed its switch from coastal defence, particularly with victory in the Battle of Britain, to training for offensive action once again. Exmoor witnessed mock infantry battles, tank manoeuvres and artillery bombardment. Neville and the rest of the RASC used their new wagons to the full, ferrying troops and ammunition. The training was thorough and extensive: the only drawback in those preparations, on those cold and frozen moors, was the contrast to where the Division had been told their services had been earmarked for: the first Territorial Division to tackle the somewhat less snowy climes of North Africa.

'I pity these poor buggers.' Neville was standing beside his wagon with Alan Such, stamping his feet and blowing into his hands to keep warm. They had just travelled fifty miles from Taunton to Frome, in Somerset, ready to transport another group of infantry to Exmoor. The journey should have taken approximately an hour and a quarter but the roads were so treacherous with ice, it had taken nearly two.

'About bloody time!' The welcome from the sergeant of the Green Howards was as frosty as the weather. 'My lads have got two days on Exmoor. They didn't need the extra half an hour waiting for you lot to arrive. Right, lads, in you get.' The infantry piled into the back of the wagons as Neville and Alan each lit a cigarette.

'And you can put that out!' The sergeant was clearly not in the best of humour. 'Now, you know where you're taking us and when and where you're picking us up?'

'Yes, Sergeant.' Alan stood to attention; this was clearly not someone to mess with. Neville followed suit. 'We're to drop you at Luckwell Bridge and pick you up again at Roadwater at 1800 tomorrow.'

'Correct. And given my lads will have completed a thirty-mile forced march, fought a mock battle, slept in the open with their bollocks freezing off and marched another twenty miles to rendezvous with their transport, that transport won't be late, will it!' He glared, clearly making a statement rather than asking a question.

At 1700 the following day, Alan and Neville were in position at Roadwater, in good time. The wagons waited in line along the roadside for the infantry to trudge wearily off the moors. The skies were leaden and grey, matching the mood of the Green Howards as they trooped off the moor in single file.

'Bet you're glad that's done,' said Neville to a private as he helped him with his kit.

The infantryman was spent. But the sag in his shoulders wasn't just from physical exhaustion.

'Lost three lads out there last night,' he said, staring at the ground.

'Hell, I'm sorry.' Neville frowned. His complaints about the cold felt suddenly inadequate. 'Exposure?'

The infantryman shook his head. 'They were sleeping too close to the road, which was covered in snow. Tank drove over them. Killed all three instantly.' He looked up at Neville, tears in his eyes. 'Nineteen years old, for Christ's sake!'

'Really sorry.' Neville knew how inadequate that sounded, but didn't really know what to say.

It was a salutary reminder that even when you were well away from the front line, the effects of war were never far away. Neville was reminded of this again when he returned home on leave the following spring. With the hard winter of preparation complete, word came through that the first units in the Division would begin embarkation for North Africa from Liverpool from 21 April. All units were granted five days' pre-embarkation leave during late March and early April.

Neville took the long journey home from Somerset on Thursday 20 March, arriving in Hull late in the afternoon. He was home and yet at the same time he wasn't: the city he'd left had suffered repeated bombing raids with German planes dropping parachute bombs, or landmines as they were known. It was a prelude to Hull becoming the second most bombed town or city in the country, after London, with 95 per cent of all buildings suffering bomb damage and 150,000 citizens from a population of 320,000 being made homeless. The buses were still somehow running and Neville looked aghast through the grimy windows as his made its way through a rubble-strewn city centre and down Holderness Road. Few buildings remained undamaged and it was only as the bus made its way out towards East Hull that the damage became more sporadic.

Despite the damage, there was resilience on display as well. Bomb-ravaged shops proudly displayed signs proclaiming 'Open for business' as their owners did what remedial work they could in between chatting with and serving customers. Neville smiled at the spirit and determination of these people – his people – as they went about their daily lives as best they could. Even so, he arrived home with some trepidation and was relieved to see that 778 Holderness Road had so far escaped the trauma of bomb damage.

It was wonderful to see his family again, but there was someone else Neville was also hoping to catch up with. On the second day of leave, Neville went to see Joan, a neighbour in Seafield Avenue.

'You don't happen to have an address or number for Joyce, do you, please?' he asked. Neville had met Joyce at a dance in Hull in December during a previous period of leave and he knew Joan was a good friend of hers.

'Yes, I do, Neville, and I expect she will be very pleased to hear from you.'

Neville hastened home with the number as quickly as he could, picked up the telephone and dialled.

'Joyce?' he enquired impatiently.

'Yes,' came the reply, guarded over the crackly line.

'It's Neville, Joyce. Remember the dance just before Christmas?'

'Neville!' He could hear the joy in Joyce's voice and his heart leapt in return. 'I'm so pleased to hear from you. Where are you?'

'In Hull, back home for a short period of leave. Could I possibly see you, today or tomorrow perhaps?'

They met outside the Regal Cinema the following afternoon. Neville was early, counting down the minutes, when he saw her approaching. Joyce was wearing a light grey, two-piece skirt and jacket which emphasised the slenderness of her figure and the richness of her shoulder-length auburn hair. She smiled, a radiant, happy smile, as she came up to Neville, rested her hands on his forearms and leaned forwards.

'Welcome home, soldier.' She kissed him on the cheek. 'I can't tell you how pleased and relieved I am to see you again.'

Skipping the film, Neville and Joyce went for a walk instead, through the war-ravaged streets, chatting and laughing, almost oblivious to the desolation and destruction. They met again that evening and enjoyed a meal and drink together in one of the few city restaurants still standing and open. Just after nine they left the restaurant and headed into the twilight, catching a bus before the rigorously imposed blitz blackout meant the buses could no longer operate for the night. The bus rattled and shook as it made its way through the streets. Neville and Joyce sat side by side, holding hands, and holding on to the moment, gazing at one another.

'I love you, Neville.' Joyce leaned forward and kissed him tenderly. Neville felt as if he had been waiting for months and years for someone to say those words. He could have cried with happiness. Never mind Edna, right now no one he had ever met could compare with the girl nestled beside him. Twenty-four hours from now, he knew, he'd be on his way back to Somerset and the final preparations before the journey to North Africa began. What would happen there, and whether he would even return, he couldn't be sure. That, though, was all for the future.

Right now, this felt the best night of his life.

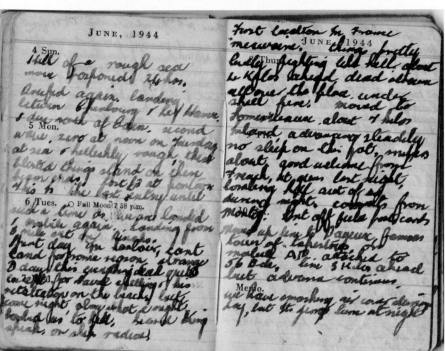

Pages from one of Neville's diaries, kept throughout the war. He recorded his experiences daily, almost without fail.

Neville at eighteen having joined up in May 1939. The surname Wood meant that 'Timber' was a natural nickname.

Charlie Spandler had a great sense of humour which he retained after the war when he became a police officer.

CERTIFIED COPY OF ATTESTATION.

No. *T/81874*   Name *Wood Neville Dalby*   Corps *R.A.S.C*

Questions to be put to the Recruit before Enlistment.

1. What is your full name and permanent postal address?
   1.   *Neville Dalby*
       (Christian Names)
       Wood
       (Surname)
       Naemere Rd. (Address)
       (Address)

2. In or near what Parish or Town were you born?
   2. In the Parish of *Lowlepops*
     In or near the Town of
     In the County of

3. (A) Are you a British subject?
     (B) Nationality of parents at their birth
   3. (A)
        (Father)   (Mother)

4. What is your trade or calling?
   4.

Under the provisions of Sections 10 (1) of the Territorial and Reserve Forces Act, and 99 of the Army Act, if a person knowingly makes a false answer to any of the following four questions he renders himself liable to punishment.

5. (A) What was your age (in years) last birthday?
     (B) Day, month and year of birth?
   5. (A) *27.6.19—* (years)
       (B)

6. Are you married, widower or single?
   6. *Single*   *No*

7. Do you now belong to, or have you ever served in the Royal Navy, the Army, the Royal Air Force, the Royal Marines, the Supplementary Reserve, the Territorial Force or Army, the Army Reserve, the Air Force Reserve, the Auxiliary Air Force, any Naval Reserve, or in any Dominion or Colonial Force? If so, state particulars of ALL engagements
   7.

8. Have you truly stated the whole, if any, of your previous service?
   8. *Yes*

9. Are you willing to be attested for service in the Territorial Army for the term of four years* (provided His Majesty should so long require your services), for the County of†
   to serve in the‡
   and to be posted to§
   9. *Yes*

10. Have you received a notice paper (Army Form E 501A) stating the liabilities you are incurring by enlisting, and do you understand and are you willing to accept them?
   10. *Yes*

†Here insert County.   ‡Here insert Corps.   §Here insert Unit

* A W.O., N.C.O., or man will be discharged on reaching the age laid down for discharge in paragraph 210, Territorial Army Regulations, unless retention is specially sanctioned.

I, *N. D. Wood* .... do solemnly declare that the above answers made by me to the above questions are true, and that I am willing to fulfil the engagements made.

Neville Dalby Wood .... SIGNATURE OF RECRUIT.
.... Signature of Witness.

OATH TO BE TAKEN BY RECRUIT ON ATTESTATION.

I, *N. D. Wood* .... swear by Almighty God that I will be faithful and bear true allegiance to His Majesty King George the Sixth, His Heirs, and Successors, and that I will, as in duty bound, honestly and faithfully defend His Majesty, His Heirs, and Successors, in Person, Crown, and Dignity against all enemies, according to the conditions of my service.

CERTIFICATE OF MAGISTRATE OR ATTESTING OFFICER.

I, ... do hereby certify that, in my presence, all the foregoing Questions were put to the Recruit above-named, that the Answers written opposite to them are those which he gave to me, and that he has made and signed the Declaration, and taken the oath at .... on this .... day of .... 19......

     { Signature of Justice of the Peace, Officer,
     { or other person authorized to attest Recruits.

I certify that the above is a true copy of the Attestation of the above-named Recruit.
.... Approving Officer.

III.

CERTIFIED COPY OF AGREEMENT FOR GENERAL SERVICE AND FOR SERVICE OUTSIDE THE UNITED KINGDOM AFTER EMBODIMENT.

I, (No.) .... (Rank) *Dvr*
(Name) *Neville Dalby Wood*
(Unit) *RASC*   (Corps) *50 (N) Dw RASC*

HEREBY AGREE that in the event of an Act of Parliament being passed for that purpose in case of a grave National Emergency I may be required to serve under the following conditions:—

*(a) to serve outside the United Kingdom after the embodiment of the Territorial Army;

(b) to be available for general service, and therefore liable to be transferred to any corps, and posted to any unit of the Regular Forces or Territorial Army after embodiment.

.... (Station.)   *Neville Dalby Wood* (Signature of Man.)
.... (Date.)   (Signature of Witness.)

*To be deleted in the case of a man enlisted under Territorial Army Regulations, 1936, paragraph 187.

Timber's attestation on joining the army. Attestation is the process of swearing allegiance to the monarch and being formally accepted into her service as a member of the armed forces.

A picture which appeared in the *Hull Daily Mail* of troops returning from the beaches of Dunkirk. Timber is just above left of centre with a cap rather than a tin hat.

TROOPS of the BEF arrive at a south-east coast port after being saved from the beaches at Dunkirk.

DRILL FOR THE STEN MACHINE CARBINE.   *Wood*

1. METHOD OF CARRYING.

   The carbine to be carried slung on the right shoulder, butt downwards, sling to the front and keep in position with the right hand grasping the butt, thumb to the front, arm fully extended.

2. POSITION OF ATTENTION.

   The carbine to be carried as above. Bring the left foot smartly up to the right into the position of attention.

3. STAND AT EASE.

   Keeping the carbine as in the position of attention, carry the left foot about 12" to the left, so that the weight of the body rests equally on both feet, the left arm to be kept in the position of attention.

4. STAND EASY.

   Grasp the centre of the sling with the right hand and relax the muscles of the body.

5. CAUTION: PARADE, PLATOON, SQUAD, ETC.

   Grasp the butt with the right hand, right arm fully extended, thumb to the front as in the position of attention and assume the correct position of stand at ease.

6. DRESSING.

   Keeping the carbine steady at the right side, turn the head and eyes to the right (or left) at the same time extend the left arm, back of the hand upwards, fingers partially closed, knuckles touching the point of the right shoulder of the man on the left, and take up the dressing.

7. EYES FRONT.

   Keeping the carbine steady at the right side, turn the head and eyes to the front at the same time cutting the left arm smartly to the side, and resume the position of attention.

8. MARCHING AT ATTENTION.

   The carbine will be carried as in the position of attention, and the left arm will swing freely from the shoulder, as high as the waist belt in front and as high as possible in the rear.

9. MARCHING AT EASE.

   Keeping the carbine in the position of attention, grasp the centre of the sling with the right hand.

10. "FOR INSPECTION PORT ARMS".

    (a) Grasp the sling as near to the barrel as possible with the left hand on the count of "One", removing the carbine from the shoulder on the count of "two-three".
    (b) Grasp the small of the butt with the right hand, forefinger along the trigger guard, to the count of "one", pause on "two-three".
    (c) Grasp the body with the left hand, at the point of balance, clear of the cocking handle, knuckles down and outside the sling on the count of "One"
    (d) Taking the time from the right hand man who will give a tap (by pushing back the cocking handle slightly with the forefinger of the left hand and releasing it) to the count of "One" pausing on the "Two-three".

Following the defeat in France, the 50th Division re-grouped and re-trained in Cheshire, in the use of the Sten gun among other things.

Before embarking for the Middle East and North Africa, Timber was stationed in the Cotswolds.

The landscape soon changed as the 50th moved with urgency into Iraq.

In a brief moment of respite from battle, the men of the Eighth Army enjoyed swimming in the sea at Alexandria in Egypt. Neville is standing on the far right of the photograph.

Timber on guard duty in the Western Desert.

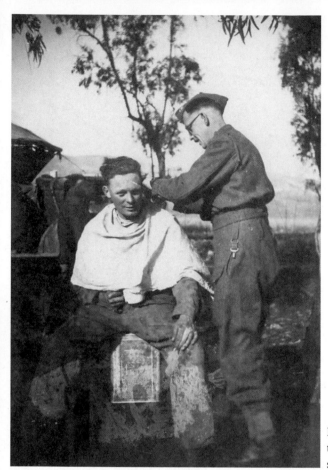

Life in camp was often routine, including the need to maintain a short-back-and-sides haircut.

Timber photographed during a secondment to Royal Army Service Corps Headquarters. He is fourth from the right in the back row.

During his time in the Western Desert, Timber visited Cairo on a number of occasions including for leave. One such memorable occasion was to Giza and its iconic monuments.

A happy group of leave-takers in Cairo. Timber is at the back on the right.

Chapter 5

Voyage to North Africa

May 1941 to July 1941

————

'Wow, just look at that!' Neville exclaimed, his eyes wide with wonder.

On the morning of Thursday 22 May, the troop ship *SS Almanzora* began its long journey from the Glasgow docks to North Africa. Neville and the rest of the RASC had arrived in Scotland the day before – retrained, re-equipped, reinvigorated and ready to take the war to the enemy. The *Almanzora* had cleared the mouth of the River Clyde by 1000 hours to begin its journey far out into the Atlantic Ocean before steaming south, clear of the prying eyes of enemy aircraft. Neville was one of those standing on the bow rail as the ship cleared the boom, when the calls came.

'Look to the front of the ship!' another soldier was shouting and pointing.

On the horizon was a phalanx of warships – an awesome array of naval power, grey leviathans bristling with menace. A sailor came to stand beside Neville at the bow rail, his eyes scanning the line of ships with an expert eye.

'You boys must be important with a chaperone like that.' He nodded to the ships ahead.

'What are they?' asked Neville.

The sailor's eyes wrinkled as he squinted into the glare. 'Six destroyers; can't tell which ones. But that brute there is HMS *Repulse*, battlecruiser, Renown class. First World War job but still a beauty, isn't she? Look at those guns! Four fifteen-inchers.'

Neville admired the sleek lines of the battlecruiser as it grew in size the closer they got.

'And the aircraft carrier?' he asked.

'HMS *Ark Royal*. A name to cherish. First carrier we've built where the hangars and flight deck are part of the whole of the ship rather than bolted on. Came out of Cammell Laird in 'thirty-seven, she did. Well, they'll look after us.' He slapped Neville on the back as he moved away to resume his duties.

Minutes later Alan Such came over and joined Neville. The sea breeze whipped past them, making them shiver and requiring them to raise their voices.

'That lot coming with us?' Alan pointed towards the warships.

'Six destroyers, one Renown-class battlecruiser, and one new aircraft carrier with an integral design,' replied Neville, letting the sailor's knowledge trip off his tongue.

'Bloody know-all, aren't we?' observed Alan. Neville tapped the side of his nose and grinned.

'Come on,' said Alan. 'Have you seen where you're sleeping yet?'

The *Almanzora* itself was an armed merchant cruiser. It had the appearance of a cruise ship with six six-inch guns bolted on wherever they could find a space. The sleeping quarters were cosy, to say the least. Cabins had been removed, with rows of hammocks strung side by side across the two lower decks. As Alan and Neville walked over, Jim Oliver was with Charlie, eyeing his allotted hammock with suspicion.

'A hammock! How the hell am I supposed to sleep in that?'

'What do you expect, Ollie, the Captain's cabin?' Charlie said. 'Stop moaning and try it out.'

Neville tried not to laugh as Jim put his foot in the air.

'It's a hammock, for goodness' sake, not a bloomin' thorough-bred,' chuckled Charlie. The three of them heaved Jim up and into the hammock a little too vigorously.

'He's in,' said Neville.

'He's out again,' laughed Charlie as Jim did a somersault with the hammock and hit the deck with a thud.

The following morning the Company were all on parade on deck. As they waited at ease, Neville glanced around him at the two lines of seventy soldiers of 522 Company. His mind drifted back two years to Durham, and then to France. Many familiar faces remained, but equally many new men had been integrated during the retraining in England. Good men at that, bright, keen to learn, comradely. To his right was Nick Jones. Always seemed to smile, did Nick, and crikey, that parting running down the middle of his hair was as precise as Moses parting the Red Sea. On his left, Joe Franklin was a good-looking fellow, darkish complexion with slightly unruly, wavy hair. Serious, but calm and determined. Then there was Harry Minchin, Peter Helmand, Stan King, Alfie Longstaffe: all good north-countrymen, just the sort to put Jerry in his place.

'Look smart there, eyes front.'

The shout came from Sergeant Rodney Stuart, standing at the end of the line with Neville's immediate NCO, Corporal Jeff Kitchen. Both were experienced soldiers, not wet behind the ears like some.

'Attention!'

Sergeant Major Arnold Taylor began his prowl up and down the lines of men on parade. His gait was slow, deliberate, each step carefully placed heel to toe like a big cat stalking its prey. His eyes flicked back and forth, scanning, critiquing, demanding. His ramrod-straight back emphasised his height, making him look even taller and more imposing in the process. He stood in front of the parade, head swivelling back and forth like an agitated owl. Beyond, Neville could see the watching sailors grinning as they went about their daily duties.

'Eyes right!' Taylor barked. Heads snapped to the right in unison as their new Captain, Raymond Norfolk, marched smartly to join the sergeant major. Bonner had been reassigned, leaving Norfolk in his previous position of command. He appeared competent – for an officer, that is. Next to the imposing figure of Taylor, he appeared slighter and shorter, a pencil moustache bristling under his nose.

'At ease, men,' Norfolk began. 'Now—'

But he got no further as the ship's sirens fired up, filling the air with their urgent warnings. 'Below deck, now!' he shouted, the rest of his sentence drowned out as the guns of the escort ships opened up. The sky filled with shell bursts as the drone of enemy aircraft grew louder. As Neville and the others hurried to the bulkhead doors, the crew of the *Almanzora* rushed past them in the opposite direction to man the guns. Around them, the sea began to erupt in huge plumes of water as bombs peppered the convoy. Then Neville was below deck and the sounds were muffled. But even here, he could feel the ship shudder as bombs fell nearby and the guns pumped explosives into the sky. They could still hear the scream of an aircraft as it plunged towards the sea, and the boom of the explosion on impact. The raid lasted no more than ten minutes, but was only the first of four that day. As far as Neville was concerned, the sooner the journey into the Atlantic took them out of range of shore-based enemy aircraft, the better.

But just because they were out of range of enemy aircraft didn't mean that the convoy was safe. Sunday 25 May dawned grey and stormy, with the ship rising and plunging through the deepening swell. It was one of those mornings where the sky started dark and seemed to stay dark. As Neville, Nick, Joe and Charlie went on deck to get some air, they noticed the crew of the *Almanzora* huddled together in small groups, many shaking their heads or looking to the heavens. The soldiers staggered, as if drunk, to the nearest railing on the starboard side of the ship near to a group of three of the crew.

'What's up? Are we sinking?' asked Charlie with a grin.

'Eh?' One of the sailors looked up, bemused.

'Are we sinking?' Charlie repeated. 'Because by the looks on your faces we should all be heading to the lifeboats.'

The three sailors shuffled closer. 'Not funny, mate!' scowled one. '*Hood*,' muttered another.

'HMS *Hood*?' queried Joe.

'Sunk,' came the morose response.

There was a moment of silence as the friends all looked at each other in bewilderment.

'There must be some mistake; she's invincible,' muttered Neville.

'Clearly not!' one of the sailors snapped.

'What happened?' Neville asked.

'Sunk by the *Bismarck* yesterday. We've heard she blew apart. Shell must have hit her magazine. Poor buggers, no one will have survived that.'

They stood in silence, heads bowed, absorbing the enormity of the news. The pride of the Royal Navy, destroyed. It seemed, temporarily at least, to shatter the belief in the invincibility of Britain's iron wall.

'Let's hope the *Bismarck* doesn't come near us,' one of the sailors said to nods from the others. It was unclear whether the remark was motivated by a thirst for revenge or a desire for self-preservation.

The following day, Neville watched as four of the destroyer escorts veered away from the convoy. Sirens whooped in salute as the ships headed west-south-west at full speed, their wakes leaving a long trail in the calm sea.

'Leaves us a bit exposed,' said Jim, who was standing by him.

'Bet they're after the *Bismarck*,' Neville replied. 'Got to be done; and hopefully they will stop the bugger coming anywhere near us!'

The answer came the next day. Neville and the rest of 522 Company were gathering for parade on deck when Neville heard a distant rumble like the threatening growl of a violent thunderstorm. But the sky appeared clear, the weather fair.

'Gunfire!' shouted a sailor, running by.

The parade was forgotten as everyone, soldier and sailor, looked towards the sound of the guns. Nothing was visible but for seventy-four minutes the deep rumble washed over the waves, increasing in intensity one minute, lapsing to relative calm the next. Then, just after 1000 hours, the gunfire stopped. There was an abrupt silence, save for the whistle of the breeze and the rhythmic beat of the ship's engines as she ploughed through the light swell. No one spoke. Quietly, and without discussion, everyone fell back into their normal routine, and 522 were ordered to a belated parade. It wasn't until 1130 hours that the ship's Tannoy crackled into life to explain what had happened.

'Good morning, this is your Captain speaking. I have marvellous news. The gunfire we heard this morning was the Home Fleet engaging the battleship *Bismarck*. The *Bismarck* has been sunk, *Hood* has been avenged and a serious threat to this convoy has been eliminated. God save the King!'

Cheers erupted across the ship. Almost simultaneously, further cheering could be heard across the convoy and the sirens whooped incessantly in celebration. It was a rare but much appreciated victory over the enemy.

'Boots, shirts, trousers! Anything you're wearing for bananas, oranges, pineapples, limes or coconuts.'

On Wednesday 4 June, the *Almanzora* passed through the boom of Freetown, Sierra Leone, at 0730 in the morning. Forty minutes later, the anchor was dropped in a harbour teeming with life and crowded with ships of all shapes and sizes. Sierra Leone was a British crown colony and the Royal Navy base in Freetown was a key staging post for Allied traffic in the South Atlantic.

Within minutes of the ship anchoring it was surrounded by hundreds of bumboats swarming like bees round a honey pot. Grinning locals held aloft whatever fruit they had and pulled their shirts and trousers to convey the terms of the trade. Unwilling to barter with His Majesty's kit, Neville and the other troops threw pennies in the water, shouting encouragement as the more audacious Freetowners dived in, resurfacing to applause as they brandished the retrieved coin.

The tops of the hills surrounding the town were shrouded in mist. June was in the rainy season and several times during the day the rain hammered down, hissing and stinging, the deck of the ship running in water. They were in harbour for two days, on board the ship. On the Friday, the *Almanzora* weighed anchor and cruised slowly through the boom with an escort of two destroyers and the cruiser HMS *Exeter*. One troop ship was missing from the convoy having been involved in a collision with a cruiser in the harbour. Those at sea set a southerly course and ramped up the knots.

Two days later, shortly after lunch, the troops were called on deck. Some were bemused, others grinned and some were heard to utter 'uh-oh'. Sitting on a chair in the middle of the deck was Chief Petty Officer Simmons, wearing just his shorts, a cardboard crown on his head and a garden pitchfork in his hand. This represented the Trident of King Neptune. As the troops were lined up, Neville glanced at a row of buckets of water warily. Once in line the stentorian voice of the bosun carried across the ship.

'Stand still or incur the wrath of King Neptune!' he thundered. He eyed the troops with a dismissive glare, then turned to the cardboard king of the sea. 'Your Majesty, King Neptune, at 1400 hours we will be crossing the line of the equator. We have a ship full of equatorial virgins, your Majesty. Will you provide your consent for these wretched souls to be initiated and transformed to Shellbacks to pay homage to your Majesty as we cross the equator?' Neptune looked at the troops in front of him and nodded.

'You! Step forward!' Neville, Joe and Alan were at the end of the line and found themselves shuffled forward to stand before the Roman god of the sea.

'In kindly consideration of His Majesty Neptunus Rex,' the bosun continued, 'you are required to swear allegiance to His Royal Highness and to cease to masquerade as men of the sea, which is a most heinous insult to His Majesty. You are required immediately to remove your shirts and place them upon your head. You will then hop on one leg as you recant and make plea with His Majesty with the words: "We honour Your Majesty King Neptunus Rex and wish to receive your blessing through baptism."'

Neville glanced at Joe and Alan. *Really?* The others looked as unsure as he felt, but they did as demanded, hopping and reciting the words, while buckets of sea water were thrown over them, drenching them from head to toe. The baptism was concluded when a hosepipe was turned on, dousing them with a further blast of freezing water.

'You may cease your dance.' The bosun grinned. 'You are initiated as Shellbacks and shall receive your certificates from His Majesty's handmaiden, Able Seaman Canham.'

The journey from Freetown was almost directly south. As the *Almanzora* left the equator astern, the weather cooled, the wind picked up and the sea welcomed the ships with an increasing swell. Training continued: Neville and the others were given daily lectures on Arabic and Egyptian language and customs, as well as lessons in desert navigation. That helped relieve the rolling monotony of being at sea, even if desert training seemed utterly out of context with the black, roiling sea. On Tuesday 17 June the convoy changed course, rounding the Cape of Good Hope. As the wind howled, the troops were confined below, banned from the deck. The ship rolled violently from side to side, throwing men and equipment into sickness and disarray.

It was with some relief that on Friday 20 June the coast of Africa once again came into view. At 0630, Durban was sighted. The convoy entered a harbour already bursting with huge ships of war, including the battleship HMS *Barham*, her four twin fifteen-inch guns pointing threateningly out to sea. After what seemed like an age, the *Almanzora* docked at 1115 hours, by which point Neville and the rest of 522 Company were lining the side of the ship staring longingly at terra firma and one of the finest, cleanest cities many had seen.

It was worth the wait. The Durban welcome was warm, with servicemen receiving special treatment, including free rides on municipal transport, special concessions at cinemas and free concerts at the City Hall. Once allowed on shore, Neville, Charlie, Alan, Nick and Joe walked off the *Almanzora* and headed into Durban to explore. Neville's legs felt strange after the weeks spent on the ship, but they recovered quickly. In high spirits, he and his friends ambled into the city.

'Well, would you look at that!' exclaimed Nick. He pointed down the main street and they all followed his gaze to a familiar sight.

'Woolworths!' laughed Charlie. 'Home from home.'

As they wandered through the store, Neville was delighted to find himself somewhere so familiar. And yet, at the same time, that familiarity found him missing home immensely.

'Smith Street,' Alan consulted some notes he had made. 'Let's check out what's on down here.' They turned right just before the Albany Hotel and headed for the Playhouse cinema – a strange building that looked like a mock-Tudor mansion, with a church spire in the middle of the roof.

'Ah, bright view.' Neville clapped his hands like a child in a sweetshop. 'Laurel and Hardy in *A Chump at Oxford*. Anyone joining me?' Without waiting for a reply he headed eagerly into the cinema. The others followed him in and they all quickly lost themselves in the hilarious antics of the great comedy duo. When the film had finished, they took the opportunity to find a pub to have a drink before returning to the ship.

'So, what's the birthday boy fancy doing tomorrow?' asked Charlie as he slapped Neville on the back. 'At least you've made twenty-first, Timber. I've got to survive another two and a half weeks yet!'

Neville smiled, enjoying the welcome taste of a pint. 'Durban will do just fine.'

Saturday 21 June 1941, Neville's twenty-first birthday, dawned bright and warm. Army duty did not stop for a special birthday, although Sergeant Major Taylor managed to growl 'Happy birthday, lad' at him. 'Don't you dare come back drunk,' he added with a wink.

At 1300 hours the Durban birthday bash began. Neville, Charlie, Alan, Nick, Joe and Harold left the ship. It was a glorious day, the

sun shining brightly in an azure-blue sky, and they decided to walk
along the beach before exploring the city further. As teatime
approached they headed for the corner of Beach Walk and the
Esplanade to the YMCA. Here, as a welcome change from ship
rations, they enjoyed a good tea of sandwiches and cake which,
following a quiet word from Charlie, arrived with a candle.

'Go on then, Timber, blow and wish,' ordered Charlie.

Neville did as bid and sat back smiling.

'Don't look so smug,' grinned Alan. 'If you can make Joyce
appear for a birthday-night celebration, then you can fetch me some
candles and I'll blow out the damn lot!'

After a whip-round to treat Neville to his tea, they headed
further up the Esplanade to the Durban Ice Arena. Several bumps
and bruised egos later they moved on again to the Durban Open
Air Amphitheatre. When the friends arrived, a band was playing
Glenn Miller's 'Little Brown Jug', and a mix of locals and servicemen
and women were dancing in the open area in front of the stage. The
birthday party danced, laughed and drank – and in Harold's case
managed to become as drunk as a lord.

'Well, it might be your twenty-first, Timber, but I expect you can
walk back to the ship. As for Harold; well, I don't think he can walk
anywhere.' Charlie looked down at Harold prostrate on the concrete
steps but still managing to slur along to 'Moonlight Serenade'.

'Rickshaw!' said Joe. 'Won't cost much and you can't come to
Durban without riding a rickshaw.'

The group heaved Harold to his feet and left the amphitheatre.
Outside, a line of rickshaws stretched down the Esplanade, present-
ing a riot of colour in the gloom of the fading light. The rickshaws
were based on a Japanese design, high-backed and beautifully
draped in multicoloured cloth. The pullers matched their vehicles,
decked out in beaded headdresses and traditional costumes. They

got Harold slumped in one with Alan as his chaperone. Joe went with Nick and Neville went with Charlie.

'Very romantic. Give us a kiss, lover boy,' grinned Charlie.

'Sod off,' laughed Neville.

Great birthday, he thought to himself, as he sat back and enjoyed the ride.

The war, though, didn't stop for birthday celebrations. The following day word came through that Germany had declared war on Russia and had launched significant attacks. This was quickly followed by the news that the war was to resume for 522 Company: the *Almanzora* would sail in convoy at 1430 the next day, destination Aden.

As the convoy headed north-north-east, the heat continued to ratchet up. The temperature of the sea reached eighty-eight degrees and the dry wind that blew off it was like the searing breath of a blast furnace. The convoy reached Aden on Friday 4 July, at which point it dispersed, leaving the ships to travel independently. The *Almanzora* left Aden the following day, passing through the Gates of Hell, the name for a narrow stretch of water flanked by two searingly hot deserts like the walls of an oven, and on into the Red Sea. Their destination was close now. Money was changed into piastres and a full kit inspection was completed under the discerning eye of Sergeant Major Taylor.

'How are you going to carry that lot, Wood?' he demanded, looking at the amount of kit Neville was carrying.

'I can manage, Sergeant Major,' responded Neville, trying not to buckle under the weight.

'Pop down to the galley, Wood,' replied Taylor.

'Sir?' asked Neville, puzzled.

'Pull up the kitchen sink, lad; it's the only thing you're missing!'

Much to his chagrin Neville had to throw his pot and plates overboard.

'He who travels lightest travels furthest, Wood.' The Sergeant Major turned on his heel to continue his inspection.

On Wednesday 9 July, the *Almanzora* dropped anchor in Port Said. The air shimmered in the heat, leaving nothing to see but sand and rocks. It was an environment to which they would become well accustomed.

Back on extremely dry land, the Company travelled by train to the largest army camp in Egypt, Markaz 33, about eighty miles west of Cairo. The journey from Port Said whistled the troops through desolate passing countryside: Neville and the others were more interested in watching the local Egyptians jumping on and off the moving train at will. The British troops were badgered incessantly by locals selling cheap watches, wallets, rotten-looking food or pleading for baksheesh. En route they passed prisoner-of-war camps crowded with Italian soldiers and numerous aerodromes with hundreds of fighter and bomber aircraft.

Once into camp they were allocated tents, given tea and a good meal, following which Alan suggested that, having been cooped up on a ship and then a train, it would be a great idea to go for a run in the relative cool of the evening. This seemed fine to begin with, until it became clear that Neville and Alan had not been giving the ship lecture about the art of desert navigation the attention the subject deserved.

'It's not getting any nearer! I thought you said you knew how far we've come?' Neville gasped, hands on knees, bathed in sweat.

'Well, this is a lesson learned,' grunted Alan. 'The distance in the desert can be deceiving.'

'Can be! Damn well *is*, you mean. No *can be* about it.'

'Can't even say it's just over the next hill,' groaned Alan. 'There are no hills, just mile after mile of sand and rocks. Come on, slacker, can't be far now. Can it?' He set off at a gentle jog, Neville trailing in his wake, muttering darkly. An hour and a half after they had begun their 'short' run, they staggered back into camp. Neville was never so grateful to see a city of tents.

Camp routine was quickly established. Reveille rent the desert air at 0630, breakfast was at 0730 and parade at 0900. During the day the temperature rocketed above 100 degrees Fahrenheit, so 1130 to 1600 hours was the time for a siesta before tea at 1730, a visit to the camp cinema, then bed by 2230. Although most days were relatively calm, Alan and Neville's run in the desert wasn't the only day to end badly.

'I'll kill the swines!' shouted Neville, his face red with anger. Alan and Joe started and looked around the gloom of the tent.

'No Jerrys here, Nev,' said Joe.

Neville was frantically patting his pockets and turning them all out systematically. Alan and Joe looked on. Finally, like a deflated balloon, Neville collapsed into a chair.

'Gone!' he exclaimed.

'What's gone?' asked Alan.

'Cigarette case,' replied Neville. 'Some swine has nicked my cigarette case.'

'Not the end of the world, Nev,' said Joe. 'You can have some of my ciggies until you can get some more.'

'Bugger the cigarettes,' grunted Neville. 'That case had the only pictures I had of Joyce and Phil.' Neville had met Phil at a dance in Glastonbury and she had quickly formed an attachment to him.

'Ah.' Joe and Alan glanced at each other, now understanding the gravity of the calamity. 'Airmail home, then?' Alan tried to be practical.

Neville snorted. 'Joyce certainly but not Phil. She's a bit too keen for my liking. If I ask for another photo it may encourage her.' Resolved to action, Neville found some paper and began his letter to Joyce.

Over the next few days, rumours were rife regarding the future deployment of 50th Division. Some had heard they were to be sent to Syria or Turkey, others Gibraltar, although they couldn't fathom why that would be. Another rumour was that it might be Cyprus. On Friday 25 July it became clear they wouldn't have to wait much longer to find out. The Division were ordered to pack after dinner, ready to leave that night or early the following morning.

At 0400, 522 Company left camp, passed through Ismailia and arrived at Port Said at 1100 hours. There, the Company and the East Yorkshires boarded the mine-laying cruiser HMS *Abdiel* and sailed with all speed for their next port of call.

Chapter 6

Cyprus

July 1941 to November 1941

During the summer of 1941, British forces had been forced to evacuate Greece. Then Crete, a bastion of the Eastern Mediterranean, had been captured by the Germans. The strategic importance of Cyprus as a stepping stone to Palestine and Syria rapidly became critical, which was why 50th Division were dispatched there with all haste to put the island into a state of defence. Their orders from General Officer Commander in Chief Middle East, General Auchinleck, were simple but unequivocal: 'Hold the island for HM Government.'

The task was huge. There were airfields and roads to be constructed, railways and docks to be reorganised. Supplies of food, water, petrol and ammunition for 34,000 troops had to be brought in and stored. Defensive positions, including some from which there would be no retreat, had to be created.

At 2345 hours on Saturday 26 July 1941, Neville and the rest of 522 Company disembarked the *Abdiel* into the chaos that was Cyprus. Once on shore, they marched twenty miles to the transit camp and prepared to fortify an island.

★   ★   ★

'Gary Waller?' asked Joe, smiling at the young Cypriot.

'That's a very English name for a Cyp,' murmured Nick with a frown.

'No, idiot!' exclaimed Joe. 'When you asked me what to call him I meant gharry-wallah, not Gary Waller. This magnificent, glorified horse and cart is called a gharry and the driver is a wallah.'

'My name Yange.' The slightly built, boyish-looking Cypriot driver stood by his vehicle bobbing his head. 'You no drive, me drive, good price,' he grinned and bobbed.

'I have no intention of driving it,' exclaimed Neville in surprise.

'Maybe not,' said Alan, 'but I gather some of the lads have been coming into town, throwing the Cyps off their vehicles and having gharry races up and down the streets.' This caused Yange to bob even more.

The starting point for 50th Division was Famagusta on the east coast, a delightful medieval walled city with the deepest harbour in Cyprus. It was Joe who had suggested taking a gharry across the city to the Cathedral of St Nicholas, which had been transformed, in the days of the Ottoman Empire, into the Lala Mustafa Pasha Mosque. Once everyone had climbed in, the vehicle set off at a trot, Yange encouraging the horses with gentle wrist flicks of his whip. They were heading down the Canbulat Yolu when the gharry slowed to a walking pace.

'Trouble ahead, by the looks of it,' muttered Alan. The road ahead was a hubbub of people and vehicles, Cypriot and British Army.

'Pull over, please.' Neville tapped Yange on the back and the five of them dismounted to the roadside. The scene was chaotic. Some Cypriots were being frogmarched away by the local police, others were a short distance away, taunting, while more locals just stood by looking bemused. An ambulance was by the roadside and British

Military Police were trying to keep the crowd back and restore some kind of order.

'Harold!' Neville spotted a familiar figure and waved for him to come over hurriedly. As he got close, Neville could see he had a gash above his left eye and a dark, dry rivulet of blood ran down his left cheek. 'Hey, what's happened to you? And what the hell's going on?' demanded Neville.

'Six of us were walking along minding our own business when we were attacked by a mob of them.' Harold winced at the memory. 'A dozen or so came out of a side street in front of us, then another dozen came up behind. Laid into us, they did. Poor Whitey has been stabbed. Not looking good, may have punctured a lung. He's in that ambulance there.' Ronald White was relatively new to 522 Company and Neville knew he wouldn't be the only one to feel both angry and saddened at the news. He turned his head towards the small remaining group of taunting Cypriots some way down the street.

'Hold your horses,' muttered Charlie, guessing what Neville might be thinking. 'Let the locals deal with it.'

'Don't know about you, lads,' said Alan, 'but I've lost my appetite for sightseeing. I'm off back to camp.'

They waved at Yange, who turned the gharry around, and they headed back the way they'd come in silence, grim and vengeful.

'And so, gentlemen, is written the eleventh commandment,' said Charlie suddenly. They all looked at him.

'Meaning?' asked Joe.

'Thou shalt not covet thy neighbour's gharry and tip Cyps out thereof or this may seriously piss them off. Learned that in Sunday school, you know.' Four other passengers scowled at him.

'Welcome to Limassol, sleeping beauty,' nudged Nick.

Over the next few days, the bulk of the Company were relocated to Limassol on the south coast of the island, about seventy miles from Famagusta. After the abortive sightseeing trip, Neville had spent most of his time there in camp. As well as the threat from locals, he'd also been feeling unwell: his back was blistered from the sun and he'd barely eaten anything for three days, bar a handful of biscuits. During the journey to Limassol, he'd felt so bad that he'd pulled over. Nick drove the rest of the way, while Neville tried to ignore the bumps in the road to get some sleep.

'Blimey, what a dump.' As Neville came to and looked around at the expanse of low, squalid houses of his new home, he was singularly unimpressed. Twenty minutes later, when they arrived at the camp, he was even less so. The tents had been pitched in a ploughed field and, even for a British Army camp, it was rudimentary. The current camp occupants were quick to welcome the newcomers: millions of ants swarmed over everything – tents, kit, boots, utensils. They were everywhere.

'Dim view of this,' sighed Neville. But, as usual with the army, he knew they just had to get on with it. In an attempt to alleviate the misery, Joe joined Neville and Nick late in the afternoon and they opened two bottles of Island whisky and cognac.

'Coming down to Limassol, Timber?' asked Joe.

'I don't feel up to it. Think I'll get to bed early,' said Neville. But though he retired shortly after 2000 hours, sleep eluded him: the ants had invaded his bed and were crawling all over his body.

The next morning Neville rubbed his bloodshot eyes, scratched the numerous itchy patches on his body and decided he needed to attend the sick parade. The Company Medical Officer, Dr Forbes, affectionately known as Dr Frankenstein, examined Neville, then gave a good hard look as he sat down and began writing on a slip of paper.

'Looks to me as if your gypo stomach is a bit like colic,' he suggested. 'You may have eaten something which doesn't agree with you, but that's a bit unlikely from just a few biscuits. Anyway, I think it will pass, one way or another. What concerns me more,' he leaned closer, 'are those patches on your arms and feet turning septic. Report to me again in forty-eight hours, on Monday morning.'

By the Sunday, Neville's arms and feet were worse, but generally he felt a little better. His spirits rose further when he took possession of a Bedford fifteen-hundredweight truck. During the morning he took it out around the outskirts of Limassol and discovered that the vehicle was not governed – in other words its speed was not limited. He left a trail of fist-brandishing Cypriots in his wake as he sped past, forcing many with more rudimentary transport on to the verge. He pulled back into camp just after 1300 hours and Sergeant Stuart waved him down.

'Uh-oh,' groaned Nick, who had been enjoying the spectacle in the passenger seat. 'Think some of the locals have been complaining already?'

Neville popped his head out of the window. 'Looking for me, Sergeant?' he asked, a picture of innocence.

'Yes, Wood.' Stuart put his hand on the cab door and pointed to a wagon a short distance away. 'Get yourself over there next to that wagon. Meat has just come in. It needs checking by a butcher, and I believe that's you.'

Relieved that he wasn't in trouble, Neville parked up, jumped down from his cab and vaulted on to the tailgate of the meat truck. Hanging inside were at least a dozen carcasses of beef. He went to each of them, checking them closely. Finishing his lookover, he came back to the tailgate and sat on the edge.

'Mycobacterium bovis,' he declared.

'Which means what, Wood?' asked Stuart patiently.

'Open lesions in the carcass, Sergeant. Means they're tubercular, so I'd condemn the lot.'

'Oh, bloody marvellous,' muttered Stuart, who had clearly been looking forward to a proper supper that evening. 'Hard-boiled eggs and bully beef again tonight then!'

On Monday at 0900 sharp, Neville reported back to the Medical Officer. Forbes examined his legs, arms and ears closely and grunted. Then he sat down, placed his spectacles on his desk and put his hands together in a steeple.

'I hope you're not praying, Doctor,' chuckled Neville.

'Not on this occasion, Wood, but I'm sure there will be many times to come when it will be the only thing I can do.' He smiled grimly and paused before continuing. 'I'm afraid it's not good news. You've got Staphylococcus aureus, breaking out all over and I don't mean just on your body. You may know it as impetigo. Those small vesicles or pustules are highly contagious. So you will need to keep yourself meticulously clean, no swimming, and will have to report daily to the orderly who will apply a bactericidal ointment, Mupirocin, for you. You may continue with your normal duties for the time being.'

For the next three days normal duties entailed a great deal of driving the Bedford. As part of the fortification of the island, petrol points had to be formed, principally for wagons engaged in troop carrying. Should there be an attack upon the island the ability to deploy troops rapidly and flexibly would be crucial. By the Wednesday Neville was on his fifth trip to and from Limassol where he collected the supplies of petrol. On this occasion he was accompanied by Harry Minchin and they were heading to Limassol with an empty wagon. Harry had his feet up on the dashboard and he was looking out at the countryside, his expression thoughtful.

'Penny for them?' asked Neville, glancing across at his passenger.

'You know, I was just thinking it's good to see you doing a full day's work, Timber,' observed Harry with a smile.

'Meaning what exactly?' Neville frowned.

'Now don't get me wrong,' Harry held up his hands. 'I'm not criticising, but let's face it, you do rather well dodging parades and drill.'

'I'm not dodging anything. I have to report to the medical orderly twice a day now. Believe me, you're better off being on parade than having this damned impetigo.' He drove on in silence until, with a jump, he felt a hand reaching over and rubbing on his ear. Neville pulled the vehicle to a halt.

'What the hell are you doing, Harry?'

Harry rubbed his fingers across his face. 'Contagious, you told me. Well, I fancy skipping a few parades myself so maybe you can help old Harry out!'

By the following Sunday, Harry's wish had come true and he had impetigo on his ears. Neville's own impetigo continued to drive him to distraction. The ointment was making little impression on the huge patches of weeping bare flesh. The condition wasn't the only problem in camp, with a nightly ritual of men being carried from their tents suffering from the effects of sand fly bites or heat exhaustion. But in spite of the flies and intense heat – often above 100 degrees – the monumental task of preparing the island's defences against attack continued unabated.

'Looks like we're on the move again.' Nick came into the tent and threw himself on to his bed, exhausted.

Neville looked up from his pen and paper, and the letter home he'd been writing. 'When and where?' he asked with a sigh.

'Place called Polemidhia,' replied Nick. 'Something to do with winter rains being due. Beats me when we're still in a red-hot August.' He glanced across at Neville, who had resumed writing. 'Important letters?' he asked.

Neville paused and considered, unsure whether to confide his innermost feelings. 'I need to write to that girl Phil in Somerset,' he said eventually. 'She's a lovely person but she wants more than I can give her.'

'Does she want to get engaged?' asked Nick, propping himself up on his elbows.

Neville nodded. 'I like her a lot, but the fact is I'm in love with Joyce.'

'Does she know?'

'Phil? That's what I'm writing to tell her. The second letter is to Joyce. I'm asking her if she would consent to becoming engaged.'

Nick whistled softly and lay back on his bed. 'It never ceases to amaze me that we're so far away from home, doing something we never thought we would have to do, fighting the bloody Germans again, and yet the heart strings are pulled from back home.'

Neville looked across at his friend. 'You understand then?'

'I like to think so. We all want something that anchors or connects us with home, something we're fighting for, something to look forward to going back for. Are you sure about Joyce?'

'Ye-e-es,' Neville replied slowly. 'Joyce is the sweetest girl I've ever met. It's not just because I need someone there at home waiting for me. Have you got someone?'

'Not bloody likely,' snorted Nick. 'Time for all that when I get back to Blighty.'

On Monday 18 August they moved to Polemidhia, from a ploughed field to stone and rocks, south of Limassol, four miles from the sea. The following day Harry Minchin was admitted to hospital with worsening impetigo. His wish of skipping parade had become much more than he'd bargained for: he wouldn't re-emerge for active duty for the best part of six months.

For everyone else, the work was relentless. Neville and Nick were tasked with driving to the ammunition dump in Nicosia to collect a wagon full of high explosives. They took the seventy-mile route over the central mountains exhilarated and excited by the wild, rugged scenery and throwing the wagon round hairpin bends. On the return journey, given the nature of the load, Neville was less inclined to be quite so cavalier. The ammunition dump at Polemidhia quickly became substantial, and also a potential target. Enemy air raids on the island were becoming heavier and more frequent. The port installations in Famagusta, in particular, took a heavy pounding from Italian bombers, although the death toll was minimal. The camp at Polemidhia and the nearby ammunition dump were heavily camouflaged and guarded against the threat of bombs and sabotage.

On a stifling hot Saturday afternoon, Neville was on guard at the dump. He was accompanied on his four-hour duty by Alan Such and two soldiers from the Durham Light Infantry. They patrolled the perimeter of the dump in pairs. Neville was with one of the infan-trymen, Jack Clarke. As they were approaching the end of their guard duty, Jack noticed that Neville was starting to lag behind.

'You okay, Nev?' he asked.

'Feel lousy, Jack. I can hardly put one foot in front of another.'

'Want me to get a relief?'

Neville shook his head. 'I can manage. Think we've only got another half an hour or so, anyway.'

Jack looked at Neville and frowned. 'Hate to tell you this,' he said, 'but your face don't look none too good.'

Blasted impetigo! thought Neville. He was aware that his face was blistering once again. During the night it began weeping and itching, leaving his sleep fitful at best. The following morning Neville reported to the Company medical officer again.

'You back again, Wood? Quite a little regular, aren't we?' Forbes said with a smile. Then he peered more closely at Neville. 'But by the look of you I'm not surprised.' The doctor completed his examination and gave Neville the news. 'That's it for you, I'm afraid. No guard duty today. You have acute impetigo and tonsillitis and a very toasty temperature of one hundred and one. I'm sending you to the hospital in Polemidhia. Report back in thirty minutes and one of my orderlies will take you there.'

The hospital at Polemidhia was one of several British Military Hospitals in Cyprus. In common with the others it was a hutted hospital with seventy-five beds run principally with Cypriot staff. There were fifteen beds in each hut and, while it may be described as spartan with its iron bedsteads and corrugated walls, it was also clean with crisp, white linen and a strong smell of disinfectant.

Neville woke the first morning with his nightwear and bedding drenched in sweat. The nurse helped him from his bed and offered him a cigarette. He slumped in a chair and shook his head, then changed his mind and let the nurse light the cigarette for him. He leaned forward, arms on knees, and inhaled the smoke slowly, watching as his bed was changed. In fresh nightwear he returned to bed and had his temperature taken.

'Has it come down, Nurse?' he asked.

'Same as before,' she gave the thermometer a shake, 'and your pulse is up at eighty-four. You must rest some more.'

Neville tried. He ate little, slept some of the time and continued to sweat profusely. Over the next two days, his temperature oscillated between ninety-eight and 103. By Wednesday both his temperature and his pulse had stabilised. His mood was buoyed further by a visit from Nick, Joe and Peter Helmand.

'How're you doing, slacker?' grinned Joe.

'You should have more respect for the sick,' croaked Neville, 'but as you ask I feel much better today, thanks. Got any cigs?'

'Right out,' said Nick, 'but I'll bring you some tomorrow.'

'And something to read,' added Neville. 'I'm bored as hell in here.'

'When are they letting you out?' asked Peter.

'Dunno, Helmy. When they're satisfied I've stabilised, I suppose. But I'll be happy to get out and get some decent food as well. I've been on starvation rations and what I've had is lousy. Cooked in coconut oil!'

The situation, though, did not get any better. Nick failed to show with the cigarettes, the food remained virtually non-existent and Neville continued to be bored silly. When the medical officer eventually appeared, Neville vented his frustration.

'I'm taking a dim view of this all round,' Neville told him. 'I want signing out of here.'

The MO looked at him over his glasses. 'Temperature one hundred, Wood. That's not good, is it? This island is known as "white man's grave" and we really don't want to be carrying you out in a wooden jacket.' Before Neville could argue, he turned on his heel and moved across the hut.

Eventually, Nick and Helmy appeared with thirty Craven A cigarettes, but Neville's temperature stayed stubbornly high, rising again to 103. And now it was accompanied by intense pain behind the eyes and severe skin irritation from bites or spots all over his body. When Alan Such came to visit on the Sunday, his expression told just what a forlorn sight he looked.

'No point me asking you if you feel better, then?' smiled Alan.

'Browned off to hell, mate. They think I may have malaria now.'

Alan took a step backwards. 'Cheer up.' He offered Neville a parcel at arm's length. 'At least I've brought you some proper bread and a two-pound tin of axle grease.'

Axle grease was the name they'd given the yellow oily margarine they ate. Neville opened the tin Alan had brought. Tearing off a hunk of bread, he ran his finger through the oily substance and slopped it on to the hunk. 'Thanks, Alan,' he said between mouthfuls. 'Feel better already.'

Neville wasn't the only one to have a problem with the hospital food. The following day he was one of a group of patients who took the law into their own hands. Those who could get out of bed made for the cookhouse. Four of them went in, swiftly followed by the sound of pans hitting the floor, shouts and expletives. Moments later the Cypriot cook was frogmarched out of the building and unceremoniously dumped on the ground.

'You no do this,' he yelled, brandishing his fist. 'I get officers.'

'Yes, we can,' one of the patients yelled to cheers from the others, 'and we bloody well will. You can call who the hell you want but we'll murder you if you do!'

Thirty minutes later the group were devouring eggs and chips and taking plates through to those still bedridden.

That was just the first bit of good news. An hour later, as the irate patients returned to their huts, they were greeted by uproar and commotion.

'Call that a bloody bed? More an open tin can! And look at those blankets and sheets. Not fit for a tramp!' Neville recognised the shouts of Sergeant Major Taylor, whose complaints were heard all over the hospital site as orderlies scurried back and forth. Neville entered his hut to see the sergeant major berating an orderly. He slid back into bed and leaned towards the bed on his right.

'What's going on?' he whispered.

The patient next to him tried not to laugh. 'Oh, please,' he grimaced, 'it only hurts when I laugh! The sergeant major has just been admitted with acute diarrhoea!'

Neville burst out laughing. A fiery pair of eyes swivelled in his direction.

'Shut up, Wood, or I'll be over there to wipe that smile off your face!'

The day after the sergeant major was admitted, the food remarkably improved. To make matters even better, a Greek medical officer examined Neville and allowed himself to be persuaded to sign Private Wood out of the hospital, on condition that he reported sick to the British medical officer the next morning.

On top of that, Neville headed back to camp to learn that he was to receive an extra three pence a day after two years' active service. He was now paying thirteen shillings and six pence a week into his Army Post Office account. *Enough to make any Yorkshireman smile*, he thought.

'We're back on ammo dump guard duty,' Nick announced as he ducked under the flap of the tent.

'You've got to be joking,' groaned Neville. 'Where did you hear that?'

'Just seen Sergeant Stuart. He said you'd be pleased with the news!'

'Very dim view,' grunted Neville. 'I thought the Cyps were doing that?'

'They've been taken off guard because they can't use a rifle.'

'Hell of a lot of use they'll be when the action starts. First shot and they'll chuck! Probably offer to make Jerry some Koupes dishes,' Neville said to laughter from Nick. 'If those meat doughnuts don't kill him nothing will. Anyway,' Neville continued, 'I've had some news. I've been told I'll get my new wagon tomorrow, but I'll have to go to the troop-carrying section. I told them they could stick their wagon in that case.'

'Anybody in? Ah, how's the malingering invalid?' Alan popped his head into the tent and ducked as a boot hurtled towards him.

'Buggered, if you must know,' snorted Neville. 'Went to the range this morning and fired rifle and Bren. I had to march four miles with the rifle and two thousand rounds. And me, a sick man!'

Alan sat down with a sharp intake of breath and a grimace. 'That boil on yer bum still giving you trouble?' asked Neville.

'Not half.' Alan winced. 'It's a hell of a size now.'

Neville reached under his chair and brandished a knife. 'Freshly sharpened today. Come on, get your trousers down.' He flicked the knife in his wrist.

'Don't you come near me with that thing!' Alan leapt to his feet, alarmed. 'I don't know where it's been.'

Two days later Neville took over a Chevrolet, thirty-hundredweight converted civilian wagon. He stood with Nick and Joe, shaking his head with incredulity.

'Damn and blast!' He patted the wagon on its side. 'It's a proper flying bedstead. Think I'll run it over the edge of the cliffs by accident.'

In spite of the worn clutch and gearbox, leaking sump and tailboard hanging off, Neville spent the day with the rest of the Company moving the ammunition dump. Against his better judgement, they filled the unstable wagons with highly volatile nitroglycerine in bottles; amatol, a highly explosive material made from a mixture of TNT and ammonium nitrate; fulminate of mercury; lyddite and wet and dry cotton. It was a potent cocktail of sympathetic explosives liable to go off at the slightest touch.

Once his wagon was loaded, Neville pulled himself up into the cab immediately. Any delay would test the nerves and courage to breaking point. As he started the engine and the wagon shuddered to life, the cargo rattled and vibrated. Neville's hands were white as they clutched the steering wheel. He could feel beads of sweat forming and running into his eyes, stinging and blurring his vision.

His mouth was dry and his heart beat rapidly. As the vehicle moved forward with a judder, he held his breath in the expectation of an eruption of explosives. As the anticipated bang didn't materialise, he breathed out slowly and began his journey. As he drove along, the fumes from the cargo seeped into the cab, heightening the tension and giving him a severe headache. No matter how many trips Neville made, the same thoughts persisted: *Could this be the one? What if she blows? Will I feel the pain before I die?*

That evening, Neville, Nick, Joe and Alan swapped stories. 'Well, I'm glad we've got that over and done with,' Alan sighed.

'I was sweating like a pig carrying that stuff over those rough roads. Thought I was going to blow at any minute,' agreed Neville. 'What?'

Alan was looking sheepish. Two days previously he had borrowed Neville's rifle for guard duty. 'Here's your rifle back, Timber,' he said as he handed the weapon over. 'Except, well, I'm not sure that it's yours.'

Neville examined the rifle and serial number. He looked at Alan aghast. 'This isn't my rifle. You know what that means, don't you? Bloody court martial. Have you reported it to the sergeant major yet?' Alan shook his head. Neville blew out, beginning to seriously regret laughing at Taylor's diarrhoea in the hospital. 'Better get it over and done with. I've often wondered what life in the glass house will be like.'

Thirty minutes later, much chastened, they returned to the tent.

'Well? Did he see the funny side?' asked Nick.

Neville shook his head. 'Open arrest pending a court martial and an immediate inquiry.'

But later that evening Neville went to see Alan, who was slumped on his bed looking utterly crestfallen.

'Guess what?' Neville asked. 'The serial number I gave you

– turns out it was the wrong one. That rifle is mine after all. Bright view all round, eh?' Neville remained close to the tent flap as he watched Alan, eyes wide, cheeks turning red, slowly raise himself off his bed.

'Bright view? I'll give you bright view, you good-for-nothing bastard!'

'Hang on a minute there,' shouted Neville as they moved nose to nose. 'Which bloody idiot misplaced his rifle in the first place so he had to borrow mine? Huh? You!' Neville prodded Alan in the chest. Alan grabbed Neville's lapels.

'And who's going to tell the sergeant major and look an idiot?' They stood together, eyeball to eyeball.

'We both are.' Neville grinned, breaking the tension.

'Then out for a drink and get pissed to celebrate?' asked Alan.

'That's the plan.'

With arms around each other's shoulders they left the tent laughing as they continued to hurl abuse at each other.

'She's been blown up once, you know, on Larnaca docks.'

'Well, it's a damn pity it wasn't a direct hit,' grunted Neville. The wagon was in the workshop again with a leaking half shaft through the rear off-side hub. It also felt as if the steering was going. Nigel Binks, who was in charge of the workshop, was far more affection-ate with the wagon than its driver.

'Poor old girl, you ignore him.' He patted the vehicle. 'Let's see if we can put you right.'

As Neville left Binksy whispering endearments to what he regarded as a piece of junk, Sergeant Stuart came marching over to intercept him.

'Private Wood,' he barked.

Neville snapped to attention and saluted.

'Get that flying fortress of yours back on the road.' Stuart nodded towards the workshop. *Flying fortress?* Neville wondered.

'You have a detail at 0400 tomorrow and it's hush-hush.' Stuart handed over his instructions. 'Here are the map coordinates where you will rendezvous with two naval launches which will require refuelling. I can tell you it will be a two-hundred-mile round trip over difficult mountain roads, so get some decent sleep before you go.'

'Yes, Sergeant!' Neville saluted but was not dismissed. 'Anything else, Sergeant?'

Stuart smiled. 'Yes, Wood, when you get back, pack up some gear because you're going on four days' leave in the mountains.'

'I'd sooner not, Sergeant,' grunted Neville.

Stuart frowned. 'Well, you're damn well going, Wood, no arguments. Now get on with it. Dismiss!'

Binksy worked his magic with the wagon and the hush-hush detail was completed over a long day of difficult driving. Neville left as ordered at 0400, located the rendezvous relatively easily, and delivered the fuel. Despite natural curiosity no questions were asked and no information provided. He arrived back at camp weary and hungry at 1630.

The following morning he climbed into the back of a troop-carrying wagon along with eight other members of 522 Company and was driven to a camp just outside the Pano Platres on the southern slopes of the central Troodos Mountains. They arrived at 1300 hours and after roll-call had some time for rest and recuperation. Neville left the camp on foot and walked to the Krios River, which crosses east of Platres, forming a rich green valley of varied flora and fauna. He walked the two miles to the Kalidonia waterfall, a cataract plunging twelve metres, and sat on a rock marvelling at the scenery. *You know, Nev,* he mused to himself, *this little jaunt ain't half bad after all.*

He arrived back in camp in the early evening. The temperature was dropping significantly and the cool mountain air drove him to his bed early to keep warm. He slept the sleep of the just. The following morning dawned bright and crisp. Roll-call was the one formality of the day and by 0900 Neville was on a hiking trail to the 6,404-foot summit of Mount Olympus. The ascent was easy to follow but relatively hard to accomplish. The higher he climbed the more he marvelled at the developing panorama, and by late morning he had reached the summit. He was alone with the gentle, cool breeze, the scent of pine and the scenery exhilarating to all his senses. He turned 360 degrees and looked across the island to the faraway shores of Turkey and Syria. He smiled at the brass plate bearing the points of the compass and ran his finger along the arrow directed towards London, 2,093 miles away. 'As the crow flies, I expect,' he muttered. 'Wish you could be here with me, Joyce.' He sighed wistfully.

Upon his return from the mountains, Neville went in search of his wagon, but couldn't see it anywhere. He looked around the workshop, asked the question again and looked from mechanic to mechanic as each shook his head. He walked around the camp and found Sergeant Stuart.

'Sergeant, I can't locate my wagon,' Neville explained.

'Think it might be bad news, lad. Your wagon and driver have been missing since yesterday afternoon. It was a mountain run and chances are they may have gone over the edge.'

Neville cast his mind back to the day before, when Joe brought him back from the Troodos. They had travelled along the Seven Sisters, a mountain road of hairpin bends. As Joe turned to talk to Neville and momentarily lost concentration the wagon teetered on the brink of a 2,000-foot drop to the valley floor below. *There but for the . . .* he thought.

He wandered back to his tent, where Nick thrust a piece of paper into his hand. 'Well, that sets the ground rules!' he exclaimed.

Neville read the two paragraphs from Major General Ramsden, Commander of the 50th Division. 'Bright view of that,' he said. 'If there is an invasion, there will be no retreat and no evacuation. Can't be much more unambiguous than that!'

'Don't know about you but I reckon we go to the pictures and make the most of it. Before Jerry arrives and spoils it.'

'Smashing job!' agreed Neville.

In the afternoon they headed into Polemidhia and bought tickets to see Dick Powell in *The Singing Marine*. The cinema was basic, with wooden upright chairs for about one hundred people and a Cypriot projectionist frantically fiddling with the old projector. Windows lined the side of the building, which were all open to allow air to flow and keep the temperature relatively comfortable. The film was about halfway through when there was a *crump*, *crump* noise and the building shook as two sticks of bombs exploded nearby. Shouts drowned out the film and chairs flew as the Cypriots in the audience dived out through every open window. Within fifteen seconds the cinema was clear with the exception of a dozen British soldiers, who looked at each other and smiled.

'Windy bastards!' shouted one at the windows. Neville turned to look at the projector. The projectionist was nowhere to be seen, but the spool continued to whirr, so he sat back in his seat and enjoyed the remainder of the film.

Neville was assigned to 17 Casualty Clearing Station, 153 Field Company Royal Engineers based at Zyyi, a small village on the south coast between Limassol and Larnaca. His new vehicle was anything but new – more half replacement, half flying bedstead. To exacerbate matters, a 400-gallon water tank had been manoeuvred on to his vehicle and he was taking it up to be refilled at the water tower on the hillside, a tower with no access road.

'Come on, girl, you old crock!' he encouraged as the wagon rocked, rattled and groaned. 'You can do it.'

Neither Neville's humour nor the health of the wagon improved when it was accidentally refuelled with water, necessitating draining of the pit tank and clearing all the feed pipes and carburettor. As he cleaned the muck and oil off his hands and arms, he felt a large hand clasp him on the shoulder and a Scottish voice booming behind him.

'Well, laddie, looks like you need a break. Come with us down to the village, aye?'

153 Field Company was drawn mainly from Scotland and they were a friendly and welcoming bunch.

'Don't mind if I do,' replied Neville, delighted with the invitation.

'Aye, as you've fixed that old bus we thought you may like to drive us down there.'

They were also a canny bunch.

Eight Scottish Royal Engineers jumped on to the back of the wagon and squeezed into the cab, and they took the short journey down to Zyyi. Parked just off the square, Neville was intrigued by the crowd of brightly dressed locals near the church. The whole group wandered over and were greeted warmly by the Cypriots. On the steps of the Greek Orthodox Church a young man, smartly dressed in dark trousers and jacket with a red sash around his midriff, was handing flowers to a young lady resplendent in a long flowing white wedding dress.

'Welcome, welcome,' cried some of the Cypriots. 'Please, join our wedding celebrations as honoured guests.' The crowd gathered round the soldiers and they were ushered, willing and curious, into the church. Each of them was given a lighted taper to hold and they took the places offered to them among the congregation, the size of which suggested it must be the whole village.

'I've never seen anything quite like this. What is happening?' asked Neville in a conspiratorial whisper, fascinated by the unfolding ceremony.

The old man to his side nodded three times and as the priest continued with his chanting and rocking, he leaned across. 'Ah, what you see is only part of it,' he replied in excellent English. 'The wedding ceremony hasn't changed for generations. Before the couple even come to church, male relatives dance around their soon-to-be marital home with a mattress sewn with five crosses and with five bells placed on it. This symbolises the couple sleeping the sleep of the blessed. A baby doll is rolled on the mattress to symbolise fertility and relatives add money to symbolise wealth.' He paused momentarily, listening to the chanting, smiling and nodding, then he leaned over again and continued, 'The bride and groom are dressed by relatives whilst musicians play. Their clothes are placed in a basket and danced around three times for blessing. The red sash you see is crossed three times to mark the journey from innocence to married life. Always in threes: God, Son and Holy Spirit.'

The ceremony moved on and the old man nudged Neville. 'You see, the rings are blessed and placed on their right hands because the right hand of God blesses us.' He patted Neville's right hand. Crowns with ribbons were placed on the heads of the couple and swapped three times. Each of them took a sip from a cup of wine proffered by the priest and they were led three times around the altar. They faced the congregation and the priest separated their hands. The old man leaned over, grinning and nodding. 'Only God can separate them now,' he said.

As the couple made their way through the church, rice and coins were thrown over them signifying wealth and fertility. Neville reached into his pocket, found a penny and threw it in their direction. The old man nodded approval and blew out Neville's taper. 'Come, join us at the feast,' he encouraged with open arms.

'I must get back,' Neville shook his head, 'but thank you for allowing me to be part of this wonderful ceremony and telling me about your customs.' As the soldiers emerged back into the square, Neville sought out the soldier who'd invited him down. 'I'm heading back to camp if that's okay with you,' he said.

As the other soldiers followed the villagers to the feast, Neville climbed into the cab of his wagon. He sat there for a few moments, reflecting on what he had just seen.

'Oh, Joyce,' he sighed, starting the engine, 'please write to me.'

Back in camp Neville returned to his tent, where he sat alone, deep in thought. He was interrupted by Alan, who had come down to Zyyi and brought the mail with him. There were several letters for Neville, but as he flicked through, he could see that none was from Joyce. He put the pile down on his bed, unopened.

'Hell, Alan, I'd sooner it finish altogether than just be half and half. I gave her credit for more decency than just to drop it and not say anything to me.'

'Write to her,' Alan suggested, 'and demand to know one way or another, Nev. You have a right to know and it's clear it's driving you nuts.'

'But what if she's ill or, God forbid, she's been killed or injured?'

'Well, write to her and if you hear nothing ask one of your relatives to make some discreet enquiries. Anyway, my friend, I've got to go. Let me know if you hear anything and I'll keep an eye out for the mail for you.'

Neville went with Alan to his wagon and waved him off before heading to the canteen. There he sat and wrote a letter to Joyce that was firm and to the point – write or it's all over. He finished, addressed the envelope and stood holding it. *Won't post it yet*, he thought. *Maybe I'll hear from her tomorrow.*

Rumours were rife about the next move from Cyprus and it was clear from the preparations that it was a question of when rather than if. The Royal Engineers started to sell the pigs they had bought for Christmas, and work accelerated at the hospital they were constructing. Neville took the opportunity to go for a swim in the sea and then came back into Zyyi where the local market was bustling. He smiled as he saw two Royal Engineers queuing for the local fortune teller. Having bought some oranges and grapefruits from a fruit stall, he noticed the fortune teller was now unoccupied. She suddenly looked up at him, curling her forefinger to beckon him over. Her dark, limpid eyes seemed to bore into his soul. *Why not?* he thought. He strolled over to her table where she was running her hands over a crystal ball. She took Neville's hand and ran her finger across his palm. She muttered something incomprehensible and rolled her eyes so only the whites were showing. Then she held out her hand palm up.

Here we go, Neville thought and paid her some coins.

'In twenty-two days and twenty-two hours you will go somewhere where it smells. Be careful; you will not be safe there.' She rolled her eyes again and continued. 'There is a girl, a beautiful girl.'

Neville sat up quickly at that and leaned in.

'She has black eyes and her heart beats faster when she sees you.'

Neville's shoulders slumped. Joyce's eyes were blue.

'You will have lots of girls,' the fortune teller added quickly. 'And in two days you will receive the letter you have been waiting for.' That perked Neville up again. 'You will go to England suddenly. You will marry and have three fine sons.' Then the fortune teller frowned. 'She is not the one,' she said as she released his hand. This appeared to be the end of the consultation.

Ah well, Neville thought, *at least I'll be able to check the twenty-two days*.

On Friday 7 November 1941, nineteen days after Neville had his fortune told, 522 Company finished four days of troop carrying to Famagusta and returning with troops of the 5th Indian Division. At 1230 hours on the Saturday they boarded the destroyer *Jackal* and steamed away from Cyprus.

What the fortune teller didn't get right was where Neville was heading. Rather than going back to England, the *Jackal* took him south, south-west to Haifa in Palestine.

The next phase of Neville's war was about to begin.

Chapter 7

Hostility in Iraq

November 1941 to January 1942

The situation was critical and speed was essential. But that was the problem. The 5th Indian Division, now based on Cyprus and using the transport of the 50th Division, had left their vehicles behind. This was transport drawn from every conceivable dump in the Middle East and it had been flogged to death. Upwards of 900 vehicles were completely unserviceable and the north-countrymen of 50th Division had a journey of approximately 1,000 miles, across inhospitable country, to complete rapidly.

The officers of the Division had been briefed by Headquarters, Middle East. Intelligence was forecasting a German thrust by up to ten armoured divisions south-east into Iraq via a corridor of level country to the east of the Caspian Sea. The 50th was tasked with rapid deployment towards the Caucasus Mountains to prevent that breakthrough and the seizure of the oil wells by the enemy.

Neville and Nick were on guard duty at the Jaffa Road camp, four miles outside Haifa, their rifles loaded, bayonets fixed, but the biggest threat seemed to be buzzing around them.

'Bloody flies!' snorted Nick, swatting a host of them away as they seemed intent on getting into his mouth and ears, up his nose and into his eyes.

'More of the damn things in one square inch here than in one square mile in Cyprus.' Neville flicked away another swarm.

'Where do you reckon we're off to next?' asked Nick.

'Damned if I know, but I'm wondering *how* rather than *where*. The wagons are total wrecks. Most have done more than twenty thousand miles already. I don't think we'll get more than ten miles down the road in those heaps of—'

'Watch out,' hissed Nick, 'Corp approaching.'

Corporal Jeff Kitchen was their immediate non-commissioned officer and was new to the Company. He was twenty-five years old, already an experienced soldier, slightly built with short fair hair. He had made a good early impression with his affable but no-nonsense manner.

'Anything doing, lads?' he asked as he came and stood beside them.

'Just officers coming and going, Corp, otherwise all quiet here,' reported Nick.

Kitchen scanned the area then started swatting, waving his arms violently. 'Bloody flies!'

'Any news about what's happening, Corp?' asked Neville.

'All I know is that the brass are running around frantically so something's up. Anyway,' Kitchen turned to look at them, 'I've got a job for you both and Joe. You three are getting some three-tonners tomorrow and will be the advance party.'

'To where?' asked Neville.

Kitchen smiled. 'Don't know yet. But, wherever, just get the lads there and camp set up pronto. That's the British Army for you.'

The following morning at 0900, Neville left the camp in a

Chevrolet, heading north, through Acre, to begin assembling a new camp about ten miles along the main road.

'Welcome to your new des res,' quipped Nick. 'All modern amenities available. Hot and cold running snakes, scorpions, mosquitoes and damned big flying beetles. No home is complete without them.' He ducked as a can of bully beef hurtled in his direction. More trucks rumbled up and a Company of Green Howards leapt out and began setting up camp across the road.

'What's that?' asked Nick, squinting at a shape further north.

'Dogs?' suggested Neville with a frown. It was hard to be sure with the heat haze shimmering over the dusty road. Neville, Nick and Joe walked up the road a short way to take a look.

'Dead camel,' announced Joe, as the shape came into focus, a group of animals surrounding it. 'And I reckon they're coyotes or jackals. I suggest we don't go any—'

The crackle of rifle fire filled the air. Instinctively the three men dived into a ditch along the roadside. They scanned the hills rising to the east as the crackle continued, but there were no tell-tale signs of exploding dust and rock to indicate they were the target. Then six soldiers of the Green Howards came running up the road and formed a semicircle, kneeling on one leg facing the hills, rifles raised, searching for flashes of gunfire. A sergeant glanced down into the ditch.

'You men all right?' he asked.

'Yes, thank you, Sergeant.' Neville peered up from the ditch.

'Not advisable to venture too far without weapons.' The sergeant smiled. 'Shall we get back?'

Somewhat chastened, Neville, Joe and Nick scrambled from the ditch and with the Green Howards crabbing along, watching the hills, they all returned to setting up camp.

The remainder of 522 Company joined them the following day. They came with a consignment of woollen underwear issued for the cold climate which, for many, affirmed the rumours that they were heading for the Caucasus Mountains. Though the mid-November days remained pleasantly warm, the nights were becoming increasingly cold. Much of the time in the days that followed was spent in the workshop in an attempt to make the wagons serviceable. In some instances, it was prudent to engage in a little subterfuge. During one tea break Neville surreptitiously removed a good spare wheel from one of the wagons in the workshop and replaced it with the punctured one from his own, *Minnie Muncher*.

'Why do you call that thing Minnie Muncher?' asked Joe.

'Well, when I'm driving along it makes a noise like it's munching a bag of spanners,' explained Neville.

'Ah, I see.' Joe smiled. 'Know what I call mine?' Neville raised his eyebrows and shook his head. 'Timber, because it's always buggered and missing parade.' Joe hurtled from the workshop with Neville in pursuit brandishing a spanner.

One Wednesday afternoon, Neville had just finished writing several letters home when he heard the scrunch of boots and saw Corporal Kitchen marching towards him.

'Orders for tomorrow, Timber,' he said. 'You, Joe, Nick and Alan are on convoy duty. Leaving 0430.'

'Where and what for, Corp?' Neville shuddered at the cold, early start in prospect.

'Ammo, place called Wadi Sabah about one hundred and thirty miles south.'

'I'm on guard at 2330 tonight, Corp. Am I to be relieved?' queried Neville hopefully.

'What do you think this is, Timber, a bloody holiday camp?' Kitchen turned and marched off in search of the others. Neville grunted, working through the timings in his head. 'Better get some shut-eye,' he murmured to himself.

Neville went on guard at 2330 and, other than the fact he felt chilled to the bone when he was relieved at 0330, it was an uneventful four hours. He breakfasted with Nick, Joe and Alan at 0400 and thirty minutes later they reported to the wagon pool. The gloom of the early morning masked the dilapidated state of the vehicles they were allocated. Each of them was handed a slip of paper about half an inch wide and four inches long. This was the designated route of the convoy of sixteen vehicles and important, should they be required to disperse if under attack.

The convoy left the camp, heading south through Haifa. The hills of Carmel rose up to their left and the glistening Mediterranean Sea was ever present on their right. They passed through small dusty towns, Hadera and Netanya, before wending their way slowly through Tel Aviv and Jaffa. A further fifty miles through brown and barren countryside brought them to Wadi Sabah and the ammunition dump. They arrived at 0930 and began the arduous and hazardous task of loading the unstable wagons with high explosives. The exhausting work was complete by 1600. Thirty minutes later, they began the return journey north, arriving back at camp at midnight.

In less than an hour they were all asleep for what felt like little more than a cat nap. At 0500 each man was back behind the wheel and delivering the ammunition to the units of 50th Division spread far and wide, or so it seemed.

'I can barely keep my eyes open,' complained Neville to Alan and Joe as they paused for a smoke beside their vehicles on the roadside having completed a delivery.

'Oh, it's not that bad,' encouraged Joe.

'It's okay for you. I was on damned guard duty before we set off yesterday. I've had barely three hours' sleep in the last thirty-six. My eyes won't focus.'

'Well, just remember you're carrying volatile high explosives,' suggested Alan. 'Maybe that'll keep you focused.'

'Would an orange help?' asked Joe from the other side of his wagon. Neville and Alan looked at each other blankly. 'Seriously, come round here,' said Joe. They followed him round the rear of the wagon, where Joe was pointing to an oasis of green. 'Either it's a mirage or I can see orange fruit hanging in abundance from yon trees. Just waiting to be sampled by three deserving drivers.'

'Think anyone will notice?' asked Alan.

'There are thousands of the bloody things,' grinned Neville, saliva moistening his dry mouth. 'So who's going to notice if a few go missing?'

'I'll stay with the wagons,' volunteered Alan. 'You lads go and grab some.' Neville and Joe gave him a look then crossed the road-side ditch, ran across a wide area of brown, barren earth and into the trees.

'Grab and twist,' said Joe as he started reaching up, checking the fruit and dropping it into a makeshift basket of his shirt. The pair were almost fully laden when a cry came from along one of the long lines of trees.

'Bugger. We've been rumbled,' muttered Neville as an elderly man in local dress stumbled towards them, brandishing his fist and yelling imprecations. They ran back across the open ground, spilling some of their plunder along the way, but they weren't followed. The ripe, luscious fruit tasted like nectar and they devoured several oranges hungrily, saving a few for later.

The wagons limped back to camp and were delivered to the Vehicle Return Depot. Neville inspected his with one of the mechanics, who stood in front of it rubbing his chin thoughtfully.

'Knackered!' he pronounced.

'Yes, I am,' sighed Neville.

'Not you,' laughed the mechanic, 'this heap of junk. Condemned, I'm afraid. Still, we're expecting some new, decent ones.'

'Heard that before,' snorted Neville.

But the following day Neville was given a Chevrolet: two miles on the clock, steel body and chassis, 3,318 horsepower with booster gears. It was just in time: soon after, the orders came in that they were to break camp and head towards the Caucasus Mountains.

Friday 28 November 1941 dawned cold and grey. Dark threatening clouds scudded overhead; a brisk wind billowed the brown, choking dust into clouds, enveloping men and equipment, and muting reveille at 0500. At 0800, 522 Company joined the rest of 50th Division on its journey east towards Lake Tiberias. They crossed the River Jordan at 1315 and passed into bleak desert country. The convoy, several miles in length, snaked through the Golan Heights, south to BetShe'An and east to Al-Mafraq. The overnight stop saw Neville and the others sleeping fitfully in or under the wagons, trying to stay warm against the cold. The quiet was continually broken by drivers starting their cold engines to warm them and to avoid potential breakdown.

They moved again as dawn broke. Crossing into the Arabian Desert, the country was flat, arid, barren and nothing but hard gravel. Mirages were frequent with the desert looking as if it was a vast sea of shimmering water. But the only real sign of life was the occasional wild camel. The drivers had no maps to guide them: Neville hoped that whoever was at the front of the column had attended the desert navigation courses and paid rapt attention.

The convoy crossed the border into Iraq and woke the following morning to snow on the ground. The landscape began to change, becoming hillier and rougher. They passed through Rutbah, held until recently by the rebel Iraqi government of Rashid Ali until bombing by RAF Blenheims caused the rebels to evacuate the town. As they approached Ramadi and crossed the Euphrates there was further evidence of the May 1941 Anglo–Iraqi conflict, which posed the threat of a German foothold in the country. The hostility of the locals was palpable, with shouts, obscene gestures and spitting on the wagons as they rolled by.

They reached Lake Habbaniya and, just beyond, the aerodrome where they were ordered to remain for one day for rest and maintenance. Although six months had elapsed, the detritus of a fierce battle was everywhere. Neville looked with a shudder at the bullet-riddled vehicles, mangled artillery pieces and spent ammunition littering the shell-pocked ground. The day of rest he was looking forward to was anything but: maintenance and repair to his vehicle were required, which he carried out during a vicious, stinging sandstorm.

The following morning, 522 Company left the aerodrome at 0530, one of the advance companies driving the fifty miles to the Iraqi capital of Baghdad. Neville tried to take in the city, admiring its monuments and statues, but was frequently pulled back to the here and now by the shouts and threats from the streets. Weapons were loaded: as they moved north to Tuz, the order was given that any threat was to be dealt with by shooting on sight.

On Saturday 6 December, 522 Company arrived at Kirkuk, a journey of approximately 800 miles completed in just under nine days. Neville was as spent as his wagon, but there remained work to be done: camp needed mapping out ahead of the arrival of the main body of the Division. The weather, though, had other ideas: the rains began, hammering down and turning the semblance of a camp into a quagmire. The roads in Iraq were rudimentary – scraped earth covered in crude oil which hardened to something like tarmac. That is, until it rained. At which point, they turned into something akin to sheet ice, and vehicles lost their grip entirely.

'We're staying put,' Joe announced as he came over to the wagons. The day after their arrival at Kirkuk was brighter and they were busy loading supplies. 'Just seen Sergeant Stuart, and we're digging in. Still need to run this lot around to the units but this is now home – temporarily, at least.'

'Damn good job,' grunted Neville. 'I got stuck three times yesterday trying to move around in this little beauty.' He patted his wagon affectionately.

Over the days that followed, Neville's dislike of Kirkuk increased significantly. The cold was intense, the locals were hostile and the weather deteriorated. The rain came down in torrents, all day and all night in some instances. The tents leaked cold, dirty water and, when he left that relative sanctuary from the elements, he found himself sinking to his knees in mud and oil. In spite of the wet and the cold, he put his overcoat to one side – it became too heavy to wear, caked in mud and saturated with water.

'I need those supplies. Quartermaster wants them at the cookhouse.' Billy Binks was a dispatch rider, although he looked like a walking mud heap. He'd been sent over to collect the payload in the back of Neville's vehicle, a request that was given short shrift.

'Well, Q can come and get them,' laughed Neville in response, 'because these wagons are well and truly stuck and going nowhere.'

Binksy looked around, frustrated. He spotted Sergeant Stuart and plodded over to him, knee deep in mud. 'Sergeant, can you help me, please?' he said as he saluted. 'I've been sent down by the quartermaster to request delivery of the supplies of Spam to the cookhouse. Those good fellows over there tell me their wagons are stuck.'

Sergeant Stuart looked from Binksy to his smiling subordinates. 'So they are.' He smiled without a trace of humour. 'Follow me.'

The pair plodded over to Neville, Nick and Joe. 'Spam needed at the cookhouse, lads,' said Stuart.

'Yes, Sergeant, but the wagons are stuck,' replied Neville, smiling.

Stuart smiled back and clasped his hands behind his back. 'In that case, you can carry it. It's only about a quarter of a mile. Box each, six trips, job done. I'll leave you in the capable hands of Private Binks.'

Carrying boxes of tins of Spam a quarter of a mile through the mud and slime was backbreaking work but they kept their spirits up by abusing Binksy all the way. And at least the job had its compensation – they managed to purloin eggs and sheep heart as a reward. Returning to their tents, exhausted, they fried these on their charcoal stove, allowing the sizzle and smell to take them away, if only temporarily, from their soggy surroundings.

Christmas Day was only four days away. The rain had relented and Neville was lounging in his bivouac when Nick popped his head through the flap. 'You look a bit glum,' he observed.

'Not a good day,' replied Neville morosely. 'I've been into Kirkuk and got fed up being pestered by the wogs, demanding baksheesh or trying to sell me some crap. I've still had no mail from Joyce and if I don't hear from her by the end of January then I shan't bother with her. Looks like I'm on guard duty on Christmas Day and I feel lousy. I can hardly walk because of an abscess on my knee. Where are you going?'

'I'm off outside to shoot myself,' said Nick. 'Other than that, everything all right?'

Neville brightened and moved a blanket. 'Six bottles of beer for dinner, Christmas night,' he beamed. 'A local brew so I don't know what it'll be like, but I intend to get pissed anyway, guard or no guard.'

The following day the heavens opened again. Neville's leg was excruciatingly painful and his mood did not improve.

'I don't believe it,' he growled, 'I've just finished cleaning my wagon and the camp is a bloody swamp again.' Moving supplies around the area continued to be treacherous. On the four-mile stretch of road between 522 Company and the East Yorkshires, twenty-six wagons were abandoned in the mud. On his second trip there Neville saw an old friend standing beside the staff car. He pulled over and rolled down his window.

'Span, long time no see,' he said with a broad grin.

Charlie waved and sauntered over. 'Timber, sir!' He saluted. 'Good to see you. Sorry I've been neglecting you boys but the old man wants driving all over Iraq, it seems to me.' Charlie was making a less than respectful reference to Major Raymond Norfolk, Commanding Officer, Royal Army Service Corps.

'How are you getting on in all this weather?' asked Neville, shaking Charlie's hand through the open window.

'The old girl glides through the mud like a ship on the ocean.' Charlie shook Neville's hand back, patting him on the arm. 'And I'm glad we have a good solid building to stay in. No bivouacs for Charles Spandler Esquire.'

'Lucky bastard!' snorted Neville. 'Maybe see you at Christmas dinner?' Neville waved, revved his engine and turned his steering wheel sharply. A tidal wave of mud plumed into the air engulfing Charlie who stood, arms outstretched like a bedraggled scarecrow, one that had clearly lost its Christmas spirit.

Christmas Day dawned bleak and grey. The rain continued to fall from the heavens in torrents. Rivers flowed through the camp three foot deep. The mess tent, thankfully, was erected on slightly higher ground and at 1300 hours, 522 Company forgot their trials and tribulations as they enjoyed a splendid Christmas dinner. 'Mother, Father, Dave and Joyce,' said Neville as he raised his bottle of beer to his loved ones at home. (Dave was his younger brother, and still lived at home.)

Immediately after the meal they all listened to the King's speech. The speech was relatively short and the King finished with the words: *'The fulfilment of the task to which we are committed will call for the unsparing effort of every one of us. I am confident that my people will answer this call with the courage and devotion which our forefathers never failed to show when our country was in danger.'*

A chorus of cheers rippled through the mess tent. Charlie nudged Neville. 'That devotion means you now have to bugger off on guard, Timber. I would save you a couple of bottles but I have some vague recollection of drowning in mud.' He grinned as he raised his bottle of beer. But when Neville returned from his stint on guard duty, he found his friends had indeed saved him some beer. The rest of Neville's memories of Christmas Day 1941 disappeared into a blur.

As the New Year approached, the rain relented. The wagons were able to move with care and Neville completed several details collecting and distributing petrol and crude oil. In between time he tried to maintain his vehicle. More often than not it took a full day to chip the mud off the wagon and make it look anything like presentable. New Year's Eve was on a Wednesday and while Neville laboured to clean his wagon, Nick and Joe disappeared into Kirkuk. They returned in the early evening with several bottles of wine. As the light faded, Neville, Nick and Joe were joined by Alan and Jim Oliver.

'Grub first?' asked Jim. 'Need to line the stomach, particularly as we don't know what's in those bottles.'

'Suggest we keep weapons loaded,' said Alan. 'Those coyotes and wild dogs are getting bolder by the day and venturing into camp. Couple of the lads in the Durhams were attacked by four of them a few days ago, before someone shot them.'

They lit the burner and Jim produced a frying pan. 'Cook will never miss it,' he pronounced. They had acquired some more sheep hearts to go with eggs and tough bread.

'Fry the bread as well,' suggested Neville.

'First things first; let's get this thing going,' said Jim as he added crude oil to the frying pan. 'Right,' he said as he clapped his hands, 'water, please.'

'Remember, just a few drops,' Alan said. When cooking with the crude oil collected from many of the pools around the area they added a few splashes of water to spread the flames. 'You have done this before, haven't you?' asked Alan as Jim was handed a mug of water.

'How difficult can it be?' replied Jim, tipping the mug into the pan. The gloom lit up as the oil exploded. They all threw themselves to the ground as a frying pan flew one way and the stove the other.

'Bloody hell, Ollie, I want to see nineteen forty-two,' laughed Neville. 'I might get bombed or shot at by Jerry but I'd prefer that than being decapitated by a frying pan in the comfort of my own camp.'

The rain relenting was not the only good piece of news for Neville. On New Year's Day he received a letter from Joyce, which was warm, loving and encouraging. His spirits soared, no longer gnawed by the desolation of thinking he had been forgotten by those he loved. The following day more post arrived and Neville was surprised to see a second letter with Joyce's handwriting.

'You look like you've seen a ghost, Timber.' Alan was opening a parcel from home as he and Neville sat having a mug of tea in the mess tent.

'Don't hear from Joyce for weeks on end then, blow me, two letters in two days. Wish I hadn't sent that nasty one a few weeks ago.' Neville slit the top of the envelope with his knife. He sat quietly and read the neat letter, taking in the rounded handwriting. He turned the pages over and then read the letter again.

'Nothing wrong, I hope?' asked Alan, noting the frown on Neville's brow.

'No, no, it's the brightest view possible, ever.' Neville gasped as he began reading it again. 'I'm engaged.'

'Great news! I couldn't be happier for you,' laughed Alan as he shook Neville warmly by the hand. 'She might have to wait for the ring, though.'

Chapter 8

Into the Western Desert

January 1942 to May 1942

The rain might have gone, but the weather wasn't finished with 522 Company. Temperatures plummeted, snow and sleet drifted down without pause and it was impossible to get warm even with a ration of rum. The wagons froze to the ground and nothing was moving.

On Tuesday 6 January, Neville was ordered to stand by for a troop-carrying detail. Sixteen wagons shuddered and lurched through the snow to the area occupied by the East Yorkshires. The infantry piled into the back of the wagons and at 0930 the convoy moved north towards Irbil. As they headed into the hills, the infantry frequently had to dismount to dig the wagons out of the snow, particularly where it had drifted. They covered thirty miles in three hours before stopping. The infantry disembarked and set about the task of digging defensive positions through the snow and ice. It was late afternoon as the gloom descended, and with the intensity of the cold increasing, the troops were ordered back to the wagons.

Poor buggers, thought Neville as he watched them drag themselves over the tailboards, faces etched with exhaustion and aching with cold. The sound of engines starting was sporadic. Some fired, some stuttered and some did nothing. Neville's started at the third attempt and tow ropes were attached to those unable to start. The bitter cold had frozen the snow and sleet on the roads and the convoy slipped and slithered out of the hills. Neville's brakes were frozen and he had to rely entirely on gears to slow his vehicle down. Halfway back to camp his wagon gave up with a shudder. The lights went out and the engine stopped. A tow rope was attached and the convoy limped back into camp late in the bitter winter night.

Two days later the news circulated that the Caucasus campaign had been cancelled.

'Well, that means a move,' said Nick as he, Neville and Joe speculated over egg, beans and toast.

'Damned waste of time being here,' grumbled Joe.

'Must've been a good reason,' munched Neville. 'Things change. Where now, though?' *Somewhere warmer, please*, he thought.

On Tuesday 13 January, 522 Company were ordered to break camp and prepare themselves for a long journey, their final destination the battle arena of the Western Desert.

One week after leaving Kirkuk, Neville and the others found themselves standing beside the oil pipeline running from Iraq to Haifa. They were following the pipeline, stopping at the booster stations on the way. They had left H4 Booster at 0700 that morning, and were en route to Mafraq in Jordan when they came across a remarkable sight: the racing camels of the Desert Patrol. The convoy halted to meet the Bedouin tribesmen, now transformed into the finest Arab fighting force, led by John Bagot Glubb.

'Glubb Pasha!' exclaimed Neville, slightly in awe. 'You know, the new Lawrence of Arabia. Lieutenant-General Glubb, I think. A Lancastrian, but no one's perfect.'

'Christ, he's coming over here,' gasped Nick.

Striding over to the stationary wagons was a well-built, imposing man, dressed in the local dish dash and keffiyeh.

'Welcome to the desert, men.' He smiled, sweeping his arm to and fro. Neville, Nick, Joe and several others who had gathered snapped to attention and saluted. 'What unit?' asked Glubb.

'RASC, sir, 50th Division,' answered Neville.

'Tykes and Geordies. Well, no one's perfect.' The men glanced at each other and laughed. 'Heading to Baalbek, I understand?' Glubb asked. He was met with blank looks, so continued, 'I'm guessing you haven't been told where you are going, then. Well, the 6th Australian Division has been recalled due to the threat of a Japanese invasion and you men will be plugging the gap. Can't have Jerry breaking through, now, can we? Not that there will be too many left after my boys have dealt with them.'

Neville looked across at the tribesmen beside their camels and imagined these brave warriors charging German armour and being slaughtered in the process.

'I know what you are all thinking,' Glubb said. 'Camels and rifles against tanks, eh? Well, men, there's more than one way to skin a cat and certainly more than one way to kill Germans. Mustn't hold you up. All haste with your journey, men.' He saluted and turned on his heel, waving cheerily as he mounted his kneeling camel.

Wow, thought Neville, as the men and camels raced away, kicking up a cloud of dust in their wake. *Wouldn't mind if he was our commanding officer.*

Over the days that followed, the division journeyed through a transformed landscape. The stone, sand, scrub and barren desert of before was left behind. Now they travelled through the verdant Jordan Valley. The drops were steep: at one point Neville grinned to himself as the cooks travelling in his wagon yelled in alarm and turned the air blue as he drove too close to a 1,000-foot drop.

Bang goes my dinner tonight, he chuckled to himself while wiping a bead of sweat from his brow.

They passed Lake Tiberias, the surrounding hilltops covered intermittently in clouds and sunshine. A glorious rainbow arced from one shore to the other as the lake narrowed towards its northern end. From Tiberias they headed north, travelling at the base of snow-capped mountains and marvelling at the sight of Mount Hermon reaching almost 10,000 feet into the azure sky. Finally they came to their journey's end, temporarily at least, at El Ain, twenty miles north of Baalbek in Lebanon.

'Nissen huts.' Neville nodded in approval. 'The ultimate in luxury.'

'Let's grab the one with the bath and ladies-in-waiting,' said Joe.

'Hallucinating again,' laughed Nick, as he smacked Joe in the middle of the back.

Once they were encamped, everyone was given a sheet of A4 paper printed on one side. It was headed 'Baalbek' and provided a historical summary of the area covering its Roman, Christian, Saracen and modern period.

When I joined the army, I never realised we would get this kind of information, Neville thought. *How to strip a gun, how to mend an engine, how to kill Germans, yes. But not a printed history of a town in Lebanon. Interesting, though.* He continued to read.

The following day he and Nick were dispatched to Baalbek to pick up rations. He drove slowly past the Roman ruins he'd read about the day before, awestruck by the magnificence of the columns of the Temple of Jupiter and Bacchus, towering forty-six feet high with the snow-topped mountains in the background. He turned to Nick.

'I can see why it's one of the Seven Wonders of the Ancient World.'

'Let's hope if Jerry breaks through he doesn't come this way,' Nick replied. 'He has a nasty habit of flattening everything.'

It was to be Neville's last detail for a couple of days. Concerned the front wheel bearings were gone on his wagon, he was towed back to camp. In the workshop he took the wheel off to discover the rollers and bearing case were ground to a pulp and the steel axle badly scored. In the absence of any spares he was effectively immobilised unless he could get another wagon. He decided to pinch the battery and the rear wheel brake drum for another truck if he could get one.

'Have you got that beast working yet, Wood?' asked Sergeant Stuart as he marched into the workshop with another sergeant beside him.

'Not this one, Sergeant; I'm looking for a replacement.'

'Well, find one quickly,' said Stuart. 'This is Sergeant Parkin, A Company, just arrived from England. He wants to visit an ammo dump, so ammo detail in thirty minutes. That means you, and Joe, Suchy and Sergeant Parkin will be going with you.'

Neville's shoulders sagged. He had been hoping to complete work on the wagon and spend some time in the mess tent catching up with his letter writing, particularly to Joyce. *I'll show the bugger an ammo dump*, he thought to himself.

Having commandeered a wagon, they drove to the dump at Balbechon. Alan and Neville went to the stacks of ammunition and pulled aside the camouflaged tarpaulins.

'Land mines first,' he whispered to Alan. 'I bet he doesn't know the first thing about setting the firing mechanism, so he'll think they're live.' Trying to keep a straight face, the pair started lobbing the mines in the direction of Sergeant Parkin, who was standing with Joe. They started kicking the mines like footballs in the sergeant's direction.

'What the hell are you two doing?' yelled Parkin as he leapt behind the bonnet of the wagon. 'They're land mines, for goodness' sake.'

'Yes, Sergeant, and these are twenty-five-pounder armour-piercing fragmentation shells,' shouted Neville as he and Alan threw the conical projectiles in all directions.

'You're all mad,' shouted Parkin. And then his anxious face broke out into a grin as he realised that his leg was being pulled. 'They're not going to go off, are they? Bastards!' he shouted back.

The Division had been tasked with constructing defences to check a German thrust south through Syria. This entailed the rapid construction of concrete pillboxes and anti-tank defences. They had been in the Baalbek area for nearly two weeks when, at 1700 hours on Monday 9 February, an emergency order was issued that all leave was cancelled, all personnel were to return to their units immediately and all ammunition was to be loaded for a move the next day. A move that would take them south, through Palestine, then west into Egypt and into the Western Desert.

Neville's latest orders had their origins two months earlier. On 18 November 1941, the British launched a surprise attack codenamed *Crusader*. It began from the Eighth Army base of Mersa Matruh (the Eighth Army being how the Western Desert Force had been renamed). Mersa Matruh was 232 miles east of Tobruk, which was under siege by the Axis forces. Over several days of heavy fighting and tank engagements, offensive and counter-offensive, the British were able to break out of Tobruk. On 6 December, General Erwin Rommel ordered his Axis forces of Deutsches Afrika Korps and Italian divisions to retreat westwards to a line between Ajedabia and El Haseia. This shortened his supply lines and he was able to rebuild his armour capability, while the British supply lines became over-extended.

On 21 January 1942, Rommel had sent forward a 'reconnaissance in force' of three strong armoured columns. The tactical reconnaissance soon became a full, surprise counter-attack. He found the Eighth Army forward elements dispersed and tired and rapidly drove the British back to a line from Gazala, on the coast and thirty-six miles west of Tobruk, to Bir-Hakeim, an old Ottoman fortress fifty miles to the south.

A stalemate ensued. Both sides regrouped and re-equipped. The British formed seven defensive boxes, each with an infantry brigade and artillery. Barbed wire and minefields extended between each box with armoured formations to the rear for counter-attack. The main strength of the Gazala Line was to the north defending Tobruk. The southern end of the line, held by the Free French, was more weakly defended but heavily mined. It was believed an attack around the flank of the southern sector would over-stretch Axis supply lines and was therefore unlikely. Even so, it was to here that the 50th (Northumbrian) Division had been summoned with haste from over 1,000 miles away, to help bolster this flank.

When the Khamsin blew from the south, it was like the hot panting breath of a dragon, spreading a smothering blanket of dust over man and machine. It choked the nostrils, filled the ears, dulled the hearing and made the eyes red, gritty and sore. Tea quickly resembled a mug of mud and meals became unpalatable. But when the Khamsin didn't blow, the sunsets etched themselves on the memory. The evening wrapped the desert occupants in a cold blanket, like a benediction after the intense heat of the day. The sky was beautiful pastel shades of light purple and pink.

522 Company crossed the River Nile on Monday 16 February to enter this landscape of extreme contrasts. As they left Cairo behind them, heading west, the graveyards of smashed, rusting wagons and tanks were ever present. The following day, they camped to refuel at a small railway town.

'Where are we?' asked Nick as he jumped down from his wagon.

'No idea. Just following Timber in front,' Joe said with a shrug.

'Good thing I keep my eyes peeled, then.' Neville stretched his arms above his head as he sauntered over. 'The sign said this place is called El Alamein. Wouldn't have minded stopping at Alex but at least I could just about see into the town.' They had passed Alexandria seventy miles back, but by-passed the city in the interests of speed.

The convoy continued west along the rough single-track road, flanked on both sides by the colourless, featureless desert. They had been warned not to veer off the road, even in the event of needing to circumnavigate broken-down or destroyed vehicles. The desert on both sides of the road was mined for miles in all directions. If they came under attack, they would make the convoy harder to strike from the air by rapidly extending the gaps between vehicles. Any stricken vehicle would be pushed or shunted to the roadside and abandoned.

The convoy by-passed Mersa Matruh and, as they progressed ever closer to the front line, air activity began to increase. Neville could only watch and hope it wasn't his turn when he heard the explosions as the tail of the snaking convoy was bombed. Several wagons were lost, along with numerous casualties, but the attack did not impede progress to the extent it would have done had the front or middle of the convoy been hit. They camped about forty miles east of Sidi Barrani.

The Germans and Italians were not the only enemy. As they progressed through Sidi Barrani and past Fort Capuzzo, darkness seemed to descend like a blanket being thrown over the convoy. It was a vicious, howling sandstorm. The convoy became strung out and fragmented as each wagon struggled to follow the one in front. The only saving grace was that enemy planes were grounded.

Closer still they progressed towards the front line. Artillery, wagons, tanks, equipment of all types littered the desert, mangled, smashed, barely protruding from the drifting sands, which were like tombs of grit with twisted metal headstones. The Division eventually camped fifteen miles south-east of Tobruk, just past Eighth Army battle headquarters and thirty miles from the front line at Gazala.

'Quite like old times,' Neville said to Alan, who was standing by his wagon scanning the sky.

'Yes, very much like France – other than the scenery,' Alan replied.

They stood watching the aerobatics of the aerial dogfights: planes swooping, rolling and climbing like ravenous birds of prey in pursuit of their quarry. The scream of mortally damaged engines assaulted the hearing as the unlucky ones plummeted to oblivion in the vast expanse of desert. Smoke trails followed them down to where death embraced them in a ball of fire, then drifted away on the breeze like spirits floating from the carnage.

'Sounds like Tobruk is getting a right good pounding,' said Alan, looking towards the rumble of guns and the percussive crump of bombs.

'Well, I hope there's some of it left,' murmured Neville. 'I've got a detail there in the morning.'

'Bad luck,' said Alan.

'Bad luck nothing.' Neville grinned. 'I've been after that detail ever since we got here. That place could be the stuff of legend.'

As the Division was digging in, camouflaging as effectively as possible particularly against incessant air attacks, Neville headed for Tobruk. The journey was relatively short and unlike the barrage he'd heard the day before, the city was unexpectedly quiet. Soldiers moved around the rubble-strewn streets clearing what they could. Military Policemen directed what little traffic there was weaving along the bomb-cratered roads. Neville was surprised by the number of buildings still intact despite the pounding the port had taken.

As he approached the dockside and the bay came fully into view, the reason for the shelling became clear: ships of different sizes, war and cargo, were entering and leaving. Others, though, were going nowhere, all but fully submerged with just a funnel or mast to betray their final resting places. Some of the bigger warships that had been sunk were more clearly visible, their decks, guns, super-structures awash with the calm blue water of the bay. Neville sat and looked, pensive, thoughtful, then jumped in his seat as the anti-aircraft guns thundered, the cacophony shaking his wagon.

Time to move, he said to himself. Through the top of his wind-screen, he could just see a series of black specks in the bright blue sky. The specks became more visible, and grew, as the Luftwaffe resumed their pummelling of the port city.

Loaded with ammunition, and knowing what would happen if he received a direct hit, Neville was happy to head out of Tobruk. As he drove along the dusty roads away from the city, he watched a dogfight in the sky ahead, Hurricanes and Messerschmitt 109s leaving vapour trails in their wake as they tried to avoid being in the crosshairs of their enemy. But three German planes crashed to earth along with two Hurricanes, the second of which erupted into a fireball 300 yards from where Neville was driving along the road.

'Poor bugger.' Neville's grimace turned into a grin as he saw a parachute canopy drift slowly through the smoke, the airman twisting and fighting to control his descent. But his relief was short-lived: he watched the canopy implode and the airman hurtle to earth, crumpling in a heap just yards from his flaming aircraft. Neville stopped and closed his eyes, the impact of flesh and blood on sand and stone ripping through him. His first instinct was to head in the direction of the wreckage, just in case. But driving across a mine-filled landscape with a wagon full of high explosives on a lost cause did not seem a prudent move.

Back in camp Neville took his wagon to the workshop. 'Brakes, springs and U-bolt,' he informed the mechanics.

'We'll see what we can do but it will take some time,' was the reply. Neville looked around at the plethora of vehicles of all types awaiting attention. Over the days that followed, Neville's frustration grew. 'I'll go mad soon,' he grumbled to Nick.

'You are mad, Timber,' grinned Nick. 'What's up now?'

'I can't stand being static. I feel useless. I don't mind being machine-gunned and dive-bombed just as long as I'm doing something.'

'Be careful what you wish for,' Nick said. 'I've heard there's going to be a big offensive soon. Plenty to keep you busy when you get the old bus back.'

Three days later Neville was part of a patrol column scouting towards Alum Hamza. He had a squad of East Yorkshire infantry in the back of the wagon. Light tanks and Bren carriers in front and behind were interspersed with the wagons.

'Jerry!' came the shout. 'Nine o'clock.'

Atop a shallow ridge barely half a mile away were two German armoured columns heading directly parallel with the British. Neville quickly pulled away to his right, taking his wagon into a slight depression. As the Churchill tanks and Bren carriers turned to engage the enemy, the infantry leapt out: Neville grabbed his rifle and raced with the infantry to the relative shelter of the armour. The noise was deafening, with shells whistling across the short distance between the opposing forces. The Bren guns, capable of firing 500 rounds a minute, opened up in short bursts. They were joined by rifle fire and the distinctive report of the smooth-bore, muzzle-loading mortar being fired by the infantry. Dust and shrapnel flew through the air as German shells exploded nearby. Sharp metallic pings reverberated as bullets hit armour. Human cries and groans became more frequent as casualties were taken. Neville tried to block out such shouts and focus on the enemy, but it wasn't easy. An armoured car took a direct hit from a German tank, punched back yards from its position. Its two occupants were thrown into the air like rag dolls, hitting the earth and lying twisted, bloodied, limbless. Medical orderlies ran back and forth, bent double, administering relief where they could as the firestorm raged.

'They're turning!' came the cry. To Neville's relief, the British tanks and Bren carriers set off westward in pursuit. The drivers and the infantry raced back to the wagons and followed within minutes. The whole engagement had lasted little more than thirty minutes but the adrenalin of battle coursed through Neville's veins for hours afterwards. The elation subsided during the evening as Neville, Nick, Joe and Alan sat in the canteen listening to the radio. Judy Garland sang a selection of songs, creating an atmosphere of tired sentimentality. Each man sat quietly, thinking of home.

'New senior officer,' informed Neville.

'What was wrong with the old one?' Nick looked up from the letter he was reading.

'Gone to RASC Central Command. Can you believe it? This bloke is a Jock. Lieutenant Bill Carton. Just met him, though, and he seems okay – for a Scotch bloke, anyway. Promised us all some beer in the canteen.'

'Doesn't sound like a Jock,' grinned Nick as he resumed his reading.

The following day, their new senior officer ordered a vehicle inspection. To the relief of Neville and the others, it lasted barely ten minutes: 'He doesn't know one end of a truck from another,' said Neville, to laughter. But not everything was amusing about the exchange.

'I'll tell you what, though,' said Alan, 'he told me that the death toll for RASC is higher than the infantry.'

'Yes, I'd heard that, too,' Neville said with a frown.

The order came in for everyone to have a fresh set of inoculations. The sight of the medical orderly brandishing the needle proved more fearsome for some than the sight of a German tank turret coming over an escarpment. The jabs for malaria and blackwater fever caused stiff arms and splitting headaches. Everyone had to endure the Free From Infection inspections, dropping their trousers to ensure their private parts were not infected by the fleas and lice that many men were carrying.

On Friday 20 March, a convoy of 522 Company left camp at 0800: there were thirteen wagons in total, each full of high explosives, which were to be taken to an advance point, east of Bir Halegh, perilously close to the front line. The convoy was travelling in extended order, a snaking dust cloud, when Neville heard a tell-tale sound from above. Like eagles searching for prey, three Stuka dive-bombers were patrolling in the clear blue sky. One by one they banked, then swooped down to attack. Neville could hear the deathly screams of their descent above the wagon engines but knew he just had to drive on, hope and pray. One bomb dropped fifty yards to the left. Even from that distance the sand and gravel rattled across the windscreen and the wagons rocked on their axles. A second bomb screamed earthwards, detonating ahead of the convoy and creating a curtain of dust. There was a pause, then the wailing of the attack resumed, along with the sharp shriek of the third bomb. This detonated feet from the offside of Harry Minchin's wagon, blowing him from the cab. Moments later the wagon, full of high explosives, erupted in a fireball. Harry had been carrying two passengers: Lew Johns, whose wagon was out of service, and twenty-four-year-old Lieutenant Jardine, a young officer who had been with the RASC less than a fortnight. Neither man was ever found.

As three Hurricanes swooped from high in the sky to protect the convoy the Stukas banked away, their job done. The hunters became the hunted as the British fighters avenged the deaths on the ground, shooting down all three dive-bombers. Down on the ground, the convoy had halted. Neville's wagon was the next in line to Harry's and he leapt from his cab, running straight towards the inferno in front of him. He grabbed Harry under the armpits and dragged him away from the heat. Harry's body was charred and he had severe shrapnel wounds in his posterior, but to his amazement and relief, he was somehow still alive.

His ear drums had burst so he didn't hear Neville's comforting words: 'First blood to Jerry, Harry, but you got off lightly.'

During March an attempt was made to get an important convoy to Malta. The plan involved the Eighth Army launching a diversionary attack to draw the attention of the Luftwaffe from the Mediterranean to the Western Desert. The British operation had the code name *Full Size* and was planned as a three-column attack. Two of the columns were to attack the enemy at Tmimi and Martuba. The third was to cover the attack and withdrawal. The attack began on the night of 20 March with the East Yorkshires advancing on Martuba. They got to within two miles of Martuba Aerodrome and opened fire. Then there was pandemonium, with the Luftwaffe flying bombing and strafing missions throughout the daylight hours of 21 March.

The second column of Durham Light Infantry captured the dominating ground at Gabr el Aleima, which was directly in their path to Tmimi. Over 150 Germans were captured and Tmimi was attacked as planned. By the time the columns withdrew, the convoy had reached Malta safely.

Neville, Nick, Joe and Alan were drinking tea. They would have preferred something stronger but after a long night and day anything was welcome. And at least they were still in one piece.

'Wonder what last night was all about?' mused Alan.

'Dunno, but that should keep Jerry on his toes,' replied Nick.

'Well, I thought it was a good day.' Neville sighed, taking a sip of his drink. 'I went out with a wagon full of Durhams and came back with a load of Jerrys. And, boy, did they look pretty beaten up, although I'm not surprised given how stubborn they were defending that Gabr place. I've heard that some of our lads in the East Yorks have been trapped by a Jerry armoured patrol. Hope they make it back.'

'Well, good evening, my merry men,' came a well-known voice.

'Span! So where were you when all the fun was going on?' grinned Neville.

'Driving our lord and master back and forth to make sure you all did your job. He said to me quite categorically, 'Charlie, we need to keep an eye on that renegade, Timber.' They all laughed as Charlie sat down with them. 'Everyone is getting one of these,' he said as he handed around small slips of paper. They all looked at the black type from Major Norfolk, Commanding Officer of 522 Company. It read: *Personal from GOC. Army Commander and Corps Commander send congratulations on magnificent fight by 50 Div. last night.*

It went on to warn them that the Germans had dropped Thermos bombs one and a half miles west of where they were based. These were anti-personnel mines shaped like a Thermos flask with a motion-sensitive fuse that would detonate at the slightest movement.

'Very nice of the old man,' said Joe. 'But I'd have preferred it if he'd popped along and bought us a beer.' They all raised their mugs of tea to that.

The days that followed seemed to the troops on the ground to be a watch-and-wait stalemate. Neville complained that he had one hell of a job digging his wagon down four feet, to make it less visible. The reality was that the British commanders knew that the Axis forces would be ready to attack before the British, so the focus was to prepare the seven defensive boxes. The consistent factors during those days were the dust storms and the aerial combat. A Tomahawk fighter was brought down near to camp and Neville, with several others, headed for the wreckage. They pulled the pilot from the mangled cockpit and brought what was left of him back for burial.

On Sunday 5 April the general alarm was sounded: the Germans were believed to be approaching the main minefields. British patrols went out, the gun rumbles increased in intensity and air combat escalated. Despite the British response, the German advance took the key points of Bir Temrad, Sidi Bregisc and Rotunda Segnali, narrowing the no man's land between the opposing forces.

The relative lull resumed, but the German bombing intensified. British wagons were lost and Forward Supply Dumps were attacked by the Germans with some success. Some of the concern was alleviated when those selected for leave to Cairo or Alexandria were allowed to go. But the train carrying the soldiers was dive-bombed and machine-gunned by the Luftwaffe, killing over forty men.

To pass the time, Neville went scorpion hunting and managed to catch several in tins. Along with Nick, Joe, Alan and a few others they poured petrol on to the ground in a circle, dropped the scorpions into the centre of the ring then lit the petrol. The ring of fire sent the scorpions into a frenzy, causing them to sting themselves to death. The man whose scorpion survived the longest won the bet.

Mid-April proved bitter-sweet for Neville. He had been selected to go on leave, which cheered him immensely. He had been confiding in Nick that he had not heard from Joyce for eight weeks, and that he couldn't understand her. On Monday 13 April, Nick was with him as he collected some mail.

'Joyce?' asked Nick, recognising the expression on his friend's face.

'Looks like it.' Neville tore the envelope open. As he read it, he paled visibly.

'She's called it off,' he said. 'Says she hasn't written to show me what it's really like not to get a letter. Blimey, I only had eight from her all year. She must have had the letter I sent telling her what I thought in no uncertain terms. I knew I shouldn't have sent it.' He shook his head. 'Suppose I'll get over it but what a send-off for leave.'

The following day Neville began the journey to Cairo. He had been assigned the responsibility of non-commissioned officer for forty 522 Company men on leave. It proved more onerous than it may have with some maladministration necessitating some sweet-talking of the Railway Transport Officers.

They arrived in Cairo on Friday 17 April and made directly for the Nelson Hotel and full board for six days. The cost was two pounds and two shillings but the proper bed, with its cool Egyptian-cotton sheets, and a bathroom with hot and cold water felt like absolute luxury after the hardship of the desert. Neville walked through the lobby eyeing the numerous pretty girls and took a look in some of the brothels nearby. But he decided to give them a wide berth and enjoyed a marvellous supper instead.

The contrast to daily life at camp was stark. He stayed in bed as long as he wanted, took a stroll, went to the numerous cabarets, watched films such as Gracie Fields in *Shipyard Sally* and enjoyed a tipple or two. Tickets were booked at the Diana to see *A Yank in the R.A.F.* and the Empire Club became a favoured haunt, the bar area in particular. He took a walk round Fatima French Brothel and although some of the lads succumbed to temptation, Neville decided a look at the menu without tasting the dishes was a better approach. He went to Giza, the Pyramids and the Sphinx.

All too soon the time to leave arrived and they all returned by train to Mersa Matruh. Despite their Company moving to a new position, they arrived back on Tuesday 28 April and resumed their duties. After a day on vehicle maintenance, and enduring a howling sandstorm, the joyous days spent in Cairo soon felt like a fading memory.

The days rolled on into May: the stalemate, waiting and drudgery continued. The company were continuing to dig pits for the wagons to bring them lower to the ground and make them less visible to the enemy. As they dug, they hit rock and tried blasting through it, taking cordite from artillery shells. The tamping proved difficult, so the blasting was unsuccessful. It was back to pick and shovel and hard labour.

The tension increased. Luftwaffe bombing intensified and everyone was aware that something significant would happen soon.

The waiting was the worst. On Sunday 24 May, 522 Company were under one hour's notice to move and everyone stood to action stations. They were all aware of the weaknesses of the defensive boxes, the lack of flexibility to support one another and the fact that the minefields between each box were not covered by firepower. The Germans were expected to attack between 150 and 151 Infantry Brigades, right where Neville and his unit were dug in.

As the hours passed, the waiting for something to happen seemed interminable. The cold, starlit night of Monday 25 May turned into a bright hot Tuesday morning. All was silent, as if the desert was holding its breath. Finally, at 1400 hours, it became abundantly clear that the Germans had re-armed for offensive action quicker than the British. Two parachute flares arced into the sky and all hell was let loose.

Chapter 9

Dancing to Rommel's Tune

May 1942 to June 1942

––––––––––

The rumble of the guns was unmistakable, a relentless roll of thunder across the desert. Neville was standing staring west, where the noise was coming from. They were too far away to see, but close enough for those sounds of war to seem as though they were getting louder.

'Sounds like a major action.' Neville turned to Nick, who was listening alongside him. 'Us pummelling them or them pummelling us?'

'All I know,' said Nick, 'is that we've got orders to be away from here. Ready by 1530: four hours.' He slapped Neville on the arm. 'Drew the short straw. I'm with you.'

Nick, Neville and the rest of 522 Company had been positioned in close support of the 69th Brigade, to the rear of their defensive boxes. Ahead of them, the 69th Brigade and the 150th Brigade of the 50th Division, along with the South African Division, were in battle with the Italians. The Italians were continually attacking, pushing and probing, but the defensive boxes had remained resolute and in position, holding firm as instructed. Meanwhile, the German 90th Light Division, 15th and 21st Panzer Divisions and the Italian Ariete Armoured Division had swung south around the open southern flank at Bir Hakeim, and turned north towards Tobruk, to the east and rear of the British defensive positions. The Axis forces had immediately begun clearing the minefields between the defensive boxes of the British brigades. It left them vulnerable to attack while they worked on the minefields but the instructions to the 50th Division were clear: hold firm.

In the heat and dust of the desert sun, Neville and Nick began the heavy lifting of loading up the wagons with ammunition. It was hot, thirsty work, and it wasn't long before Neville could feel his shirt sticking to his body with sweat. But just as he felt they were on top on the situation, he saw Sergeant Stuart running along the line of vehicles, a look of panic across his face.

'Jerry's broken through!' he shouted. 'Emergency move 1230. You've got thirty minutes – anything not loaded, leave it!'

Now Neville and Nick really began to shift. Thirty minutes was nothing, and they still had a lot of loading to do. The pair of them worked so quickly that by the end they were barely able to breathe. But somehow, with the clock ticking down, they managed to load every box. Jumping into the cab, Neville grabbed an oily cloth and wiped the sweat off his face. He passed it over to Nick.

'Ready?' he asked, as he fired up the engine. Neville gave a silent prayer and to his relief, it stuttered and shuddered to life at the first time of asking.

'So where are we going?' Nick asked, as the convoy of trucks began to move out in open order.

'Sure as hell ain't going west,' Neville said, following the wagon in front of him. 'Not today, anyway.'

The convoy headed north and east, sweeping away from their

original position, away from the rumble of the Italian guns and down into a shallow valley. They passed through that and drove up on an escarpment. For a moment, all was quiet, the shadows on the sand casting different shades and relief from the sun across the convoy. But as Neville drove the wagon over the top of the depression, everything changed. As if out of nowhere, the convoy was plunged from calm into the thick of battle. All around them were strewn the smashed-up wrecks of tanks and trucks, metal casing ripped open like tin cans. On opposite sides of the valley ahead, Neville could see German/Italian and British positions pounding each other. In the middle of this, as shells whined overhead, sand and stone erupted like geysers blowing.

'I'm going straight!' Neville shouted above the din as the convoy split apart, vehicles weaving and stalling between the plumes of flame and smoke. He rammed the accelerator to the floor, forcing him and Nick back as the wagon picked up speed. Neville could feel the full weight of the vehicle as he wrenched the steering wheel left and right, zig-zagging between blazing wagons and smoking shell holes. His face was set, teeth grinding, eyes wide, as he tried to focus on the end of the valley ahead. But he could barely see or hear – blurs continually whipped across his field of vision as shells screamed past in search of their targets. The noise, meanwhile, was so deafening that he could barely hear Nick shouting next to him, his face ashen beneath the grime and sweat, lips mouthing some unheard words.

'What?' shouted Neville.

'You're heading towards Jerry!' yelled Nick, pointing at the armour three or four hundred yards to the right.

'Bugger!' Neville's expletive was lost in the assault of noise as the British artillery opened up with concentrated fire. He yanked the steering wheel sharp left and drove hard. The noise abated slightly as they moved away and he started panting as he realised that for most of the ordeal he had been holding his breath.

The ten minutes it took to negotiate the valley seemed like hours. As the convoy began to regroup on the other side, it was in a much-reduced number. Some never made it, incinerated under the fierce heat of the enemy attack. Others veered too far west and ran into the enemy armour to be destroyed or captured. As the sound of battle receded, Neville knew they had been lucky. He and Nick sat in silence, ears still ringing from the sound of the shells, and continued to drive towards Sidi Barrani.

'Any idea what's happening, Sergeant?'

Early the following morning, Sergeant Stuart was doing a check on men and vehicles. Before he could answer Neville's question, Lieutenant Carton emerged out of the darkness and sat down on the tailgate of Neville's wagon. The tip of his cigarette glowed orange as he inhaled and blew out slowly. As Neville waited for an answer, several members of the Company gathered round to hear the news.

If the previous day had been long, the night had felt extremely short. The gloom of the evening had transformed to darkness like someone flicking a switch, but the pitch-black offered no cover from German attack. The Luftwaffe overhead bombed continuously and indiscriminately, hoping to hit their target. Somehow Neville and the other drivers snatched two hours of exhausted sleep. At 0300 the following morning, they moved north-westerly towards Tobruk. It was here that they had paused, and where Carton was able to give them an update. The news wasn't good.

'Aye, well,' he began with a grimace, 'word is 7th Armoured is in a bad way near Knightsbridge and the 150th are, to all intents and purposes, cut off. Lot of casualties but we expect to counter-attack and drive the bastards all the way back to Tripoli. The situation is under control.' Knightsbridge was the name given to one of the line of British defensive boxes.

Neville glanced across at the doubt etched on the faces around him. It certainly didn't feel like everything was under control. But they moved on: what was left of the convoy travelling southwards a few miles from Gambut. As darkness lightened into dawn, they could see the airfield was taking a pounding from the Luftwaffe and steered well clear. To the south, the sound of battle intensified. The Cauldron, the area of battle near to the 150th, was living up to its name. The German armoured offensive, which had stalled due to fuel and ammunition shortages as they extended their lines around the southern flank, now resumed with venom as the British minefields were cleared north of Trigh Capozzoli, a route between the 69th and 150th boxes.

The bitter, attritional fighting continued without pause. But 522 Company could only await orders. They remained in position, stood to, in anticipation of an enemy breakthrough. Neville was frustrated at the temporary inactivity, wanting to be doing something to ease the nerves which were taut with the tension. As the morning dragged on, he and Nick found themselves watching the skies where the battle between the Luftwaffe and the RAF continued. Planes were turning, rolling, climbing, firing and evading in quick succession. Neville followed one particular dogfight between a German fighter and a British Kittyhawk. The German plane was right on its tail, bobbing and weaving and firing short bursts of cannon fire. *They're close*, Neville thought. *They're low*. Then, with the Kittyhawk barely thirty feet from the ground, it took a direct hit in the engine. It was down, crashing flat to the ground, sliding and lurching in a cloud of sand and smoke towards Neville's truck.

'Run!' he shouted. Neville and Nick dived for cover as the Kittyhawk's guns went off, peppering the canopy of Neville's truck and filling it full of holes. It screeched to a halt just twenty yards from the truck, covering Nick and Neville with a stinging shower of dust and stones. Instinctively, the pair ran towards the stricken aircraft, leaping on to the wings, Neville coughing as he inhaled the thick black smoke. He pulled back on the cracked canopy. The pilot was struggling with his straps but by some miracle he didn't appear badly hurt. With Nick's help, Neville pulled him from the smouldering aircraft. The Kittyhawk, he knew, could blow up at any second. They dragged the pilot to a safe distance, where a team of Company medics ran across and took over.

'Gather round!'

Neville had barely time to catch his breath before Lieutenant Carton was barking at them. He was standing on the tailgate of a wagon and bellowed to make himself heard above the noise. 'Stop mollycoddling the RAF, you two,' he chided, as Neville and Nick joined the rest of the group.

'Okay, boys,' Carton continued, once everyone had come over. 'Our lads have a major shortage of ammo in the boxes. We're splitting the Company in two. Half of you will take ammo to the 69th and half of you will head to the 150th. As we're not sure what we hold and what Jerry holds, and to avoid their aircraft, we will be taking it in under cover of darkness, no lights. Be ready to move at 2100.'

Another night, another gauntlet to run. As darkness fell, Neville was among twelve wagons heading south-west to the 69th. In the gathering gloom, he strained his eyes to look for any distinguishing landmark in the barren terrain. All he had to guide him were the flashes of gunfire, tracer and bombs detonating that punctuated the darkness with temporary windows of light. The wagons reached the Durham Light Infantry positions just before 2300.

Neville stopped near the artillery positions and jumped down to help the exhausted artillerymen to unload.

'Bring us some more, will yer?' one shouted as Neville turned his wagon around and headed back the way he'd come. He arrived just after midnight and waited for the return of the second convoy, which had been assigned to the 150. When they finally returned at 0300, three of the wagons were missing. Neville ran over to see Jim Oliver slump down from his cab, his face etched with misery and his voice cracked with frustration.

'We couldn't get through,' he explained, close to tears. 'We tried, but lost three of the lads. Jerry has them in a stranglehold, pounding them to bits. The East Yorkshires are running out of ammo, poor bastards. We must be able to do something for them. It's sheer bloody murder in there.' He ran an arm across his eyes. 'Sitting on our arses in boxes. My God, what are they thinking?'

'That will do, Oliver,' snapped Carton. But there was compassion in his admonishment. 'Get some rest,' he added.

Jim, though, wasn't finished. 'East Yorkshires and Green Howards aren't getting any bloody rest, Lieutenant.'

And rest was not forthcoming in the days that followed either. On 30 May, the defensive box of the 150th Brigade was attacked again. It was defended resolutely by the East Yorkshires and Green Howards, but dawn the next day brought with it the banshee-like wails of the Stuka dive-bombers. They pummelled the defensive positions prior to a concerted attack by German and Italian infantry and tanks. As hard as the 150th defended, they could only hold out for so long. By the end of the day the box was overrun: 3,000 prisoners had been taken and 101 tanks destroyed. The Germans now held a consolidated position in the middle of the British Gazala Line. To the south only the box at Bir Hakeim, defended by the Free French, continued to thwart the enemy.

Back in 522 Company, Neville, Nick and the others tried to digest the news.

'So damned much for everything being under control,' said Neville through gritted teeth. 'The Desert Fox is leading us a merry dance.' Nick and Joe nodded in agreement.

'Battle's still going on at Knightsbridge and Bir Hakeim.' Alan tried to stay hopeful. 'Maybe that will turn the tide.' But the silence to his response said everything. The men stayed near the wagons, deep in their own thoughts, smoking and waiting for fresh orders. They didn't have to wait long.

'Heads up,' snapped Sergeant Stuart as he marched towards them. 'Ammo details, Tobruk to El Adem.'

'What for, Sergeant?' Neville asked, trying to keep the anger out of his voice.

'Not yours to reason why, Private Wood. But as you ask, we're building a new defensive box around El Adem.'

'Never mind defensive boxes!' It was Alan who was to snap first, his hope switching to frustration. 'Why can't we just go and stick it to the bastards?'

'Enough!' Stuart's voice was sharp in response. 'You've got your orders. So move.' Before anyone could disagree, he marched away.

That evening, Neville was in a slow-moving snake of wagons when the attacks started. Even in the fading light, it wasn't long before the Luftwaffe spotted them. As the night wore on, and they ran detail after detail, the losses mounted up: 240 men, numerous wagons. But the details had to continue. Without sleep or respite, Neville drove throughout the night and the following day. It was only that evening that they finally paused; hungry, thirsty, weary, but unbowed.

★　★　★

'Fancy something a bit dangerous?'

Neville was scraping the last bit of bully beef he could extract from a tin when Alan sat down beside him, a glint in his eye.

'Dangerous? Meaning that driving on that bloody road for two days, being bombed, shelled and strafed wasn't?' replied Neville. But his interest was piqued. 'Go on.'

'Company is looking for volunteers for some sort of hush-hush detail,' Alan explained. 'Six wagons, tomorrow night. I've volunteered and I've told Carton you and Nick are sure to be up for it.'

'Oh, that's great!' snorted Neville, giving him a withering look. But just as Alan started to seem worried, he broke into a grin. 'Okay. I'll go see him.'

Alan was right when he said the mission was dangerous. The detail, Neville learned, was to load up with mines and take them to the forward boxes defended by the South Africans on the road to Derna. It would take Neville right into the jaws of the enemy, but it was a challenge he didn't feel he could turn down. Taking the fight to the Desert Fox seemed too good an opportunity to miss.

For once, the gods seemed to be with them. The following night, as they set out under the cloak of darkness, the moon shone clear in the sky, lighting their way. The drive seemed almost suspiciously straightforward, with the only discord the rumble of distant guns getting louder the further west they drove. But then, halfway into their journey, the moonlight was suddenly obliterated as if a curtain had been yanked across it. Seconds later, the cause became clear as a howling sandstorm engulfed the small convoy.

'Blast and blazes!' groaned Neville as he slammed on the brakes.

'Just keep going,' said Nick, next to him.

That, though, was easier said than done. The convoy slowed to barely a crawl and Neville struggled to keep Alan's wagon in front in sight. The storm was a fierce one, wind and sand shaking and rattling the wagon as they continued forwards. But thirty minutes later, as quickly as the sandstorm had whipped up, it disappeared. Neville's wagon emerged into the moonlight once more. They could see the desert ahead, but only Alan's truck out of the other vehicles. The pair of them pulled to a stop. Neville jumped down and walked over to talk to Alan. Not only were they four trucks down, the moonlight showed that they were not on any discernible track or road. The only things visible were the silhouettes of a number of smashed-up tanks and wagons, the remnants of a previous battle.

'I thought you were on the road,' Neville said.

'I lost Bob in front almost immediately we went into the sand,' Alan explained.

'Well, where the hell are we?' asked Joe, who was travelling with Alan. They all looked around the featureless landscape.

'I can't tell if they're ours or theirs,' said Nick, squinting at the moonlit hulks all around.

Joe tilted his head to one side. He'd heard something. 'Engines?' he asked. 'Maybe the other lads?'

Neville shook his head. He could make out another sound he recognised. 'That squeal is tank tracks.'

'Weapons,' snapped Alan. The four of them ran back to their trucks. Neville and Nick pulled their rifles from their cab and dropped to one knee beside the front wheel arches, ready to fire. No sooner had they crouched down than two leviathans roared over the top of a shallow depression. Neville gasped. Two Panzer Mark III tanks had them lined up in their gunsights. As they held their position, two armoured troop carriers emerged from the crest and moved towards them.

'*Legen Sie ihre Waffen ab!*' came the shouts from the first carrier, followed in guttural English: 'Put down your weapons!' Neville knew they had no choice. He, Nick, Joe and Alan dropped their rifles and got up slowly, hands raised.

'*Engländer?*' A German officer walked towards them. As Neville glanced round, he could see he was covered by at least a dozen German infantrymen, the carriers and the tanks. '*Der Krieg ist für Sie vorbei.*'

'What's he saying?' whispered Neville. Another German soldier approached, who was able to translate.

'The battle is over for you, Tommy.' He grinned. The officer, meanwhile, was checking their wagons.

'*Mitkommen,*' he gestured to the four British soldiers, '*und uns folgen.*' Neville looked across to the other German soldier for an explanation.

'You will follow us in your wagons,' translated the soldier. 'And I will ride with *you.*' He jabbed at Neville with his pistol. It was meant to be threatening, but Neville felt strangely calm. Yes, his first reaction had been one of panic and fear at the array of weaponry pointing at him. He had heard the stories of German atrocities, gunning down prisoners mercilessly, booby-trapping corpses. But not on this occasion, at least not yet. *So, this is the enemy*, he thought as he stared into the eyes of the German soldier. *Arrogant bastards.* The German soldier smiled at him and nodded his head towards the wagon. *Bide your time*, Neville told himself. *Your chance may come.* He was followed to his cab and watched intently as he got in, the gun pointing at his back. The German came round the front of the vehicle and climbed in beside him.

'So let us drive.' The soldier leaned back against the inside of the passenger door, his gun resting in his lap. Neville breathed deeply to maintain his calm and started the engine. It was a strange convoy: the two British trucks sandwiched between the German carriers and tanks. After driving across the desert for twenty minutes, they crested a slight rise. In the moonlight, Neville took in a mass of men and machines, of German infantry and armour. The vehicles came to a halt, the German soldier barking at Neville to dismount. Along with the others, he was made to march with his hands behind his head, guided at gunpoint to a clearing in the middle of a corral of vehicles. Another German soldier gestured downwards with his rifle.

'*Hinsetzen und bewegen Sie sich nicht.*'

'I think he wants us to sit down,' said Neville, trying to interpret the German. He glanced over at his three comrades. They too looked resolute, watchful, wary. The four of them sat in a line, with the German soldier keeping guard. In the background, guns rumbled in the distance and flashes lit the horizon. As the darkness receded to a grey dawn, Neville realised how much he was aching from the cold and from sitting in one position.

'What time's breakfast, Fritzy?' Joe asked, only to be met with a stony stare down the barrel of a German rifle. They sat there without speaking, the sound of aircraft growing in volume, feeling increasingly menacing.

In the thin morning light, Neville tried to take in their surroundings. About twenty metres away from them was a staff car, where three German officers had stopped to scrutinise a map placed on the bonnet. The middle of the three removed his cap and ran his hand over his pate. He turned slightly, showing the black iron cross around his neck. Neville double-blinked. It couldn't be, could it?

'Look,' he hissed to the others. 'Over there.'

Alan gasped. 'Is that who I think it is?'

The four British soldiers looked at each other in disbelief, each nodding slowly. They were barely twenty yards from the legend of the German Army: Erwin Rommel, the Desert Fox.

'Almost makes it worthwhile being captured,' said Nick.

Almost, Neville thought. It was certainly a surreal situation. There they were, captives of the enemy, held at gunpoint, in mortal danger in the middle of a battle. And now they sat, awestruck, looking at the man many considered to be unbeatable.

'Oh, for my rifle now,' said Neville.

His attention was distracted as an ambulance pulled over to their right. Two German medical orderlies jumped from the front, leaving the engine ticking over as they headed to the rear. There, they helped out half a dozen men, bloodied and bandaged, leading the wounded to a tent dressing station. Now everything happened quickly. First there was a noise overhead, then the earth shook as the bombs from the RAF began to hit home. Then the German anti-aircraft guns responded and Neville put his hands to his ears to protect himself from being deafened. The air was by now thick with choking sand and dust. All around them, as the explosions came closer and closer, everyone was running for cover. Wounded men stumbled, crying in pain, for the dressing station. Rommel, to Neville's disappointment, was straight into his staff car and was driven away to safety. Their guard had taken cover. That gave Neville an idea.

'Quick,' he hissed, 'the ambulance.'

Under the cover of dust and confusion, the four of them moved as one. Despite the stiffness they half ran, half crouched towards the vehicle. Neville jumped in behind the wheel, Nick sitting beside him. The others dived into the back.

'Christ, where to?' he gasped.

'Just drive and keep your head down,' said Nick.

Neville released the brake and eased down on the accelerator. Slowly, and then more confidently, he turned the ambulance round and moved away. The pair of them glanced round, keeping a sharp eye out for any sign of an alarm being raised or someone in pursuit.

'They'll notice it's gone any minute,' Nick said.

'Yes, but in this mayhem they won't know who's taken it.' Neville sounded far more reassuring than he felt. 'We won't need to go far before they can't see us.'

They weren't the only ones on the move. Tanks, wagons, armoured cars and troop carriers were all driving away as bombs continued to rain down. Neville saw a group of Germans near an overturned armoured car trying to wave them down, but he drove straight on.

'You're going west!' Nick shouted, his voice full of panic. 'You need to go east, east towards our lines.'

'For God's sake, Nick, shut up, I know what I'm doing.'

'No!' shouted Nick. 'Turn around.'

But Neville said nothing, just gripped the wheel and focused all his attention through the grimy windscreen. Nick, though, had other ideas. He tried to grab his arm and the steering wheel, to get Neville to turn around.

'Bloody calm down,' Neville snarled, his eyes blazing. 'Right now I'm banking on Jerry thinking we're running wounded to the rear. At some point we'll be in the open and *then* we turn towards the coast and east from there. I need you watching and helping me, not getting into a flap and pulling my bloody arm.'

Nick sat back and Neville continued to weave his way through the German army, who were more preoccupied with the ongoing battle than with an ambulance moving to the rear. He watched tanks on the move, troops mounting wagons, heard artillery firing, ack-ack guns peppering the grey sky with explosions of flak. As they headed further west, so the concentration of men and materials began to lessen. Neville looked out of the corner of his eye and saw Nick beginning to relax.

'Think we're out of the woods yet?' Nick asked.

'I'll say no more than I'm hopeful.'

But they were far from out of the woods. Just as it seemed as though they'd got clear, on the road ahead a wagon was on its side. Two German soldiers were on the ground, being treated for injuries. Several others were languishing by the roadside, smoking. A lone German stood in the middle of the dusty track, feet apart, facing the oncoming ambulance. He began waving his arms to flag it down. Neville banged on the partition behind him.

'Trouble!' he shouted for the benefit of Alan and Joe.

'What do we do?' Nick's eyes were wide with fear. Neville weighed up his options. He was barely twenty yards from the enemy. Whether they could see his uniform he would never know, but as he continued to drive forwards, the German in the middle of the road began to lift his rifle.

'Decision made.' Neville slammed his foot down hard on the accelerator. The ambulance surged forward and ate the yards of track. The German tried to take evasive action, but took a glancing blow off the side of the bonnet, spinning him into the dust. The other Germans looked up, bewildered.

'We haven't got long,' said Neville. That was an understatement: moments later, bullets started to hit the ambulance. Neville hoped Alan and Joe had hit the floor, but his main concern was to put distance between them and the enemy as quickly as possible. Without pausing or looking back, they pushed on. After two miles, they came across a track to the right. Neville made an instant decision to turn and head north towards the sea. The primary battle action was taking place around the British defensive boxes inland, so they were untroubled as they crossed the barren landscape. When the sea was in sight, he turned right again and headed east.

'You okay?' he asked, glancing over at Nick. He was motionless, pale and drawn and Neville frowned. 'You haven't been hit, have you?' Nick shook his head. 'Well, we're going east now,' Neville said. Nick nodded, almost imperceptibly, but said nothing.

For almost forty minutes they drove on in silence, no sign of any other vehicles. Until, that is, Neville saw something in the distance, heading straight in their direction and instantly recognisable.

'Tanks,' he said, nodding ahead and slowing the ambulance down.

'Theirs or ours?' asked Nick.

'Not sure,' replied Neville, squinting and trying to see what they were. 'But we're running out of options. We can't go back, we can't go into the sea, into the minefields.' His mind was made up. 'We go ahead and take our chance.' He drove the ambulance on slowly now, as the tanks loomed larger and gun turrets swivelled in their direction.

'They're Valentines!' exclaimed Nick, springing up in his seat and coming alive.

Thank goodness, Neville thought. Fifty yards short of the tanks, he pulled over. They sat for a few moments, looking at the six-pounder guns pointing at them directly.

'Okay, on foot from here,' shouted Neville, banging on the partition behind him. Nick and Neville dismounted from the ambulance slowly and Alan and Joe joined them.

'Let's take it steady,' Alan said. 'Their nerves could be shredded, so let's do nothing to provoke them in case they're feeling trigger happy.'

'Agreed. Hands up and slowly towards them,' said Neville.

The four of them moved forward cautiously. Nothing stirred, just the breeze and the Valentines' guns bristling with menace. By the time they were fifteen yards away, they stopped, unsure what to do next.

The turret top of the lead tank flipped open with a clang. A head and torso appeared. In heavily accented English a voice said, 'You can come through now. We just wanted to scare the shit out of you.' Soldiers of the 3rd South African Division emerged from behind the Valentines. They had bayonets fixed but appeared relaxed.

'Who are you?' demanded a sergeant.

'RASC 50th Division, Sergeant,' responded Neville.

'Bloody hell, *rooineks*, and what are you doing coming from that direction?' He used the Afrikaans expression for an Englishman from the days of the Boer War, when the British soldiers invariably had red necks from the sun.

'Escaped from captivity, Sergeant,' said Neville.

'In *that* thing?'

'What else, Sergeant?' Neville smiled.

'Come on, bloody English,' the South African smiled back, 'let's get you fed and watered and back to your unit.'

As Neville followed the South Africans, he suddenly felt incredibly weary and weak. The adrenalin of the previous few hours had carried him through, but now the lack of sleep, food, water and above all the tension and fatigue that came from fearing for their lives caught up with him. He was exhausted but relieved. Despite everything, they had made it back. The battle, it seemed, was over.

But for these four soldiers of 522 Company the battle was not yet over, after all.

During the early days of June, the battle continued to rage at Bir Hakeim, where the Free French resisted heroically, and around Knightsbridge where the armoured forces pounded each other. As deadlock threatened, Rommel rapidly reinforced his positions to provide fresh impetus to his attack and press home his advantage. He took his next decisive action on Friday 5 June when he split his forces in the south, sending the Ariete and 21st Panzer divisions east and the 15th Panzer division north towards the Knightsbridge defensive box. His eastward thrust threatened the tactical headquarters of two British divisions who were once again on the defensive against the speed and aggression of the Axis attacks. By 13 June the British were down to seventy tanks. They were being pushed back north and east, leaving the 50th Division isolated on the Gazala Line to the west, behind the German lines.

'Okay, boys, listen carefully.' Lieutenant Carton gathered the group of drivers in close, speaking quietly, almost conspiratorially, as the order for the 50th to withdraw came through. 'We're breaking out tonight. The position is we can't go east or we'll run directly into Jerry armour. We can't go south for the same reason and we can't go north and east because the South Africans are withdrawing that way.'

'Why are we withdrawing at all, Lieutenant? Jerry hasn't beaten the 50th. Two of the boxes are still fighting.' Alan's question was greeted by grunts and nods.

Carton did not look pleased to be pulling back either. 'We're isolated, boys, with precious little armour left. We have to go back to new defensive positions. A Company will take the 69th Brigade and B Company will take the 151st. We move at 0300 tomorrow and here is the tricky bit,' he glanced round the group as he revealed the plan, 'we're heading south-west straight through the Italians.'

'That'll please them. Mama mia, notta them again,' came a comment greeted by laughter.

'They'll be too busy drinking wine and sleeping it off,' said someone else.

'Better drive through the Eyeties than Jerry,' muttered Neville.

'Pipe down,' snapped Carton. He was serious. 'Once through enemy positions we'll turn south then east around Bir Hakeim. Rendezvous will be Fort Maddalena about one hundred and twenty miles east at the Egyptian border. Now, leaving at 0300 it will be dark. We will travel without lights to maintain the element of surprise for as long as possible. All wagons will have a small white patch painted on the back. Follow the white patch in front and just keep going. The infantry will cover fire and clear out as necessary. Everything but the wagons and the infantry will be left here and destroyed. Any questions?' There was a moment of silence.

'What if we get separated, Lieutenant?' asked Joe.

'Then it's bloody good luck and every man for himself. You have petrol and rations for three days. After that . . .' The unsaid words were left to their imaginations.

Early morning of Sunday 14 June was still and cold. Neville blew into his hands to keep warm as he climbed into his cab, part of a snaking convoy of wagons, two or three abreast. Around him, in the silence, the infantry clambered into the back of the vehicles. Engines coughed to life, merging into a single low rolling rumble: beyond, Neville could hear the incessant sound of artillery towards Tobruk. At 0300 the convoy moved south-westwards, nose to tail, towards the Brescia and Pavia divisions of the Italian X Corps. Neville's vehicle lurched and shuddered over the rough terrain, as he struggled to maintain sight of the white patch in front. That patch was his sole focus, concentrating the mind and preventing thoughts of what may lie ahead.

A graveyard of rusting, mangled, smashed-up vehicles was left behind. Instead, serviceable vehicles of war and tanks loomed all around in the darkness, silent but threatening. Then, a curious noise. Neville leaned towards his open window, hardly believing what he could hear. But it was what he thought it was: the East Yorkshires up ahead were singing 'Rule Britannia'. Leaping from the forward wagons to attack the sleeping Italians with bayonets, they were supported by first one explosion, then another, small supply dumps being blown to create unbridled panic and chaos. Italians tumbled from tents and vehicles semi-dressed but suddenly wide awake, panicking, confused. They grabbed their weapons and began firing indiscriminately, at each other as much as the 50th. In the midst of all this confusion, the 50th fought their way through into the desert. The breakout had been achieved and the Italians had been given hell as a parting gift in the process.

Neville could still feel the adrenalin coursing through him as he continued the drive south. 'Smashing job! What a glorious scrap,' he muttered to himself.

They pushed on in the darkness, the sky no longer lit by fires and tracer. The journey was punctuated by trucks breaking down, more often than not the one following close behind crashing into the back of the stricken vehicle, smashing its own radiator. At which point, the infantry leapt out of the disabled vehicle, piling into those still moving. At one point, Neville slammed on the brakes as he heard an explosion close up ahead: the convoy had made contact with a minefield and one unlucky wagon had taken a direct hit. He sat and waited, tapping his fingers against the steering wheel while the sappers cleared a route through for the rest of them. As the night went on, the convoy itself was no longer a column, more a splinter of smaller groups of vehicles, fighting their way through to the open desert. It was a long night and Neville was never more grateful to see the dawn. He watched the sun reaching above the horizon with layers of mist in the hollows of the desert. The effect was to create an ethereal landscape as if the wagons floated on clouds – a brief moment of beauty to savour among the devastation.

The group of wagons Neville was now with passed Bir Hakeim with caution. They moved south-east through a desert that was barren and trackless, and with no navigable features. The cold of the night was soon forgotten with the stifling heat rising in tandem with the sun climbing higher. Water supplies were both precious and dwindling, eked out among the remaining men. As more trucks broke down and were abandoned, those that were still working were rammed fuller with soldiers and what supplies they could carry. No one was complaining, though: as hot, thirsty and cramped as the conditions were, everyone knew they could easily have been among those left to perish in the merciless desert. As much as Neville had been grateful to see the sun that morning, he was equally relieved to watch it close with the horizon once again. Somehow, they'd made it through the day. The scattered remnants of the convoy began to come together again as they closed within miles of the rendezvous. Route finding became easier, Neville following the tyre tracks of those who had passed minutes or hours before.

Around mid-morning the following day, Neville spotted the crenellated white-washed walls of Fort Maddalena.

'Boy, am I glad to see you,' he said as he peered through his grimy windscreen at the small fort atop a slight rise in the desert.

Neville had two privates from the East Yorkshires with him in the cab. 'You've done bloody wonders, mate,' said the East Yorkshireman next to him, slapping him on the back. Behind them, the shouts and cheers of relief reached a crescendo from the back of the truck.

They had made it. Just. The dispersed convoy arrived in dribs and drabs during the day, the vehicles in a sorry state; the infantry without kit, ammunition or stores; everything had been jettisoned to ensure the men of the Division had priority.

The following day they all moved again, this time to Bir el Thalata just south of Sidi Barrani for some much-needed rest. For Neville and 522 Company the rest looked like lasting less than twenty-four hours. He had spent the day on maintenance of his wagon, as far as he was able to with limited spares. Somehow,

though, his workhorse had kept going. Neville had his head under
the bonnet when the familiar Scottish brogue of Lieutenant Carton
caused him to look over his shoulder.

'Gather round me,' shouted Carton, arms in the air gesturing
everyone towards him. Neville and a group of about twenty or so
drivers moved in closer. Carton's lips closed into a grim, tight line
as he relayed their situation.

'The position is this, lads: the Division has lost about nine
thousand men and is being pulled back to Mersa Matruh to re-form.
That is with the exception of us lot. We are going to head back
towards Jerry to Buq Buq with what's left of the 69th Brigade. We
will take up a defensive position there and fight a rearguard action
along the coast road. Our flank will be formed by 7th Armoured.
We will hold the bastards as long as we can to allow a defensive
position to be established from Mersa Matruh.'

Neville waited for the call. Action was preferable to the waiting
and the tension. Rumours abounded, some with substance, some
hearsay. On Saturday 20 June, the day before Neville's twenty-
second birthday, the bombs rained down.

'He must be getting close again,' observed Nick. He was right.
The Germans had broken through, taken Bardia on the coast and
were advancing rapidly. The emergency order was issued and only
just in time.

'Get back! Go on, outta here!'

The shouts followed Neville as he ran full pelt back to his wagon.
In front of him was an enormous pile of stores and abandoned
equipment. Royal Engineers scurried around it, trailing wires as
they backed away quickly. Neville turned the engine over and
pulled his wagon round and away towards Sidi Barrani. Behind
him, an almighty boom made his wagon rock. In his side mirror, he

saw a huge plume of fire and smoke reaching up into the sky as the supply dump was blown up. On his passenger seat bounced tins of pears and pineapple: everything he could salvage from the food stores before they were added to the impending conflagration.

The rearguard was pulling back towards Mersa Matruh, turning and fighting the advance of the German armour. Neville joined what remained of the wagons as they reached the outskirts of Mersa. The convoy was scattered as German planes swooped overhead, machine-gunning and bombing anything they could see, a relentless attack of attrition. The unlucky wagons careered off the road, bullet riddled, men dying or blown apart as they took a direct hit. There was no time to think about that, though. Neville knew he just had to focus, and hope. Somehow he escaped the bombs to make it into the coastal town, but here was no respite.

'Well, you can't stay here.' An officer of an East Yorkshire brigade walked down the line of wagons that had made it. 'You'll be sitting ducks.' Neville had been at Mersa less than two hours watching the exhausted infantry and decrepit equipment limp into the town, helping where he could. 'German armour by-passing,' the officer continued to shout, 'you can't go back by the coast road. You'll have to find a ravine or wadi.' His warning was that the German armour was by-passing Mersah Matruh, cutting off those in the town from their line of retreat.

'Do we take anything or anyone, sir?' asked Neville.

'The troops stay here,' replied the officer. His expression was grim, summing up what they were likely to expect in the coming hours. 'You should head for Fuka the best way you can. Go on, before you're trapped here as well.'

'Good luck, sir,' said Neville, saluting, but the officer had turned and was shouting, trying to create some order out of the chaos. Nick and Alan ran up, breathless.

'Looking bad, really bad,' gasped Nick. 'What's to do?'

'We're ordered away sharp, so let's go.'

Neville's reduced column of eight vehicles now moved east, away from Mersa Matruh. They kept the coast road to their right, just out of sight, and lurched over the uneven, stone-pitted earth into a shallow wadi. Then, inexplicably, the convoy stopped. Neville leaned out of his windowless cab door and peered ahead. Shells whined overhead, explosions were all around but nothing obvious seemed to be stalling their advance. He got out of his cab and jogged to the head of the column fifty yards ahead.

'Why have you stopped?' demanded Alan as the drivers quickly assembled into a group.

'Soft sand,' came the reply of the lead wagon. 'I'm stuck.'

'Oh, great!' snarled Alan. 'Sitting ducks in a valley just waiting for Jerry to pick us off.'

'Give him a push,' Neville tried to be practical. 'See if we can shift him. Once he's moving again it may be okay.'

The driver got back into the cab of the stuck wagon and started the engine. Four others went to the back and the rest pushed at the sides. The wagon revved and the wheels spun spewing out hot sharp sand, but they just sank further. Alan walked ahead down the wadi.

'Look, he's walking to bloody Fuka,' said Joe. But he and Neville watched as Alan went forward about thirty yards, before turning and coming back.

'It's firm beyond that rock,' he said, pointing to where he had stopped.

'Tarpaulins!' shouted Neville. They all looked at him. 'We need something firm to drive on. Get the tarps off the wagons and lay them across the soft sand. They can work like a makeshift bridge.'

'Bloody brilliant!' Joe turned and ran back to his wagon. They removed the tarpaulins from the first four wagons and laid them lengthways down the wadi and across the soft sand, pulling the edge of the first one under the tyres of the leading vehicle. Then with a shout, they all pushed the lead vehicle again. After some more wheel spinning, the tyres gripped the tarpaulin and the wagon lurched forward down the wadi. The driver drove on to the solid earth and gave a thumbs-up out of his cab window. One by one they all navigated the wadi and pulled away towards Fuka.

They reached the village late on the afternoon of 27 June. Here they camped overnight, sleeping soundly for a few hours despite the rumble of the guns and the drone of aircraft. The following day they pulled back again to El Daba, loaded this time with what remained of the 151st and 69th Brigades. The column of vehicles limped further east, driven back by the advancing Germans.

But on 1 July the retreat came to a halt. They were on Ruweisat Ridge and the *Gazala Gallop* (the ignominious retreat of the British) was over and what was left of the 50th Division and the Eighth Army was ordered to turn and face the enemy. This, it had been decided, was where the enemy would be stopped: Ruweisat Ridge, just south of a railway town called El Alamein.

Chapter 10

Digging In

June 1942 to October 1942

The 50th Division had acquitted itself well in the Gazala battle but sustained heavy losses to men and equipment in the process. They had been pulled back behind the Alamein Line, near Amiriya, an airfield ten miles south-west of Alexandria. Should Rommel break through the Alamein defences, however, the 50th would have to hold the Nile delta.

In the meantime, the plan was to re-form and re-arm. In those early days of July Neville watched, helpless, as the Bostons, Kittyhawks and Hurricanes took off from Amiriya in sortie after sortie, flying to the front-line action. The Africa Korps was attacking Deir el Shein in an attempt to achieve a final breakthrough to Alexandria, Cairo and the oilfields beyond. They had to be stopped.

'Bullshit! In fact, I'd sooner have bombs than this complete and utter bullshit.' The frustration and anger were palpable, exacerbated by the pause in the weeks of battle and retreat, draining away the adrenalin. The news, filtering through, continued to be grim, and Neville's overriding impulse was to be at the front line with the lads. There were promises of patrols and action, and then orders were changed. In the meantime, they maintained what vehicles were left as best they could and muttered and cursed at what they perceived to be the vacillation of the officers. Neville vented his anger to anyone who would listen. Tommy Oates, a newcomer to the Company, had drawn the short straw on this particular day. Everyone else had made themselves scarce.

'What's up, Timber?' asked Tommy, frowning.

'What's up? What's up?' Neville spluttered with incredulity. 'Well, I'll damned well tell you what's up.'

'Must you?' groaned Tommy quietly. Neville frowned and decided that he must.

'What are we doing back here? We should be up there giving Jerry hell.' He pointed dramatically to emphasise his point. 'Instead of which, we don't know what the hell we are doing. Moping around in dust and stone, pestered by flies and scorpions like the bloody plagues of Egypt.' To add insult to injury, Neville had been told they'd be having daily foot and rifle drills. 'Those brass hats,' he fumed, 'those Cairo canaries will have us polishing the silver next. Are you listening to me?' he snorted as Tommy's head rolled off his palm and he nodded off in the dusty heat of the day.

The first Battle of El Alamein continued throughout July. The 69th Brigade moved south to join with the 7th Armoured Division, and the East Yorkshires and Green Howards of the 151st attacked and took Taqu Plateau, before being repulsed by German counter-attacks. The line held and the opposing forces, having punched themselves to a standstill like two heavyweight boxers, paused to resupply in the race to be ready to take the initiative.

If Neville couldn't fight, he could at least take the opportunity for some rest and recuperation: together with Nick, Joe and Tommy, they headed for Alexandria. They swam in Stanley Bay before eating, heading to the Bella Vista Cabaret and eyeing up the local girls. Neville was less interested than the others, having received a letter from Joyce telling him that she'd like to start again. He still wasn't quite sure what to do with that, so he let the sights and sounds of the cabaret take his mind off it.

'Mood's definitely changed,' commented Nick.

Neville had noticed that too. Last time he'd been to Alexandria, the place had felt friendly and welcoming to the British troops. Now, however, the response of locals was one of hostility. Throughout the city, German flags had started appearing, draped from windows and balconies, in anticipation of the arrival of Rommel and the Axis troops.

Distracted from the show, Neville heard a commotion to his side, and looked across to see several people running from the club.

'Uh-oh!' exclaimed Tommy. 'Trouble, I reckon.'

The group got up from their table and headed through the double doors to the street beyond. A crowd had gathered, and as the four of them pushed through, they could see a small group of British soldiers were faced with a semicircle of Egyptians, their knife-blades glinting in the moonlight. Neville had no idea what it was about but when he saw some mates in trouble, he wasn't going to stand by and let them be threatened.

'Started pulling down the Jerry flags,' gasped a soldier from the Green Howards as Neville stood by his shoulder. 'They didn't like that.'

'You're telling me,' grunted Neville. Swelled by the addition of Neville, Tommy, Nick and Joe, the two groups were now almost equal in size and eyed each other warily. The soldiers broke the impasse by screaming battle cries. Lunging towards the Egyptians, the majority of the aggressors took flight. But a couple stood their ground, accepting the challenge and thrusting forward with their blades. There were gasps, grunts and shouts as knives flicked through the air, flashing in the moonlight as the soldiers closed round the smaller group. The situation quickly became confused. Among the scuffles, an Egyptian screamed and collapsed with a knife wound to the chest. His grubby white gallabiyah stained red as he fell to his knees. Agony was etched on his face as he looked up at the soldiers, who stepped back. The Egyptian's remaining partner grasped the stricken man under the armpits and dragged him away as he screamed in pain. Neville looked across at the British soldier who'd stabbed him. He was barely out of his teens, clutching his bloodstained knife and sagging. His mates put a protective arm around him.

'Life's cheap here, Frank,' they reassured him. 'It was you or him.'

'It's a lot of rot, utter bloody stupidity,' Neville snarled. Nick looked across at Joe and raised his eyebrows. 'The same old thing, as soon as we come out of action, discipline again.' Neville snorted to emphasise his point and glared at Nick and Joe who were busy cleaning their equipment.

'Maybe you should apply to be an officer, Timber,' smiled Nick. 'I've heard Winston has flown over from England and is meeting the brass in Cairo. Big chance for you.'

Neville grunted.

'Anyway, we've got the footie match this afternoon. Couldn't do that while we're in action. Should be a lark giving the Green Howards a good kicking,' said Joe encouragingly.

The football match was completed by the time the Luftwaffe hit the aerodrome half a mile away from the stony, make-shift pitch. Everyone dived for cover as the bombs fell and the air rained shrapnel. At 2000 hours, with the sky quiet once again, Neville took his rifle from his cab and reported for guard duty. He was assigned the western perimeter of the camp in closest proximity to the nearby aerodrome. He began his patrol around the perimeter and stopped to look at an overturned, mangled armoured car. Neville thought he could see something in the gathering gloom. As he moved closer, the shape formed into a body half buried in the sand, its arm raised in the air, the hand open as if waving to plead for help. The body was charred, blackened.

'Poor bugger,' muttered Neville. He stood for a few minutes, considering whether to move the dead soldier. As night drew in rapidly the temperature began to drop dramatically. Neville started and instinctively raised his rifle across his chest. As he stared, transfixed, the charred hand began to curl its fingers and balled itself into a fist. It was eerie to behold as the cold of the night caused the hand to contract.

'Stupid,' chided Neville to himself, but he moved away along the camp perimeter, resolving to let the medics deal with the corpse. As he came off duty in the early hours of the morning and slumped in his cab, he knew he didn't feel right. His head was bursting and he was shivering violently. In the building warmth of the early morning he stumbled from his cab and reported to the medical officer.

'One hundred and two, Wood; not good, eh?' smiled the MO without humour. 'I think you may have a mild dose of malaria. I'm putting you on C1 and suggest you get yourself back to bed and rest.' C1 dictated the duties that were allowable and required daily reporting to the MO for further assessment. For the next three days Neville slept and tried to recuperate.

On 13 August it became clear why Churchill had been to Cairo. Lieutenant Carton called the men together in the early evening to announce a change in Middle Eastern and Eighth Army command.

'I have a communication from headquarters to read to you.' His eyes scanned the semicircle of expectant men in front of him. 'A new Commander of Middle East Operations has been appointed. He is General Alexander and he has replaced General Auchinleck.' He paused for the audible murmur. 'In addition,' he went on, raising his voice to get everyone's attention again, 'we have a new Commander of the Eighth Army. He is General Montgomery.'

'Who?' shouted someone.

'Shut up and listen.' Carton fixed the men with a glare then glanced back down at his paper. 'General Montgomery has said that we will ready ourselves for an offensive which will knock the enemy for six—'

'Is he a general or a bloody cricketer?' came a blunt northern accent followed by general laughter. Carton waited patiently for the laughter to die down before continuing.

'The message from General Montgomery reads: "We would fight on the ground we now hold and if we could not stay here alive we would stay here dead."' Carton folded the paper and looked at the sea of faces staring back at him intently.

'No more retreat,' came a shout and the whole group erupted with cheering.

Maybe we're now going to see some action, Neville thought.

'Who's the new bloke with the stripe?' asked Alan innocently.

'Dunno, but he looks like a bit of a stickler for spit and polish and discipline,' said Nick.

'Looks a bit wet behind the ears, if you ask me. Come on, Monty's little favourite,' grinned Joe.

Lance-Corporal Wood looked sheepish. 'You can take the piss as much as you want. I can stand it,' he snapped in his most stoic voice.

'You're an NCO now, Timber. No more moaning about drills and brasses,' chided Joe.

'Still a lot of tripe: Russia retreating on all fronts and we're sat here polishing bloody brasses. Anyway, I know you lot won't care, but I've been ordered to number one platoon with Tommy Oates.' Immediately their faces fell.

'Damn! Let's hope it's temporary,' exclaimed Nick. The posting meant that Neville would leave his pals behind and promotion to lance-corporal did not seem to be a cause for great celebration.

In late August, Neville and his sub-section of five vehicles found the drudgery of drill was replaced by the requirement for urgent disposition of twenty-five-pounder and six-pounder armour-piercing shells. They broke camp and moved south-west to link up with the 10th Armoured Brigade to the east of Alam Halfa Ridge. Here they spent the next two days moving ammunition from one dump to another, then back again.

'Can't you find out what we're supposed to be doing?' Tommy Oates asked Neville. 'I'm fed up of running around like a headless chicken.'

As Neville marched off in search of an officer, he saw eight more trucks arriving, and some familiar faces driving them. Nick and Joe were waving frantically at him from their cabs.

'Bright view!' gasped Neville, catching sight of his mates. 'What are you lads doing here?'

'Knew you couldn't get by without us,' Alan said as he climbed down from his cab, 'so we've come to join you to form 552 Company.'

'You know more than I do,' laughed Neville. 'But, boy, am I glad to see you.'

The newly formed 552 Company continued to move six-pounder armour-piercing shells by the wagon load. *Must be expecting some serious trouble with the Panzers*, thought Neville as a further 300 rounds were unloaded.

On Sunday 30 August, his thoughts were proved right. At 2230 the Battle of Alam Halfa began. Rommel sent his panzers through the south of the British line, much as he had done at Gazala. His battle plan was to drive north and secure the Alam Halfa Ridge to give him a dominating position behind the British front line.

But the new commander of the Eighth Army was determined to stop Rommel and drive him back, proving to his men that the Desert Fox could be beaten. The British were aware of Rommel's plan through *Ultra* intercepts. The designation *Ultra* referred to military intelligence emanating from the Government Code and Cypher School at Bletchley Park, where encrypted German communications were intercepted and broken. The information was so critical to British military intelligence it went beyond *Most Secret* and was classified as *Ultra Secret*. The work of the code-breakers meant the British armour was placed ready and waiting. The German tactics of speed and surprise were thwarted further as the panzers were the victims of poor reconnaissance and became bogged down in the British minefields. As they struggled through they were pounded by the Desert Air Force.

Behind schedule, the panzers broke through the minefields and headed at speed to the ridge. The Stukas screamed in to attack the defences but were met by the Hurricanes, against which they were no match, and instead plunged to the ground in balls of flame. The panzers ground to a halt, assaulted by the six-pounder armour-piercing anti-tank fire and the British armour, hull-down for protection. Then the news came through to Rommel that his long-promised fuel supplies were now at the bottom of the Mediterranean Sea.

All the while, 552 Company had no real idea what was going on. 'Bit of a flap on,' was Neville's observation as he watched the dogfights whirling above him, and listened to the rumble of the guns. The twenty-five-pounders were being used as tank busters and they ferried the shells forwards to the guns, which continued to pound the enemy positions.

'I've counted at least fifty,' said Neville as they unloaded the ammunition at a forward ammunition point in the front line.

'I've lost count,' said Joe, hefting boxes down from the tailgate of his wagon. 'Just smashed-up Jerry tanks everywhere.'

'Royal Engineers are finishing the job.' Tommy Oates came round a truck, lighting a cigarette. 'Dynamite to finish them off good and proper.'

The pounding had had its effect. On 5 September, word came through that Rommel had ordered his forces to retreat. The turning point in the desert war had been reached.

The Company moved back to the area around Amiriya and Neville was immediately assigned to the headquarters guardhouse as provost corporal. There was one prisoner in the guardhouse and, along with two subordinates, they kept the detainee occupied. In addition, they were ordered to keep the camp clear of locals looking for easy supply pickings. Neville couldn't believe anyone would risk breaking into a military camp, which was strictly out of bounds, but then one of his subordinates, Frank Owen, found him in the guardhouse with news of someone heading towards the slit trenches.

'They've just been filled, haven't they?' asked Neville, grabbing his rifle. The slit trenches at the rear of the camp were the ones used as toilets and, on a daily basis, they were filled with petrol and set alight to burn the waste and prevent disease.

Neville and Frank ran over to the back of the camp, slowing to a walk as they spotted an Egyptian squatting over the slit trench. He was smoking happily as he relieved himself.

'You there, stay where you are!' shouted Neville.

The Egyptian looked up in alarm, took the cigarette from his mouth and threw it down into the slit trench. Big mistake. There was a brief pause, then a whooshing noise as the petrol ignited into a wall of flame. The percussion of the explosion threw the man into the air, arms and legs waving wildly. He landed spread-eagled on the ground, face down, his robes smouldering. He looked up, painfully and warily, at the two approaching British soldiers and began muttering imprecations with increasing volume and intensity.

'I've no idea what that little lot means,' said Frank, as he and Neville stood over him, 'but I bet he won't do that again.'

By early October, General Montgomery was in the final phase of preparing to take the Eighth Army on to the attack. The 50th Division was assigned the centre of the El Alamein battle line near to Alam Niyil. The Division was attached to XIII Corps covering the middle and south of the line with XXX Corps to the north.

On Tuesday 6 October, Neville led his sub-section away from Amiriya as part of a vast convoy of trucks heading south on desert tracks. The wagons were full of explosives – Amatol, wet and dry gun cotton, slow matches, Baratol and various mixtures of TNT. They reached camp as darkness closed in. Ready for sustenance after a long day's drive, they left the wagons, heading straight to the NAAFI. As they entered the tent a captain stopped them.

'What are you doing here?' he demanded.

'RASC, sir,' Neville said. 'Just arrived with 50th Division.'

'Are they your wagons over there?' enquired the captain.

'Yes, sir,' confirmed Neville.

'Carrying what, may I ask?'

'High explosives, sir.'

The captain's eyes opened wide. 'Then, Lance-Corporal RASC, you can bloody well sod off. I don't want those things within half a mile of here. Move them now.'

What do you know? Neville grumbled to himself. But they moved the wagons to the perimeter of the camp and trudged back to finally have some dinner. Once he'd eaten, Neville then returned to his wagon, where, given the hour, he was now going to have to sleep that night. He went to the back of the truck and climbed up on to the tailgate. In the darkness he could just make out the boxes of high explosives and detonators piled high, leaving a gap of about eighteen inches between the boxes and the underside of the wagon canopy. He climbed up the boxes and wriggled into the gap, working his hands and arms free so he could tighten his greatcoat against the cold and light a last cigarette of the day.

Neville lay on his back as he lit the cigarette, blowing out the smoke in a long, contented sigh. But then his hand and arm, with the cigarette between his fingers, came down on top of the boxes. 'Ouch,' he winced, as a splinter pierced his hand. To his horror, the lit cigarette dropped between the boxes of high explosives. Eyes open wide with alarm, his body tensed as he lay, transfixed. *I'm sitting on top of a huge bomb*, Neville thought, *one where I've just, inadvertently, lit the fuse. What a way to go. After everything the Germans have thrown at me, I'm going to die from dropping a cigarette.*

Neville held his breath, waiting to be blown to smithereens. But nothing happened. He breathed out deeply, looking around in the gloom as he quickly assessed his options. *Not many*, he thought. *Get out and run like hell or somehow make sure I put the cig out.* He knew he had no time to spare and decided that there was only one viable option. Unbuttoning his flies, he pushed up on the canopy, allowing him to roll over almost on to his front. As he looked down through the gap in the boxes, into the darkness, he could just make out a light glow flickering beneath him. Quickly he adjusted his position, raised slightly on his knees, and took careful aim. 'Thank goodness for tea,' he murmured as he proceeded to piss down into the gap in the boxes. He cursed as he missed his target but contracted his muscles, adjusted his aim and tried again. The glow was extinguished just as he dribbled to a stop. He turned on to his back and lay there, listening to his heart thumping. Maybe that captain had been right to make him move his wagon to the perimeter after all.

For the next few days, the troops were tasked with the back-breaking work of digging defence pits and slit trenches, using their picks and shovels to battle with the arid, stony earth.

'What's up, Timber?' gasped Tommy Jackson, wiping the sweat from his face with a sweep of his hand but leaving it grey and grimy.

'I'll tell you what's up, we've been digging defence pits and slit trenches all day and, bugger me, they want us to move up two hundred yards and start again.' Everyone leaned on their tools and groaned.

However, normal duties soon resumed and at a pace. Mortars, shells and other supplies were moved to appointed dumps and it was obvious that something was brewing. On Tuesday 13 October, Neville and his sub-section were assigned troop-carrying duties and it was made clear that the whole manoeuvre had to be as discreet as possible. They drove to the 69th Brigade marshalling area where the Green Howards piled into the back of the trucks, fit and eager. They arrived at the front line as darkness was falling, little more than 2,000 yards in front of the enemy. There was no talking, no smoking, just quiet, efficient organisation.

Over the days that followed, deception tactics began with hundreds of wooden and inflatable dummy tanks and vehicles arrayed in sight of the enemy. Chains were attached to the back of the RASC wagons and Neville spent two hours a day driving north with the chains raised and south again with the chains dragged behind, creating a huge dust cloud. To the enemy it must have been evident that the British were concentrating their forces in the centre and south of the Alamein Line and the attack, when it came, would be from that sector.

Convoy after convoy carried the twenty-five-pounder shells to the field regiments. Speed was essential. Normally the boxes of shells would be taken to the tailgate of the wagon and lifted down carefully. Now the boxes were pushed down the wagon straight off the end as artillerymen rushed backwards and forwards to collect them.

On Tuesday 20 October, Neville and the other NCOs were summoned at 1300 hours for a battle briefing by the GOC (General Officer Commanding), Major General Nichols. The 50th Division was to attack the Munassib area frontally, led by the 69th Brigade. The excitement was palpable until the GOC confirmed what they had all expected with the diversionary ploys: the main attack was to be in the north, near the coast. The assault by the 50th was to be a feint to hold the German Panzers in the south. The sense of disappointment was huge, barely tempered by the understanding that they would all have a part to play in the greatest battle fought in the Western Desert. But the plans were already in motion: the Long Range Desert Group was behind enemy lines ready to cut his lines of communication.

Smashing job! thought Neville as he left to cascade the information to his subordinates.

On Thursday 22 October, all was quiet. Neville and many other men sat writing letters home, silently praying it wouldn't be their last. Some were chatting quietly, expectantly, others just waited in silent contemplation. Neville finished his letter and took a final detail to headquarters in the Nile delta area. He stopped his wagon, marvelling at the constant stream of tanks and guns, rumbling leviathans taking up their positions.

Friday 23 October dawned sunny and clear. The heat of the day built and the men of the Eighth Army rested and stayed in what shade they could. They ate full rations, some gobbling hungrily, others picking at the food as anxiety blunted their appetite. The anticipation grew, the tension increased. At noon the alarm sounded and at 1315 hours the 50th Division moved up to the left and right of the Munassib Ridge in full view of the enemy's observation posts. There they waited and watched.

As the sun disappeared and twilight gave way to night, the scorched ground cooled and the moon shone brightly. The ever-present flies had disappeared and the desert was still and silent, as if holding its breath. Neville, like others, stood and stared at the invisible enemy in the darkness, and he repeatedly checked his watch. The hands seemed to crawl – 2100; another check, 2110; and another, 2130.

Then at 2140 Neville's ears were assaulted by what felt like a deafening roll of thunder. The earth shook and the skyline erupted in a wall of fire as if the gates of hell had been opened. The barrage had begun.

Chapter 11

The Tide Turns

October 1942 to April 1943

At 2155 hours the infantry came to their feet. The tension of waiting, wondering, praying had seemed interminable. Now they slid their bayonets out of their sheaths and they glinted in the fire of the guns as they were fixed at the ready. The infantry faced forward towards the enemy lines, staring into the darkness, illuminated sporadically by gunfire or searchlights. Some chewed nervously, others adjusted helmet straps or just watched intently. All had a look of grim determination. This time the only way was forward. At 2200 the order came to advance. Rifles and bayonets were lifted at the ready and the steady walk into battle began as the barrage crept forward.

The whole of the Eighth Army line was advancing. In the north, XXX Corps advanced into the minefields with the sappers clearing the anti-tank mines in twenty-four-foot channels to allow the armour to advance in single file. In the south, XIII Corps made a secondary attack, with the 44th Division and the Free French on the left of the 50th. The 69th Brigade, the Durham Light Infantry, probed to the north of Munassib. Within five and a half hours,

529,000 shells had pounded the German and Italian defensive positions, but their resistance remained determined. In the darkness, dust and confusion of battle only half of the infantry objectives were taken. None of the armour succeeded in breaking through the enemy to cause havoc to his rear.

Neville and the rest of 552 Company had spent the night driving back and forth, resupplying the ammunition required urgently at the forward ammunition dumps. The amount they transported felt huge, but Neville knew it was only a drop in the ocean in the context of the barrage that the Axis troops were facing. In the grey light of dawn, they dismounted from their vehicles and tried to make sense of how the battle was going. The fact that they were tasked to dig pits to be used in the event of a German counter-attack and breakthrough didn't immediately bode well.

'Wonder what's happening,' mused Nick as he leaned on his shovel and wiped sweat from his forehead.

'Can't be going too well if we're digging defensive pits,' said Joe.

'Precautionary,' said Neville, feeling more upbeat than his friends. 'You know what these things are like, beating the shit out of each other. Let's face it, Jerry's not likely just to roll over and wave us through.' The others nodded and resumed the digging.

Despite the onslaught, the Axis positions were barely changed. The battle now entered its 'crumbling' phase – the sappers continuing to clear paths through the minefields and the Desert Air Force adding over 1,000 bombing sorties to the incessant artillery fire to progressively crumble the enemy positions. On the night of Sunday 25 October, the East Yorkshires and Green Howards attacked two small hills called *Cape* and *Moor*. The Green Howards achieved their objectives but the East Yorkshires were pinned down by heavy counter-fire.

'Urgent detail, Wood.' Sergeant Thompson appeared and handed over a small sheet of paper to Neville with handwritten instructions. 'Follow up the East Yorks and Howards to the forward ammo dump. Anti-personnel and Smoke.' (The anti-personnel shells were shrapnel shells that would explode and send bullets over a wide area, and smoke was used to conceal your movements from the enemy.)

At 2330 Neville, Nick, Joe, Tommy and Alan headed into the darkness of the desert. They were illuminated sporadically by gunfire, flares and searchlights as they travelled as rapidly as they could without lights. As they moved further forward, the bitterness of the fighting became ever more apparent. Bodies lay contorted in their death throes. Equipment smouldered and the faint cries of the wounded and dying could be heard through the darkness. As they unloaded the ammunition, the sound of rifle and machine-gun fire was punctuated by the heavier percussion of mortars, grenades and supporting artillery fire. On the return to their positions they brought back some wounded and dejected Italian prisoners – conscripts, relieved that, for them, the war was over.

Further north, the main British attack was stalling. Montgomery decided to create a reserve to throw forward and catalyse the attack. The 151st moved from the 50th to XXX Corps in the north, and the costly secondary attacks in the south, which had achieved only small gains, at great cost, were suspended.

Deception, once again, was the order of the day. On Saturday 31 October the forty-one wagons of 552 Company joined with 160 other supply vehicles to drive in convoy, in full sight of the enemy observation points, to create the ruse that manpower and equipment was being moved south rather than north. They repeated the manoeuvre the following day, relatively unmolested by the enemy on the ground or from the air.

At 0055 hours on Monday 2 November, *Operation Supercharge* began with an artillery barrage of such ferocity and intensity as to surpass anything previously witnessed. At 0105 the infantry advanced. Within 500 yards, the soldiers of the 50th Division were engaged in hand-to-hand combat with German gun and tank crews. By 0400 the 50th had reached their objectives on the Rahman Track and the armour poured through like vengeful cavalry pursuing the fleeing enemy.

'Patrol cancelled. It's a general advance.' Neville felt like punching the air at the breakthrough.

'Hun on the run,' laughed Alan.

'Not before bloody time,' grunted Joe.

They moved forward seven miles through carnage. All the way, the stench of the dead was overpowering. Corpses littered the battlefield, crawling with flies, partially enveloped by shifting sand and dust. Shuffling in every direction were thousands of Italian prisoners, abandoned by the Germans who had commandeered their transport and fuel.

'They look a sorry sight,' observed Neville, as his sub-section stopped for a smoke, awaiting further orders.

'Aye, but sooner them than us,' reminded Nick.

New orders were issued. Salvage operations were to start, the wagons of 552 Company commandeered to travel thirty miles through the minefields to see what they could find. Neville found a German armoured car that seemed worth investigating.

'Amazes me we even shifted him,' he commented to Alan. 'I've never seen an army so well dug in.' Alan was looking out at the vast expanse of desert, now a graveyard of vehicles, guns and other military equipment.

'Never thought really,' he said. 'But yes, I can see what you mean with the gun emplacements and the defence pits. Any swag?'

'Just a photograph. Jerry and his girl. Wonder if she's going to have to find another bloke?' Neville put the photograph back in the wreckage and continued rooting around. 'Notice something else?' he asked after a short while.

'What?' asked Alan.

'Absolute dead quiet. Seems funny.'

Alan grunted but stopped and listened to the silence punctuated only by the occasional wagon engine or distant aircraft.

The Germans and Italians were now in full retreat. Fuel was required for the pursuing Eighth Army and Neville's was one of twelve trucks detailed to take petrol from the salvage dump towards Mersa Matruh. It was a perilous undertaking: many of the petrol cans were Italian, in a poor state with fuel weeping out of the sides and the bottom. Halfway through the journey to the front line the convoy came together for a brief rest and parked on some farmland. The drivers dismounted and gazed skyward to the wave upon wave of bombers of the Desert Air Force heading west to pummel the retreating enemy.

The petrol was unloaded on to the roadside to prevent a significant leak into the wagons. Neville unloaded his last can, wiped his hands in the dust and grit of the desert then grabbed his rifle and fixed his bayonet. While the wagons remained stationary, he was Guard Commander and he moved away in a wide circle around the perimeter checking his line of sight in all directions. The bombers had passed and were now a rapidly diminishing drone. He stopped and cocked his head to one side. His hearing became more attuned to the silence and he frowned as he heard a buzzing intermingled with muffled conversation. Something was troubling him and he couldn't put his finger on it.

'Blast them!' he snarled as realisation dawned. He ran back to the line of vehicles, the cans of fuel seeping beside the road, and came to the front of the leading truck, where a group of drivers were huddled together.

'What the hell are you doing?' he demanded.

'Making a brew,' said one with a frown as he sat pumping the primer stove. 'Do you want one?'

'Damned idiots! You'll blow the lot of us to kingdom come. That petrol is leaking out and you start larking about with naked flames. One spark and . . .' He shook his head, incredulous. 'Put the bloody thing out before I put you all on a charge,' he snarled.

Some of the group scowled at Neville, but others looked at the ground, realising their folly. The stove hissed as it was extinguished, a catastrophic accident averted.

The remainder of November was spent on salvage operations. The whole 50th Division had been moved back and unbeknown to all except senior officers, was in great danger of being disbanded. Losses had been significant and it was no longer a going concern as a fighting division. In the end, another division was chosen to be stood down instead and the 50th was reinforced with units from the 44th.

'Heard the griff?' asked Neville one afternoon, knowing full well the four other drivers in his sub-section would be in blissful ignorance.

'Bet you bumped into Charlie and he had plenty of beans to spill,' smiled Alan.

Neville tapped the side of his nose. 'Walls have ears,' he said, causing them all to look round.

'No bloody walls here,' grunted Nick. 'Just sand, rocks, flies and scorpions. So come on, smartarse, you've milked it enough. What's doing?'

'Not even any Jerries to have fun with any more,' sighed Joe.

'No, but still taking casualties,' said Neville. They all looked at him quizzically. 'Arthur Symes has been blown up by a mine.' They all looked pensive, reflecting on the dangers of working through minefields, some of which they were unaware of. 'We also lost a stretcher party. Moving a Jerry corpse and it had been booby-trapped. Bastards.'

'Anyway, that can't be the top-secret news,' observed Alan.

'We're heading west back into action,' Neville revealed. 'Picking up the Green Howards in the next few days and back to El Adem. We'll be carrying some mortars as well. Not fired one before so I'm going to see if I can have a go.'

On Monday 30 November, they arrived at the Green Howards' marshalling area with the rest of the Company. Neville got his wish, firing the 4.2-inch mortar and its twenty-pound bomb into the desert.

'Heads down, friendly fire,' shouted Alan. 'Timber's on the mortar.'

The following day they were on the coast road to Mersa Matruh by 0800. They passed Dala Aerodrome and paused to look at the hundreds of smashed enemy aircraft, destroyed on the ground by the Desert Air Force. They left the main road and headed across the desert towards Thalata. The terrain was rough, causing innumerable delays with tyres blowing out, springs breaking and the odd wagon having to be abandoned or towed. The Green Howards were dropped off near to Tobruk and the wagons headed back towards El Adem on a secondary road. Shortly after leaving Tobruk, Neville pulled over. Nick, who was following, leaned out of his cab window.

'Another breakdown?' he shouted.

'Pee!' Neville shouted back. 'Catch you up. Just don't go too fast.'

Neville relieved himself to the accompaniment of jeering drivers passing by. As he finished, his eyes were drawn to a burnt-out wagon about fifty yards off the road. He watched the rear wagon of the convoy moving away in a trail of dust, then walked quickly over to the wreckage. He checked the back, which was empty. From a flag on the side of the cab he knew it was Italian. He climbed up and looked around. Between the driver and passenger seats he spotted something and reached across for it.

'Well, well,' he murmured as he turned the gun over in his hand. 'Beretta, I think.' The Beretta Model 1934 was the standard service firearm for the Italian army. The pistol was semi-automatic and had a full chamber of seven rounds. 'Nice souvenir,' he purred as he pocketed the pistol and ran back to his wagon.

Within half a mile he had caught up with the column, which had stopped close to at least a dozen British Bren carriers, all smashed and mangled. Neville dismounted to join his comrades as they moved from one wreck to another. As he drew near, he ground his teeth and braced himself, aware of why everyone's faces were so grim. Once you smell burning human flesh it ingrains itself into the senses: the sweet, acrid odour mixed with the smell of burning fuel. Neville looked in the first carrier, which contained two bodies, burnt and charred beyond recognition, their jaws wide as if silently screaming in agony.

'Same in all of them,' said Tommy Oates as he walked back towards his wagon. Alan also came over.

'Shovels, Timber,' he sighed. 'Burial party. Poor sods, and left here to rot.'

All the drivers took picks and shovels from their wagons and split into parties working alongside each of the carriers. They dug graves as deep as the hard, stony earth would allow and gently removed the bodies from the vehicles. Charred clothing and flesh stuck to their hands. Body parts fell away from the corpses and had to be retrieved. Within an hour all the bodies had been interred, makeshift crosses erected and dog tags collected in a helmet. The drivers stood quietly beside the graves, then turned and went back to their wagons.

Over the days that followed petrol had to be moved the 229 miles from Tobruk to Benghazi. Supplies were arriving by ship and twin-engine American supply planes. Neville took delivery of some new Ford Specials to replace the unserviceable wagons in his sub-section. It made the tiresome journey to Benghazi and back more bearable.

'Lieutenant wants you, Timber,' announced Joe as he came by. It was Sunday 13 December and Neville was preparing his wagon for another round trip from Tobruk to Benghazi. He grunted, straightened his uniform, put on his cap and went to the command tent.

'Lance-Corporal Wood reporting, sir,' he said as he saluted Lieutenant Carton. The Scotsman looked up from his paperwork and smiled.

'No Benghazi today, Wood,' he said.

Neville looked at him, confused. 'Sir?'

'You're going on a course. A ten-day NCO course. Start tomorrow 0700. You need to report to the HQ of the 2nd Cheshires near Sidi Rezergh. Carry on.' Neville saluted, turned on his heel and left the tent. He spent the remainder of the day completing his normal duties and ensuring he would be presentable the following day.

On the opening morning of the NCOs' course, Neville found himself one of thirty men standing to attention near to the war-ravaged buildings of Sidi Rezergh. He watched as Colonel Arthur Cookenden marched purposefully to the front of the men, his aides trailing in his wake. Neville was to the right of the line of men and he moved his eyes to the left, but not his head, watching the colonel turn to face them, feet apart, hands behind his back. They were stood at ease and listened to a fifteen-minute lecture on the traditions of the British Army and its need for effective leadership from its officers. Then the colonel turned on his heel and marched away, replaced by Sergeants Verity and Simmonds from the Green Howards, and Sergeant Major Slaughter, Captain Dole and Sergeant Brown from the Durham Light Infantry. They immediately launched into a day of foot drill, weapons training, grenades, map and compass reading, mines, general discipline and how to make out a 252 charge sheet. Thirty exhausted men were dismissed at 1730 hours.

'Think I'd sooner face the bloody Jerries,' snorted Neville as they made their way to the mess tent for a welcome meal.

The first part of the course finished in time for Neville to return to El Adem for Christmas Eve, where he was welcomed heartily by his comrades. 'Welcome back, Timber,' slurred Joe. 'Here, have some wops' blood.' He pushed a bottle of Italian red wine into Neville's hands who happily tipped it down his throat, wiping away the crimson dribbles from his chin with the back of his hand.

'Good to be back.' Neville grinned happily. 'But back to the course on Boxing Day.' They all groaned.

The following day dawned bright and reasonably warm, with all ranks working together to ensure a Christmas celebration to remember. Neville helped rig up a makeshift mess, made from Italian wagon sheets. Then he quickly wrote some letters home before assisting the cooks as they cut up the pork and carved the goose. The food was served by the non-commissioned officers and it was a veritable feast, with wine and beer flowing freely. Neville puffed out his cheeks as he put down his knife and fork on an empty plate.

'Stuffed!' he exclaimed. 'As my dad would say, I wouldn't give you tuppence for it now.' He patted his stomach.

The raucous atmosphere tended to drown out the radio playing Christmas carols. At 1400 hours, midday in England, the noisy chatter and laughter gradually died down as the radio played the church bells from Westminster Abbey chiming for Christmas Day. There was quiet as they all listened to the eight bells of the abbey, strident and then soft. The atmosphere quickly became reflective, even sombre. The bells ceased and quiet prevailed for a few poignant moments. Then from the other side of the mess, someone started to sing 'Silent Night'. One by one, the men joined in, Neville sure he wasn't alone in remembering both lost comrades and loved ones.

'Making me feel homesick as hell,' he muttered as he looked down at his empty plate. Alan nodded and smiled sadly.

The carol finished and there was silence once more. Gradually conversation began again, a quiet murmur this time, accompanied by the sound of dishes being cleared.

'Think Jerry is doing the same as us?' asked Nick.

'Assuming he's not using it as an opportunity to retreat faster than we can catch him,' smiled Alan. 'Probably singing "Silent Night" too.'

'*Stille nacht, heilige nacht*,' sang Neville quietly. 'It's Austrian. I remember Dad telling me about it from the last war. The Christmas truce and they're singing, "*Stille nacht, heilige nacht*", while we're singing, "Silent night, holy night". Really quite ironic. Probably thinking the same things we're thinking, the same things they were thinking back in 'fourteen to 'eighteen. History has a habit of repeating itself.' There was a reflective silence. 'It's probably one of the few things that bind us together at the moment.'

Neville returned to the Cheshires on Boxing Day. The day was cold and wet, sobering after the brief Christmas respite. He completed the course that day and upon his return to 552 Company he was immediately assigned the petrol detail to Bir Hakeim. He left at 1500 hours the following day. There was no improvement to the weather, making the bleak landscape even more forbidding. The journey was through the battlefield advance of the Eighth Army after the break-out from El Alamein. The whole landscape was littered with smashed-up tanks; war equipment and dead bodies were everywhere. His mood was solemn, grim, influenced not just by the weather but by the contrast between the Christmas Day celebration and the bodies scattered across the battlefield rotting in the dirt.

'Not a good Christmas for some poor families,' he muttered. 'Them or us.'

He was back in camp at El Adem on Monday 28 December and as he leapt down from his wagon it was clear that the 50th Division was preparing to go into battle again.

Towards the end of December the Axis forces abandoned their positions around El Agheila. They had retreated westwards to Buerat, a village fifty-six miles west of Sirte. The 50th Division were ordered forward from El Adem to force the Buerat position.

'Happy New Year!' snorted Neville, as he wiped the rain from his face.

'Oh, yeah,' said Nick reflectively, 'so it is. Not the best we'll ever have.'

The weather was still wet and cold. The rain was torrential and the terrain, usually fine sand and stone, became a morass of mud.

'Maybe next year we'll be home,' grunted Neville, with little conviction.

The left-hand U-bolts had broken off Neville's wagon. They were in the area of Msus, on the way to Ajedabia, and the whole convoy of over one hundred vehicles was at a standstill. The majority of the wagons were in a poor state but those still capable of travelling were stuck in the clinging mud and tow chains were being rigged to pull them across the wide areas of quagmire. The rain hammered down, hissing and making a tremendous pounding din on the canvas of the wagons. The drivers, mechanics and troops trudged through the mud, covered from head to toe in muck and soaked to the skin. Food was meagre, just biscuit and porridge. Overall it took several days for the Division to dribble into a bivouac area in the Regina Hills, fifteen miles east of Benghazi.

The Axis forces continued to retreat westwards, but the Eighth Army's pursuit was stalled. Benghazi was severely damaged by flooding and a savage storm had sunk several supply ships in the Mediterranean. The only way to resupply the forward units of X Corps was to transport petrol, ammunition and rations by road from the Tobruk railhead to the Marble Arch area of Benghazi, a distance of just under 300 miles. The Marble Arch, also Arch of the Philaeni, was a monument built in Libya during the time of Italian occupation. All units of X Corps were ordered to create improvised transport platoons to fetch the supplies. To provide extra encouragement, a competition was devised. Marks were awarded for the quantity of stores carried, freedom from accident, maintenance of vehicles and fitness of crews. The prize was £20 for the winning platoon. Neville's platoon of fifteen wagons was designated A1.

'Money's at stake. Bound to be a Yorkshire platoon wins it,' quipped Joe.

They worked hard on vehicle maintenance with the limited spares and supplies they had. On Monday 11 January they journeyed eastwards once again, by-passing Derna, through Tmimi to the railhead at Tobruk. The platoon loaded up with petrol and moved to just outside Tobruk to sleep in their vehicles for the night. They left early the following day, the rain lashing down again, the howling wind rocking the wagons despite the weight of the load. The darkness was closing in as they parked up fifteen miles east of Barca, in an old Italian fort. They had covered 145 miles, which, in the atrocious conditions, was some achievement. Tea was brewed, cans of bully beef were opened and consumed hungrily with biscuits.

Ping! Ping!

'What the hell's that?' Alan frowned as everyone instinctively reached for their rifles and crouched close to the ground. Eyes strained into the darkness, searching for any tell-tale sign of where an attack was coming from. But it didn't make sense. They were in the middle of nowhere. The pinging noises increased in rapidity, coming from the direction of the wagons.

'It sounds like we're under fire,' said Nick, 'but it can't be Jerry, surely?'

Neville loaded a round into his rifle. 'Better go and check.' They crawled through the mud in a wide circle around the wagons but could see nothing. No gun flashes, no movement, nothing. Pinging persisted from inside the wagons. Neville and the others edged to either side of the rear of the first wagon. He used hand signals to direct two of them to pull the tarpaulins aside while the others aimed their rifles into the interior. With a nod, the flaps were yanked aside. Three rifles pointed into the interior, the light of the moon penetrated the darkness of the wagon, stacked high with cans of petrol.

Ping!

'Ahhhh!' Neville sighed in relief. 'It's the cans. They get hot during the day and the metal expands. The cold makes the metal contract causing it to make that noise. Probably wouldn't notice it at other times but it's so damned quiet here.' He shook his head. 'Fancy thinking we were under fire.'

The following day the column completed the journey and unloaded at Number 3 Petrol Depot just south of Benghazi. Day after day, week after week, Neville's team continued to run the 600-mile round trip. In total, millions of gallons of petrol and tons of

The men of the Royal Army Service Corps, 50th Division showing their pride at their achievements in the Western Desert when the Axis forces were in full retreat towards Tunisia and ultimate annihilation.

Back in England in 1944, in East Anglia, and preparing for the great assault on the continent of Europe which began with D-Day. Timber is standing second from the right.

NOTES TO DRIVERS.

Remember :-

1. Your petrol must be switched thro' to the tank with the extended breather.

2. Your engine must be HOT before wading, otherwise it will stall on contact with the cold water.

3. Engage 4 - wheel drive and lowest gear.

4. Let your vehicle run down the ramp SLOWLY on the handbrake, keeping your engine revving HARD; in gear; clutch depressed.

5. As soon as your radiator disappears under the water let your clutch full in and put your foot FLAT on the accelerator and KEEP it there. That's all.

6. Don't get wind-up - THERE'S NOTHING TO IT !

ON SHORE.

1. Remove groundsheet and lower blanking flap.
   Later - remove ALL waterproofing and prepare for normal running.

2. Don't forget after wading you have not any brakes until the drums dry out.

3. If vehicle is not to be used for some time work all pedals and controls repeatedly to prevent salt drying on them and seizing the bearings. Warm up engine thoroughly every few hours to dry out dynamo, starter motor etc.

4. These simple precautions may save you serious trouble later.

Instructions to drivers for driving their trucks ashore though the water on D-Day.

Timber and another soldier with the Belgian family with whom he was billeted towards the end of 1944.

The farewell photograph from the Belgian family with whom Neville was to stay in touch for many years after the war.

PERSONAL MESSAGE

FROM THE C-IN-C.

(To be read out to all Troops)

1. The operations of the Allies on all fronts have now brought the German war to its final stage. There was a time, some years ago, when it did not seem possible that we could win this war; the present situation is that we cannot lose it; in fact the terrific successes of our Russian allies on the eastern front have brought victory in sight.

2. In 21 Army Group we stand ready for the last round.

There are many of us who have fought through the previous rounds; we have won every round on points; we now come to the last and final round, and we want, and will go for, the knock-out blow.

3. The rules of the last round will be that we continue fighting till the final count; there is no time limit. We know our enemy well; we must expect him to fight hard to stave off defeat, possibly in the vain hope that we may crack before he does. But we shall not crack; we shall see this thing through to the end.

The last round may be long and difficult, and the fighting hard; but we now fight on German soil; we have got our opponent where we want him; and he is going to receive the knock-out blow; a somewhat unusual one, delivered from more than one direction.

4. You remember the poem written by a soldier of the Eighth Army in Africa before going into battle, in one verse of which he described what he considered we were fighting for:

> "Peace for the kids, our brothers freed,
> A kinder world, a cleaner breed."

Let us see to it that we achieve this object, so well expressed by a fighting man of the British Empire.

5. And so we embark on the final round, in close co-operation with our American allies on our right and with complete confidence in the successful outcome of the onslaught being delivered by our Russian allies on the other side of the ring.

Somewhat curious rules you may say. But the whole match has been most curious; the Germans began this all-out contest and they must not complain when in the last round they are hit from several directions at the same time.

6. Into the ring, then, let us go. And do not relax till the knock-out blow has been delivered.

7. Good luck to you all - and God bless you.

(signed) B.L. Montgomery,
Field Marshal
C in C 21 Army Group.

Holland
Feb. 1945.

General Montgomery's message to all troops ahead of the final push into Germany.

(above) Timber drives across the Rhine on the newly constructed bridge, many of the materials for which he had transported.

(right) A safe conduct pass to enable German soldiers to surrender safely.

SAFE CONDUCT

The German soldier who carries this safe-conduct is using it as a sign of his genuine wish to give himself up. He is to be disarmed, to be well looked after, to receive food and medical attention as required, and is to be removed from the danger zone as soon as possible.

PASSIERSCHEIN

An die britischen und amerikanischen Vorposten: Der deutsche Soldat, der diesen Passierschein vorzeigt, benutzt ihn als Zeichen seines ehrlichen Willens, sich zu ergeben. Er ist zu entwaffnen. Er muss gut behandelt werden. Er hat Anspruch auf Verpflegung und, wenn nötig, ärztliche Behandlung. Er wird so bald wie möglich aus der Gefahrenzone entfernt.

The British Army were left with no illusions about the dangers they would face once they had crossed the Rhine into Germany.

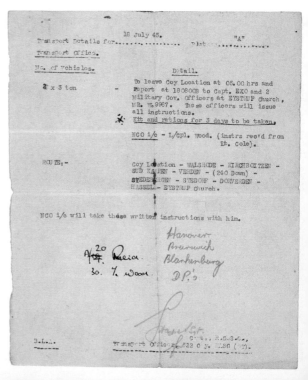

YOUR FUTURE OCCUPATION.

FOREWORD

It is probable that during the occupation we may meet extensive/organised resistance and sabotage by individuals and by groups.
Information contained here has been compiled primarily for the Military Police, but it will be needed also by every soldier in Germany,-just in case.

It is a compilation of the experiences and recommendations of men of Dutch and Belgian groups. These men resisted German occupation of their countries. They know the tricks and all the answers; that's why they are alive to pass the information on to you in this form.

DON'T BELIEVE IT.

Dont believe that there are any "good" Germans in Germany.
Dont believe that it was only the Nazi government that brought on this war. People have the kind of government they want and deserve. Very few people resisted the Nazis. After the war you won't find a German who will admit to being a Nazi. They'll all be "good" Germans.

A Belgian major whose battalion is serving with the Allies, who was twice wounded in two wars with Germany, who was stationed in Germany from 1918 to 1929 as an officer of the Belgian Army of Occupation, knows the Germans better than most of us ever will. He says:
"A German is, by nature, a liar."

HEROES?

The German people may appear to be friendly and docile as you move into Germany and compel them to live differently and govern themselves differently.

Are they?

A small portion of Germany has been occupied for several months. Twice, at night, Germans have strung wires across the main road through Aachen to tear off the head of some jeep driver.

After occupying a little German village for two months, and long after proclamations had been posted calling on Germans to turn in all arms, a house to house search found more than 20 assorted firearms.

Would you be friendly to a foreign force that occupied your country?

If your kid brother shot one of those men, wouldn't he be a hero to you and your whole community?

Germans have kid brothers too.

BADGES AND CACHETS.

In the Netherlands, the people used to wear a little flag of their country in their lapel or on their dress to show their loyalty to their country. A razor blade or piece of glass was concealed in it. When the Germans tried to remove the emblems, they cut their fingers.

If the Germans begin to wear some sort of badge as a symbol of resistance, and we want it removed, they may try the same trick.
Make them remove it with their own hands.
A Belgian resister says:

The German is a genius of destruction; he invented the most diverse arms to kill or injure his enemies. Some Nazis are such fanatics they wouldn't hesitate to blow themselves up if they thought an Allied soldier would die with them.
"Everything found on a suspected person may be dangerous.

"Dont open fountain pens, cigarette cases, spectacle cases or any other container. Such articles may be small grenades. If you want it opened make the person being searched ... open it. Remain at a distance, covering him with your weapon
2/so that you can

18 July 45.

Transport Details for................... Plat .... "A"
Transport Officer.

No. of Vehicles.   Detail.

2 x 3 ton   To leave Coy Location at 05.00 hrs and report at 180800B to Capt. EXO and 2 Military Gov. Officers at EYSTRUP Church, MR. W.9967. These officers will issue all instructions.
* Kit and rations for 3 days to be taken.

                    NCO i/c - L/Cpl. Wood. (instrs rec'd from Lt. Cole).

ROUTE:-   Coy Location - WALSRODE - KIRCHBOITZEN - SUD KAMPEN - VERDEN - (240 Down) - STEDEBERGEN - STEDOW - DORVERDEN - HASSEL - EYSTRUP Church.

NCO i/c will take these written instructions with him.

                              Hanover
                              Brunswick
    ....20 ....   Blankenburg
    30. 7. Wood.   DP's

                              ....
                              ....
                              O.C., R.E.S.Co.
3.L.I.   Transport Officer, 522 Coy. R.A.S.C. ('...').

Orders given to Timber for a special mission in Germany which involved the transportation of die-hard Nazis.

The war with Germany was over and Supreme Commander of the Allied Expeditionary Force in Europe, General Dwight D. Eisenhower bade farewell to all Allied troops.

SUPREME HEADQUARTERS
ALLIED EXPEDITIONARY FORCE

TO ALL MEMBERS OF THE ALLIED EXPEDITIONARY FORCE:

The task which we set ourselves is finished, and the time has come for me to relinquish Combined Command.

In the name of the United States and the British Commonwealth, from whom my authority is derived, I should like to convey to you the gratitude and admiration of our two nations for the manner in which you have responded to every demand that has been made upon you. At times, conditions have been hard and the tasks to be performed arduous. No praise is too high for the manner in which you have surmounted every obstacle.

I should like, also, to add my own personal word of thanks to each one of you for the part you have played, and the contribution you have made to our joint victory.

Now that you are about to pass to other spheres of activity, I say Good-bye to you and wish you Good Luck and God-Speed.

Dwight D Eisenhower

Timber returned to civilian life with a glowing commendation from the British Army – 'a good type of man'.

Mike Wood photographed in 2006 with his parents, Peggy and Neville. The photograph was taken on Father's Day on the weekend Mike presented his father with the full transcript of his wartime diaries and anecdotes.

This photograph was taken on the last occasion Mike's parents were able to come down to Norwich, in September 2002. Following a visit to Anglesey Abbey, near Cambridge, the journey back to Norwich passed Mildenhall and from the back of the car Neville suddenly said he remembered it, that he used to go there to shower. This was the first time Mike knew he'd been in East Anglia. Neville is standing in front of the Desert Rat Memorial at High Ash in Thetford Forest and subsequently Mike discovered that, although the 50th were spread across East Anglia, Neville had stayed in a Nissen hut right behind where he was standing in the photograph.

ammunition and rations were stockpiled. Punctures were vulcan-
ised, spares scrounged or pilfered, anything to keep the wagons
rolling.

'Do you want the good news or the bad news, lads?' asked
Sergeant Thompson. He had gathered the platoon together after
their last ammunition drop. They all looked at him expectantly for
news of the competition. 'The good news is 50th Division has five
platoons in the top six for Ten Corps. You lads are in the top six but
the twenty quid has been won by A3. I would say you'll find them in
a bar in Benghazi but you won't. That's the bad news but there is
more good news to come. You will find them in Benghazi because
we're under orders to prepare for action.'

The date was 26 February and the 50th were on their way to the
Mareth Line.

The Mareth Line was eighty miles inside Tunisia from the
Libyan border. It crossed a semi-arid, scrub-covered coastal plain
between the sea at its north-east end to the Matmata Hills at its
south-west end. It was like a mini version of the Maginot Line, built
by the French as a line of fortifications. The line followed the wadi
called Zigzaou, a formidable ravine with steep banks rising up to
seventy feet.

The objective of the Eighth Army was to advance and capture
Sfax, then on to Tunis. To achieve this, the army had to smash
through the Mareth Line, an attack codenamed *Operation Pugilist*.
On 6 March 1943 Rommel launched a spoiling attack on Medenine,
south-east of Mareth, designed to delay the British attack. Through
Ultra intercepts, the British were aware of the German plan and part
of 50th Division was rushed to the defence of Medenine, while the
remainder faced the grim task of a frontal assault on the formidable
defences of the Mareth Line.

Neville, usually desperate for action against the Germans, found himself struggling with fatigue. 'I'm completely washed out, no interest or energy,' he told Tommy as they rested up at Bengordin, eighty miles east of Mareth. 'This flamin' war's lasted too long and it's time this Division had a rest. I'm tired and so is everyone else.'

'We've got him well and truly on the run, though,' Tommy encouraged.

'Yes, and we've got the dirty work to do again. Move him from the Mareth Line and all his strong positions. A nasty job but one fitting for the Division that gets all the nasty jobs.' Neville threw his cigarette on the ground and looked up at Tommy. 'Still, I suppose we shall do it.' He moved away to take up guard.

They advanced close to the front line the following day and began moving ammunition, particularly twenty-five-pounder shells. The shells were taken from the forward ammunition points to the guns. The twenty-five-pounders were dug in frantically, ranged on the enemy at 18,000 yards.

'When this action starts we shan't chase Jerry out, we shall blast him out,' panted Neville as he unloaded boxes of shells.

'Leave it to us, mate,' grunted a gunner.

Neville slept little, ate little and fought fatigue. There was no time to bathe so clothes were hastily washed through with petrol and hair washed with paraffin. In a brief, lighter moment, Neville said to Alan as he finished cleaning his hair: 'If you need some light just put your cig near me. I'll light up like a Roman candle.'

The Germans did all they could to cause chaos. The Luftwaffe flew sortie after sortie, but suffered crippling losses at the hands of the Desert Air Force. Bombs rained down, planes crashed in balls of flame and gunfire rumbled incessantly. Patrols went out regularly, including the Ghurkhas, with orders to silence the guns firing on Medenine. The cold steel kukris, the Ghurkha fighting knife, were drawn and bloodied. The soldiers jeered as Lord Haw Haw, the American-born British Fascist politician and Nazi propaganda broadcaster, announced that the British Army was now using savages.

By 19 March all was ready. Neville finally managed his first proper night of sleep for several days and he woke refreshed, alert and determined. 'I'm getting up to the guns tonight,' he confided to Nick.

'How do you know it's tonight?' asked Nick, his interest piqued.

'Heard a rumour. I'll wangle it somehow.'

At 2120 hours, 200 twenty-five-pounders led the medium guns into action. Neville was with the Cheshires and he watched and marvelled as round after round was loaded and fired. His ears were ringing and his eyes were dazzled by the flashes. He could feel the heat from the guns and discarded shell cases as the battle unfolded around him. Surely German forces couldn't survive this battering? The shout came for three battalions of the Durham Light Infantry and Green Howards to advance into the inferno. But the constant calls for artillery support indicated the advance was meeting stern resistance from the fortified, and dug-in, enemy.

The infantry took their objectives but with considerable loss. They weren't helped by the terrain and the filthy weather, which prevented the deployment of support tanks and anti-tank guns. The 15th Panzer Division counter-attacked and took back much of that which had been taken. Fighting was bitter, hand-to-hand and bloody.

Although it felt as though they were achieving little, the frontal assault had the effect of fixing the German defences as the New Zealand Corps blitzed Wilder's Gap, a left-hook route through the Matmata Hills that would allow the Eighth Army to attack rapidly north-east behind German positions. The 50th continued the fight, a desperate action in the centre. Some Italian forces gave up and crossed the British bridgehead, fired at by those who remained on their own side. Neville was assigned escort duty and, as he marched alongside 200 defeated soldiers with his sub-machine gun, he saw how all the fight had gone out of them.

They weren't the only ones where the mood was low. The Durham Light Infantry had been driven back to the edge of the wadi. They had taken appalling casualties and in many cases had lost most of their officers. The decision was taken to withdraw them, leaving the 5th East Yorkshire Regiment on the enemy side of the wadi where they came under repeated attack. Accurate and persistent artillery fire and aerial bombing helped them to fight off the enemy, but they too were withdrawn on the nights of 23 and 24 March. The whole of the Division was now back to its start point.

The Eighth Army lost 4,000 men in the Battle of Mareth, most of them from the 50th Division. The cost had been high, but the bloody frontal assault was the key enabler for the successful flanking movement and victory. Thanks to the work of the 50th Division, the New Zealand left hook pushed the enemy back, leaving the Axis forces with no alternative but to abandon their positions on the Mareth Line. They moved thirty-five miles north-west, further and further towards Tunis and total annihilation.

On 29 March Neville went forward through the Mareth Line to recover lost equipment. The adrenalin of battle and the euphoria of another victory were soon wiped out as he smelt the familiar odour of the dead lingering across the landscape. He stood and watched the burial parties with a heavy heart.

'We've pushed Jerry back to Sfax now, I gather,' he sighed. 'And we're stuck back here, mopping up.'

'Thought we were supposed to be resting. Wasn't that what you wanted?' asked Tommy.

'Yeah, well, I'm browned off with all of this. I want to be up with the lads.'

'Be careful what you wish for.'

Alan's reply proved to be prophetic. The 50th Division was called forward. The Germans had dug in at Wadi Akarit and they had to be defeated again.

Wadi Akarit was a strong defensive position north of Gabes, secure on both flanks. The Germans knew that if the Eighth Army could be held there the Axis forces could focus on stopping the Allied First Army approaching from the west. But if the British could break through to Sfax and form a continuous front between the Eighth and First Armies, they could squeeze the Axis forces into a shrinking pocket, trapped in and around Tunis. The attack on Wadi Akarit would begin with the 51st Highland Division on the right, the 4th Indian Division on the left and the 50th Division once again in the centre.

On 6 April, the 7th Green Howards on the right and the 6th East Yorkshires on the left attacked Hachana Ridge and Jebel Romana. They made good progress: Neville watched as thousands of prisoners were led away before beginning his next ammunition detail. He moved off and bumped and rocked over the rugged tracks, weaving left and right in an attempt to evade the enemy dive-bombers.

Smashing job! he laughed to himself as he threw himself about in his cab.

The following day the 6th Green Howards passed through the 7th Green Howards to press home the attack. By 1100 hours it was clear the enemy had been broken and the armour and infantry of the remainder of X Corps poured through the gap. From the heights Neville looked down across the Plain of Tunisia to watch it all unfold.

'Flamin' marvellous!' he exclaimed at the sight of the Eighth Army fanning out in clouds of dust.

'He can't keep fighting much longer, I wouldn't have thought,' said Nick, standing beside him. 'Meanwhile, we're chock-a-block with prisoners. Don't know what we're going to do with them.'

'At least the Green Howards have helped there,' said Tommy. The others looked at him. 'They had a real set-to with the Italian Marines, lost several officers and over a hundred men. So when they took the slit trench they shot any of the bastards that were left.'

'Doesn't surprise me,' murmured Neville, his mind drifting back to burning Bren carriers and burial details.

On 12 April news came through that Sousse had fallen, ninety-three miles from Tunis. The following day the 50th moved forward. The contrast in the landscape was both startling and welcoming. The dirt, dust and scrub they had been used to was replaced by greener groves of olive trees, grass and flowers.

'I must be dead and gone to heaven,' grinned Neville, as the platoon stopped near to the colosseum at El Djem. 'This countryside is almost unbelievable. And look at that Roman ruin. Would have liked to look round that. Maybe one day.'

'Tunis next,' said Nick. 'Major General Nichols has promised we'll be one of the first divisions into the place.'

'We deserve it,' they almost said as an echo.

Orders came through that the Division was to replace the New Zealanders for a frontal attack on Enfidaville. Neville and 552 Company moved the ammunition from Sousse to Enfidaville, approximately forty miles. There they waited for instructions. On 21 April they were called together by Lieutenant Carton.

'I expect you're wondering what the delay is,' he began. Neville glanced at the others. Was this going to be good news? His experience of the war by this point was to expect the unexpected.

'We have a change of command,' Carton continued. 'Major General Nichols has left for another command and our new CO is Major General Kirkman, CBE, MC.' He articulated the letters slowly. 'Major General Kirkman has ordered his staff to prepare to move . . .'

'Tunis, here we come,' muttered Neville.

' . . . to Alexandria.' There were gasps of incredulity.

'But, sir,' came a voice from the back, 'we're only forty miles from Tunis and finishing him off.'

'Yes, sir,' shouted another, 'surely after what this Division has been through they can't stop us finishing the job now?'

Carton remained silent a moment as the murmur grew. *Typical,* Neville thought. *We've done all the hard work and someone else is going to march in and take all the glory.*

Carton put his fingers to his lips and the soldiers went quiet.

'It's recognition for what we've achieved that we are allowed to go back, re-fit and rest, and . . .' He paused for effect before continuing with a smile. 'We are to prepare for the invasion of Sicily.' There was a short silence as the troops took in the news. *Sicily?* Neville thought. *Isn't that in . . . ?*

'That's right, boys. We're going back to Europe to take the fight to Jerry there.'

'Smashing job!' Neville punched the air, as cheers erupted all around.

Chapter 12

Back to Europe

April 1943 to December 1943

'What on earth is that smell? It stinks!' Neville wrinkled his nose in disgust. He was standing outside the NAAFI tent in camp just outside Alexandria, his hunger for lunch diminishing rapidly.

'Maybe our chefs have already taken the decent food on ahead to Sicily,' offered Nick.

Both were covered in sweat. The mid-July temperature had soared and their shirts and shorts were soaked and stained from working on the wagons. The Division had just completed its arduous journey of over 1,000 miles from Tunisia. They had returned through the gap at Wadi Akarit, on to Benghazi and Mersa Matruh, though as Neville remarked, 'At least this time we're not going back with Jerry hot on our tail.'

They had paused for a time at El Alamein, by the new cemetery. Hundreds of graves, some of the dead of the 50th Division, were laid out in neat rows, each bearing a simple cross. The hot breeze had created swirls of dust as they stood there in thought, like spirits emerging from the earth. Otherwise there was silence, such a contrast to the cacophony of battle just a few months before.

Alexandria had provided the briefest respite – a snatched chance to swim in the sea, rest and recuperate. Now they had been ordered to move again, to Mena just north of the Great Pyramids of Giza. But not before lunch, or so they thought.

Nick and Neville entered the NAAFI tent to discover it was empty.

'Not surprised,' muttered Neville. 'That smell is enough to ruin any appetite.'

On a table was the cause of the sulphurous stink: a tray with a pyramid of peeled, hard-boiled eggs. Such was the oppressive heat that the eggs had turned a strange shade of grey and purple. Neville gulped, Nick went pale.

'Don't think I'll ever be able to touch a hard-boiled egg again,' Neville said. 'Take our chance on the way to Mena?' Nick nodded and they left the tent quickly.

The convoy of wagons set off later that day, driving into a beautiful golden sunset. Darkness was setting in rapidly as they arrived at Camp 30 at Mena. The following morning Neville emerged from his tent to watch the sun rise, setting the pyramids alight with a golden glow.

'Can you believe it?' Neville said to Alan. 'We're back at a camp opposite the one we first came to when we arrived two and a quarter years ago.'

'Yeah,' snorted Alan, 'and in between time we've covered just about every grain of sand and damned rock in North Africa.'

Operation Husky began in the pre-dawn of 10 July with 150,000 troops, 3,000 ships and 4,000 aircraft converging on the shores of Sicily. The invasion force was supported by paratroopers who were to seize some of the main bridges on the island. The 50th Division landed in the south-east corner of the island, one and a half miles north of Avola.

The landings were met with only light resistance, with the Germans and Italians successfully misled into believing that the Allies would invade Crete or Sardinia. The Division quickly established a bridgehead, moving inland rapidly. The coastal plain was cultivated with vineyards, olive groves and citrus orchards. Stone walls bordered roads and fields and the land was criss-crossed with numerous dry water courses and ditches. Up to 2,000 yards inland the ground rose slowly, then more steeply with hills about 1,000 feet above sea level. The hills were rocky or covered with scrub, a very different theatre of war to the barren desert of North Africa.

The 50th consolidated in the Floridia–Solarino area prior to a push northward through the foothills to Lentini on the southern edge of the Plain of Catania. But not everything went to plan. By the third day of the invasion only fifteen RASC vehicles had been landed. The loss of motor transport ships had been heavy and 234 vehicles were at the bottom of the sea, lost to German air and naval attacks.

There was only one road north, running adjacent to the coast. Paratroopers had successfully prevented the Germans from blowing up the 400-foot Primosole Bridge over the River Simeto. The northern side of the bridge was now defended by German paratroopers and the attack by the Durham Light Infantry was bloody and protracted. The bridge was taken at great cost and the Division assumed an active defensive position just south of the heavily defended Catania Aerodrome. There they battled the Germans, Italians and the onset of malaria – a trio of enemies that lay in wait for Neville and his friends.

★ ★ ★

'We're off!' exclaimed Neville as he ran over to tell the others the news. 'Orders being issued. Back to Alex tonight and off to Sicily.'

Joe grunted as he finished a mug of tea and threw the dregs across the sand. 'I was getting quite comfortable here,' he mumbled. The rest of the drivers were jubilant.

'Anything but the heat, the flies and the boredom,' grinned Tommy Oates.

'Heat and flies in Sicily, Tom,' said Alan.

'And biting ones at that,' continued Neville. 'We're to collect mosquito nets and Mepacrine tablets. We're Ammo Company S22, petrol is S23 and rations S24.' He spoke quickly, his excitement palpable and infectious.

They drove in convoy to Alexandria and almost immediately were directed aboard the landing ship and tank HMS *Boxer*. The ship slipped its moorings on 26 July, laden to its maximum capacity of twenty-seven vehicles. She steamed westward at a steady fifteen knots in a convoy of twelve ships, protected by destroyers of the Royal Navy. As the sun began to rise in the early morning of 29 July, the fort of Vittoria emerged from the mist, the ship dropping anchor off Augusta on the east coast of Sicily.

Several ships were called in for unloading at once, some using the available jetties and others dropping their ramps at the water line. HMS *Boxer* did the latter and Neville was sitting in his cab, engine running, as the ramp slowly descended and the blinding sunlight flooded in. As soon as the ramp came to a stop with a heavy metallic thud, the first vehicle drove off the ship. Neville fol-lowed. The Royal Navy beachmaster, hands cupped round his mouth, bellowed instructions: 'To the right, lively now. Get that heap of junk away from here. LCT 146, get the hell out of here. You there, push that bloody truck out of the way. Do you want to be dive-bombed? Then get cracking.' Neville waved cheerily as he drove by, but was acknowledged only by a scowl.

Once assembled a quarter of a mile from the waterfront, S22 were ordered north towards Catania, over the Primosole Bridge to the front-line defensive positions of the 50th where the ammunition was needed the most.

'Looks like we've got something to shoot the buggers with now,' announced a Durham Light Infantryman with a broad Geordie accent and a friendly wave as Neville and the rest of the Company turned off their engines and dismounted from their cabs. With the ammunition unloaded, orders came through for S22 to proceed immediately to Syracuse to collect further supplies. As the last boxes were being lifted off, Neville leaned on the front of his cab and lit a cigarette. Tommy Oates joined him.

'Impressive, huh?' Tommy nodded in the direction of Neville's gaze.

'First time I've seen anything like it. Quite a sight.' Neville smiled.

In front of them loomed Mount Etna, rising majestically from the Plain of Catania to a height of 10,990 feet. Its huge conical shape dominated the island landscape, a plume of smoke billowing from its summit and drifting westwards in the gentle breeze.

'Looks like it's having a smoke too,' grinned Tommy.

The journey to Syracuse entailed a return trip of eighty miles. Over the next two days, S22 put the miles in, journeying up and down the coast road to bring tons of ammunition forward. As the German mortaring and shelling began to lose its intensity, it seemed a strong indication that the enemy was pulling back. On 4 August the Division was ready to move again. The advance began with the 69th Brigade on the left and the 151st on the right. The enemy had withdrawn and the 50th set off in pursuit.

On 5 August the Mayor of Catania surrendered the city to the British. The convoy of wagons carrying the ammunition, petrol and rations began making its way northwards around and through the city – a route that was less exposed to enemy fire than the westward route through the low foothills of Mount Etna.

Driving through Catania, Neville and the other drivers were greeted by a pitiful sight. The city stank of squalor and the rubble-strewn roadside was lined with Catanians emerging from the shelter of the city's catacombs. Both young and old were filthy, ragged, emaciated, their eyes dark and sunken above hollow cheeks. Some waved warily, others held their arms out, palms up in supplication.

The convoy stopped, Neville watching as army biscuits were thrown from a couple of wagons in front of him. Barely had the packets hit the ground before screams and wails turned to violence. Young and old pounced on the food. They kicked, scratched and punched as they fought desperately. One old lady staggered back from the melee clutching her chest, collapsing, motionless. Military Police appeared to try to restore order, clearing the way for the wagons to move forwards.

The convoy crawled on, clearing the city and moving north-wards, but progress wasn't any easier. The plain gave way to the lower slopes of Mount Etna, which fell away steeply into the sea. This left the main road running north as the only viable route for vehicles. Cross-country wasn't an option: the dry riverbeds criss-crossing the countryside were steep or sheer and many of the vineyards and olive groves were terraced, supported by lava walls twice the height of a man. The minor roads, meanwhile, were more like rough tracks bordered by similar lava walls, pro-viding good cover but equally trapping men and equipment in the equivalent of a shooting gallery, particularly from the higher ground to the north-west. The main road was the only way to go, but had to be cleared of mines by the sappers, which slowed progress further still.

By 9 August the infantry had made contact with the enemy. As the Germans withdrew they didn't go quietly, blowing the bridges over the Mangano and Leonardillo rivers. The riverbeds were dry but the banks were steep and impassable for motor transport. With the wagons unable to progress, alternative arrangements had to be made to keep supplies going forwards.

'Driver required for a new type of transport, Timber,' shouted Alan. Neville was in the back of his wagon checking the ammunition boxes. He moved to the tailgate and looked out the back of the wagon to see Alan waving at him. He double-blinked – what was that with him?

'Meet the army's secret weapon.' Alan was walking up alongside a train of mules. 'C'mon, Timber, it'll be like one donkey leading another.' Neville threw an oily rag at him.

'What's going on?' he asked.

'As I understand it, we can't go straight ahead, we can't get round by sea, so we're sending the poor bloody infantry across those slopes up there.' Alan pointed towards the Etna foothills. 'These fine beasts are going to do the, well, donkey work, to carry the ammo and supplies.'

It was a quick fix to the immediate situation. The mules carried the essential supplies along rough tracks in rugged, precipitous countryside that the vehicles couldn't use. Neville and the other RASC drivers kicked their heels and waited while the engineers and the bulldozers cleared the road and made the riverbeds crossable. Progress continued to be made: by the evening of 14 August the infantry had occupied Taormina, just thirty-two miles from the ultimate objective of Messina. But as the Germans continued to blow up roads, tunnels and bridges, it was a frustrating march forward.

'At least in the desert we could get to where we needed to be,' grumbled Joe.

'Yes, apart from the wadis, the rain, the mud and the Luftwaffe,' Neville reminded him.

Frustration among the men was growing. When the move finally came, it was once again by sea. The wagons were loaded back on to another landing ship, tank (LST) to the south of Taormina at Cape Schiso and ferried to the north to Cape d'Ali – as far as the Royal Navy could realistically transport them. Neville was one of the first to disembark from the ship and he was immediately ordered to stockpile the ammunition. A sergeant major of the East Yorkshires informed him and the drivers of another seven vehicles, that they were now part of the 4th Armoured Brigade and would be re-assigned to troop-carrying duties. The advance of the infantry had, so far, largely been on foot, but the British now needed to advance rapidly in pursuit of the fleeing enemy.

As dawn broke on 17 August the soldiers of the 5th East Yorkshire Regiment climbed into the wagons. As soon as it was fully light, and the mines on the road could be seen – Neville hoped – the small convoy set off. He'd worried what the response might be, but other than isolated rifle or machine-gun fire, the convoy was untroubled. At 1000 hours they reached their objective of Messina. The town was eerily quiet; as Neville drove through, the thought of ambush was ever present. But there was nothing but the by-now-familiar detritus of war: rubble, smoking buildings and destitute locals asking for food.

Then the convoy came to a halt. Soldiers ahead. The infantry jumped out, ready to engage. Neville braced himself for conflict. But then came a shout, and an accent that he hadn't expected to hear.

'Hey, what kept you guys? We've been here waiting since last night for you. Looks like the good old US of A got here first . . .'

* * *

Compared to the travails in the desert, the campaign in Sicily had been short, sharp and successful. Neville and the rest of the Division were moved back from Messina to the Cape d'Ali area, halfway between Messina and Taormina. There they rested, swam and wondered what – and, indeed, where – they'd be assigned next. On Monday 30 August, Neville thought he'd got his answer. He was working on vehicle maintenance when the voice of Lieutenant Carton made them all turn.

'Over to the NAAFI area sharpish. We have a visitor,' he shouted, marching through the RASC vehicles. Neville wiped his hands on an oily cloth and joined the crowd heading towards the NAAFI. As he got closer he saw a familiar figure standing on the bonnet of a jeep, hands in pockets, scanning the growing number of troops. He was waving his arms, encouraging everyone closer to him. *Could it be . . . ?* Neville thought. *It was.* General Bernard Montgomery, better known to all as Monty, began to speak. His voice was high-pitched and his accent clipped and crisp. To Neville and the other soldiers of 50th Division his presence was mesmeric. This was the man who had led them to victory after victory at a time when it seemed success would never come. Neville squeezed through, close enough to hear his speech.

'I shall read to you a letter I sent to your Commanding Officer, Major General Kirkman.' Montgomery paused as he carefully unfolded a sheet of paper. '"Now that the campaign in Sicily is over I would like to tell you how well I consider you and your division to have done. One somehow never imagines that 50th Division can do otherwise than well, and in this short campaign it has lived up to its best traditions. The Division has been in the forefront of the battle for the whole thirty-nine days of the campaign, and has had no rest. Please tell all your officers and men how pleased I am with what they have done."' He paused, folded the paper back up and replaced it in his right breast pocket. 'I have come today to tell you that myself.' He spoke for five minutes more about the campaign, promising great deeds to come for the 50th, before jumping down from the bonnet. He waved as he climbed into the back of the jeep, smiling at the cheering troops as he moved on to other parts of the Division.

'No word on what next exactly, though,' observed Joe as they returned to their duties.

'No, but he was talking about future great deeds for the Division. It must be Italy,' Neville mused.

The invasion of Italy began a few days later on 3 September at 0430 hours. But the 50th Division were not involved, still idling around Cape d'Ali. Word got through to them that a bridgehead had been established and they expected the call to action, but it never came. On 10, 11 and 13 September the Divisional Commander, Major General Kirkman, addressed some 3,000 officers and men at a time in the ancient Greek amphitheatre at Taormina. The vast open-air amphitheatre, which could seat 6,000, had remarkable acoustics. A scale model of Sicily had been constructed in front of the stage and Kirkman gave the troops an outline of the campaign as a whole and the part of the 50th within it.

He finished by reading an article from the Special Correspondent of *The Times*: "'But I always had the feeling that the sheet anchor of the army was the veteran 50th Division. They had the hard, dirty work at Lentini and Primosole, and the long slog up the coast from Catania past Etna. They got less public mention than some other divisions because theirs was the unspectacular flank of the front. They plugged on, learning the new warfare the hard way, taking their punishment and coming on for more. Tyne and Tees may well be proud of them, for they are a grand division."'

A grand division. Neville, like the others, found Kirkman's presentation rewarding. It was always nice to feel appreciated and recognised, but it left them no closer to knowing what they were going to do next, or when the move to Italy might come.

It wasn't until 19 September that the eagerly anticipated signal to move arrived. But when it did come, it was not with the expected orders. Rather than heading to Italy, the Division was to return to England. When Neville heard the news, he wasn't quite sure what to think. There was joy at the thought of a return home after so long away. But it was tempered by the sense that they were missing out as the remainder of the Eighth Army advanced northwards through Italy.

Even the return home wasn't straightforward. Equipment was handed in but then the move was postponed. The waiting continued.

Here we go, thought – hoped – Neville. *Things are probably starting to go badly so they're keeping us back to go over to Italy and sort it out.* But the call to arms still didn't come: they idled and waited some more, finally receiving orders to move to Augusta for embarkation for England late in October.

On Saturday 13 November 1943 Neville said goodbye to his wagon, a quarter of a mile from the portside of Augusta. He slung his kitbag and rifle over his shoulder and joined what was left of the 50th Division aboard the *Empress of Canada*. They sailed later that day. After dropping anchor off Algiers for a short time and some minor excitement with destroyers dropping depth charges, the journey home was relatively smooth.

The *Empress* sailed into Southampton on Saturday 11 December. It was the first time Neville had seen England since Thursday 22 May 1941 – 993 days. Neville had been on deck to watch as the south coast emerged from the early-morning mist. He continued to watch as the sailors scurried around the decks preparing to dock. The morning was damp and chilly, particularly after Sicily. *Welcome back to England*, he thought, blowing into his cold hands and stamping his feet to keep warm as the ship glided into its moorings and the ropes were secured. Looking out at the docks, he was surprised, and a little disappointed. He hadn't been expecting a hero's welcome, but he also hadn't been expecting the quayside to be empty.

Strange, isn't it? he reflected. *In nineteen forty, we scramble home from Dunkirk in a hurry with our tails between our legs and there's flags waving and crowds cheering. Now we come home having given Jerry what for and not a bloody soul in sight.*

Chapter 13

Preparing to Make History

December 1943 to June 1944

Part of the reason for the quiet welcome was because the return of 50th Division to England had been arranged under stringent security. Some of the Division had returned some days earlier, sailing into Glasgow and Liverpool. Divisional Headquarters had been established at Chadacre Park near Bury St Edmunds in Suffolk. The 69th Brigade was based around Thetford and the 151st around Sudbury.

Even so, it was a sobering experience. Neville and the rest of 552 Company left the ship, kitbags slung over their shoulders. From here, they were marched along West Bay Road towards the Southampton West Railway Station. Few people were about at this early hour of the morning but they were greeted with curious looks and some friendly waves.

'No point talking to the locals,' nudged Alan. 'Southerners – they'd never get the accent.'

At least the transport arrangements were seamless. Neville and the others were boarded on to waiting trains. Within forty-five minutes of leaving the ship they were on their way.

'Where do you suppose we're off to?' asked Neville as they watched the countryside race past in a blur.

'No idea. Every station so far has had no signs. How the hell are you supposed to know where you are?' grunted Nick.

'That's the point.' Alan sighed patiently. 'If Jerry had managed to cross the Channel there would have been no point making it easy for him. All the road signs and general signage have been removed. Mind you, now he's not coming over so you'd have thought they would have put them back.'

'Wherever we end up, I bag the telephone,' said Neville. Back in Britain, his thoughts had turned again to Joyce. It had been so long since they'd spoken, and he couldn't wait to hear her voice.

They changed trains in London and travelled across country. Neville nodded off, lulled by the rocking of the carriage and the monotonous rhythm of the rails, and was nudged awake by Alan. Through bleary eyes, he looked out of the grimy window at a magnificent cathedral with a central octagonal tower.

'I think I've seen a picture of that,' said Alan. 'I reckon we're in East Anglia and that's Ely Cathedral.' The train moved slowly through the unnamed station and twenty-five minutes later it slowed down to a halt with a hiss of steam.

'This is it; everyone out,' came the shout down the train. They took their kitbags from the rack and dismounted on to the platform.

'Where are we?' asked Neville, looking around the relatively small station.

'Thetford,' snapped a waiting Military Police sergeant. 'Trucks are outside so move along smartly now.'

In total, just over 200 soldiers, mainly 552 RASC, spilled out of the station and into the waiting wagons. *Nice to be driven for a change,* thought Neville. Twenty-five minutes later they were waved through a fenced and guarded perimeter.

'Lancs!' exclaimed Neville, looking out of the rear of the wagon at a line of Lancaster bombers. 'We must be at an RAF station.'

'And Stirlings,' added Alan, craning his neck round the side of the canvas. Although they didn't know it, they had arrived at RAF Mildenhall. The truck came to a stop and they leapt down from the tailgate, looking around at the awesome display of air power with row upon row of Wellingtons, Lancasters and Stirlings. The stop turned out to be relatively brief but sufficient for the soldiers to be fed, showered and telephone calls to be made. Neville was hungry but went straight for the telephone, desperate to hear some familiar voices. First, he telephoned home and spoke with his stepmother. Then, as no one else was waiting, he dialled again, his heart in his mouth as he heard the voice that answered.

'Joyce, it's Nev! I'm home, back in England!'

There was a pause and a silence.

'Joyce? Are you there?' Neville frowned.

'I'm so pleased you are safe,' Joyce finally replied. 'Where are you?'

'Some RAF place near Thetford.'

'Where's that?'

'No idea, East Anglia somewhere.' There was another awkward silence.

'It's been so long,' breathed Joyce.

'I know, but I'm back now, although I don't know for how—'

'Things have changed, Neville,' Joyce blurted out. 'I'm sorry.'

Now it was Neville's turn to pause. 'What do you mean?' When the words came, they sounded like a menacing growl.

'I'm so sorry, I've met someone else.'

'Who?'

'Does it matter?'

'It damned well does to me.' Neville was having to fight hard to keep control of his feelings.

'There's nothing I can say to make this any easier. Please, let's still be friends.'

'I can't believe what you're telling me. After all this time. After everything I've been through.'

There was another prolonged silence. Neville felt a tap on his shoulder: another soldier waiting to make his call. The anger flared within him. 'And you know what? I don't give a damn.' As the line went dead, Neville replaced the receiver.

'Sorry,' said the waiting soldier. But Neville grunted and walked away.

It was cold, dark and damp by late afternoon as Neville and the others completed their journey to High Ash in Thetford Forest, where they would be encamped for the foreseeable future. Through the deepening gloom they could see numerous Nissen huts erected between the trees. The accommodation was basic, with each damp and draughty hut having ten occupants and each man allocated a bunk and a locker.

'Absolute luxury.' Nick smiled as he inspected the external Elsan chemical toilet. 'Saves having to go and pick my own tree.'

'We've slept in worse,' said Neville. His anger had cooled and he was now more philosophical. Alan gave him an encouraging slap on the shoulder.

'It'll be all right, Timber.'

552 Company had been billeted with the 7th Armoured Brigade. Camp life was quickly established; after everything they'd been through it felt like a comfortable routine. Early in December, Neville was one of many in the Company to receive notification of his Leave in Lieu of Fighting: four weeks' leave for those who had served abroad for four years.

'Christmas at home. Bright view of that,' he beamed. On Friday 10 December, Neville and many other RASC comrades boarded the train at Thetford and journeyed north to Hull. The family welcome Neville received back at 778 Holderness Road was something he'd always remember. But his delight there was tempered by the knowledge that some of his comrades would come home to rubble and death, and others hadn't been fortunate enough to come home at all.

His mood was tempered, too, by the fact there was no Joyce any longer. But that disappointment didn't last long. In fact, the break-up with Joyce was quickly forgotten when he met Sheila Mills at a dance in the city. Over the four short weeks of his leave they went on to meet a number of times. Sheila took Neville home to Hornsea and introduced him to her parents. The following day Sheila came to tea to meet Neville's father and stepmother. It was a rapidly blossoming relationship. There was one complication, however: Neville had also struck up a friendship with Jean Nichols, Freddie Nichols' sister. She was a strikingly beautiful woman, but was engaged to an infantryman in the East Yorkshires. Neville couldn't help but fall in love with her.

On Friday 7 January 1944 Neville returned to his unit in Thetford Forest, completely torn: he was very fond of Sheila but was also very much in love with Jean. On top of this, he felt utterly bereft and wretched, once more having to adjust to army life having been back at home.

'You do get yourself in a pickle,' chided Alan as they sat drinking a pint in a pub in Brandon.

'I know, I know.' Neville looked down at his beer. 'Sheila's a nice kid, but Jean—'

'Is spoken for,' Alan reminded him. 'Think how you felt when Joyce dropped the bombshell. I reckon they need to bring the invasion forward to give you something else to think about.'

Neville managed a weak smile. 'I know, it's not playing the game. Doesn't help with the usual bullshit here. I'll sort it out,' he said firmly. 'Thanks, Alan, you're a good pal. In fact, so good you can buy me another pint.'

To relieve the tedium of waiting for whatever orders they were given next, 552 Company arranged cross-country runs against the 7th Armoured Brigade. Neville spent some time, too, on the firing range with Sten, Bren and rifle. As January drew to a close he was issued with a detail to Benacre near Kessingland in Suffolk. The fact that it was nearer the coast meant the invasion rumours became rife. Vehicle maintenance was accelerated: it was still tedious but at least it felt as though it had a purpose.

'This Benacre place is one hell of a dump,' complained Neville. 'Stacks of mud and trees and not much else.' Someone mentioned there was a dance in Kessingland, and Neville persuaded the others to go. There would be 'plenty of Wrens', he cajoled them, with one Wren in particular he ended up taking a shine to.

'So, who was she?' asked Nick as they were preparing to leave the dance that evening.

'That, my friend, is a good Yorkshire lass from Leeds,' Neville said with a grin. 'Lavinia, Vin for short. I'm meeting her again on Thursday.'

'You might get yourself into a pickle again,' warned Alan.

'I might be dead next week,' countered Neville.

Neville and Vin met as arranged and spent a happy couple of hours walking and talking. Neville was in good spirits: Vin was a spontaneous, happy girl and he felt relaxed in her company. All was going well until she told him that she was getting married in five weeks. Neville's face fell momentarily, but he smiled again.

'Congratulations,' he deadpanned, 'he's a lucky man and I'm very pleased for you both.'

What the hell, he thought, *we're only friends*.

On Sunday 6 February, all the officers and NCOs of the Division were summoned for a briefing by their new commander, Major General Graham. The early stages of the planning for the invasion of mainland Europe had been on the basis that the 50th Division would go ashore as part of the second wave. But Graham now explained the plans had been changed: XXX Corps would now be the assault force and 50th Division would be the spearhead.

Last to leave in 1940, first to go back in 1944, Neville thought.

Training and detailed planning wasn't the only thing to be accelerated. Over the next few weeks, Neville and Vin met each other almost daily. Inevitably the relationship blossomed, despite Neville chiding himself for being either a martyr or a bloody fool. Whichever it was, he was falling in love again.

On Thursday 17 February, he was on an ammunition detail to Lowestoft. He loaded his wagon as rapidly as he could and went to the WRNS' quarters in St Mary's Convent, South Lowestoft. His heart sank when he found out that Vin had already left to go north for her wedding day. No goodbyes, but maybe it was better that way. He trudged back to his wagon utterly miserable.

Neville's final period of leave began towards the end of February for nine days. With Vin a forgotten memory, he spent much of his time with Sheila. When he returned to his unit, now at Braintree in Essex, it was with the belief that Sheila was his true love and Jean, Joyce and Vin were just good friends. That felt resolved at last; and with his mind clear and focused, it was time to get ready for war again.

The former cavalry barracks looked like an old schoolhouse: red brick with yellow-brick bands, stone lintels, grey slate roof and brick ridge stacks. This was Le Cateau in Colchester, where Neville had been sent for what was described as a twenty-one-day toughening course.

'I could have refused it, but I didn't want to give anyone the pleasure of saying I couldn't take it,' he said to Nick and Joe as he packed to go.

'Tough as an old army boot when you've finished that, Timber,' laughed Nick. 'I've heard something about it from one of the lads in 7th Armoured. Rather you than me!'

Neville was one of over a hundred soldiers from different units, including some Americans from 82nd Airborne. He wasn't quite sure what to expect, but the first day set the tempo with fifteen- to twenty-foot logs picked up in teams and thrown in the air at various angles to encourage teamwork. This was followed by the first of several speed marches. They began with a three-and-a-half-mile forced march in thirty-five minutes followed by a mock battle. The soldiers were made to carry kit weighing twenty-two pounds along with weapons.

I'm buggered, groaned Neville to himself at the end of the first day. *And that was just a warm-up!*

As the course continued, the marches became more taxing: seven miles in less than seventy minutes followed by digging a defensive position; nine miles in less than ninety minutes followed by firing practice; twelve miles in less than 130 minutes followed by an assault course and weapons drill. Everyone worked as a team, encouraging stragglers, in some cases dragging them by their armpits. Neville got on particularly well with the Yanks and was disappointed when, one week in, they were recalled to the American Army.

Interspersed with the forced marches were cross-country ones. The remaining soldiers were dropped in the middle of the country-side with supplies, equipment, a compass bearing and maps. They then took it in turns as pairs to lead. Caution was essential, with the instructors acting as enemy snipers and setting ambushes. Weapons training and firing practice included the rifle, Bren, Thompson sub-machine gun, Boys anti-tank rifle, revolver, grenades, Vickers machine gun and three-inch mortars. In addition, Neville received basic instruction in mines and demolition. He was given lectures, demonstrations and practice in field craft – ground cover, camouflage and concealment – unarmed combat and close-quarter fighting, first aid, health and hygiene. The three weeks concluded with a mock battle.

The course had been losing around two casualties a day, so when they had their final parade on Tuesday 28 March, fewer than seventy of the original intake were able to take the salute. Neville had done well; he'd passed all his PE and weapons tests and completed the final twelve-mile forced march fifteen minutes under the required time.

Relieved it was all over, but proud of what he had achieved, Neville returned to 552 Company, which had now relocated to Bournemouth. The remainder of 50th Division were in Weymouth for collective training with the Royal Navy and RAF. The invasion of Europe was drawing ever nearer.

The Germans knew the Allies were coming, but they did not know where or when. Major invasion rehearsals were completed during April: SMASH 1, 2 and 3. Vehicles and men were loaded on to LSTs – landing ship, tanks – and men and machines assaulted the beaches of the south coast of England, usually under fire from live ammunition and with inevitable 'friendly fire' casualties. The anticipation among the troops was rising to fever pitch.

On Thursday 27 April, Neville and six other trucks from 552 Company were ordered to prepare to load on to 2829 LST II serial 58080. He was sitting in camp with Alan, Joe, Nick, Josh Mackinsey, Tommy Oates and Tommy Jackson.

'This has got to be it, surely?' He glanced from face to face. 'Sooner the better. I'm fed up of being in and out of boats and bobbing up and down on the damned Solent.'

'Reckon they know we're coming?' asked Nick.

'Must do,' said Tommy Oates. 'But if we don't know where and when, I guess they can't know either.'

'But you can't miss the ships,' commented Neville. 'Thousands of 'em.'

'There's so many, I reckon if they stuck them side by side from here to France we could probably hop across without getting our feet wet,' said Alan to chuckles from the others. Neville noticed that Joe wasn't laughing and was looking more serious than the others.

'Let's just get over and finish the bastards,' he snapped. 'Bloody Germans, I hate the bastards. Kill them all.' Neville reached out and put a hand on Joe's shoulder. Joe put his face in his hands, his shoulders rocked as he wept silently.

'Come on, Joe.' Neville gave his shoulder a rub. 'It'll be over soon.'

'All this damned waiting,' sobbed Joe. 'I can't stand it. I can't go.' Neville glanced across at the others, who all looked as alarmed as he felt.

'We're your mates, Joe. We'll look after you,' Alan tried to reassure him. Joe nodded then shuffled to his feet and left the tent. No one said anything for a while.

'I usually look forward to going into action,' Neville said. 'What will be, will be; but I have a bad feeling about it, too.'

'Give over, Timber,' said Nick.

'That might be something to do with Sheila?' suggested Alan. 'Listen, everyone,' he clapped his hands, 'we've come this far and we're going to get the job finished. Everyone will be fine as soon as we get the order to go. Trust me.' Alan got up and left the tent.

At 1200 hours on Sunday 30 April, the trucks boarded the LST, which pulled out into the Solent at 0200. Hundreds of similar ships began to gather, like bees round a honey pot. The one bonus for the soldiers was that the food on the ships was surprisingly good compared to camp. As the dawn broke, Neville sat eating breakfast, looking at England emerging from the mist. It was almost pleasant.

'Joe okay?' asked Neville as Nick came over to join him.

'Seems to be. Very quiet, but he's checking his truck, then rechecking, then checking again. Anything that keeps him occupied.'

'It's strange.' Neville was looking back at the coastline. 'Despite all the time we've been back in England, I don't feel like I've been home.'

'That must mean you've never met Sheila, then. Just a dream.' Nick grinned.

'She is that,' said Neville with a smile, thoughts of war briefly pushed to one side.

This wasn't the call to arms just yet. After four days bobbing on the Solent, the ships returned to dock in Southampton and 552 Company were sent to Cadlands A Transit Camp in the New Forest. Here they were given new trucks, Ford F6oL FWD, which they set about waterproofing: they had received orders that they had to be able to negotiate six feet of water.

'Have you read this bloody rubbish?' snorted Neville, reading the instructions they'd all been handed. The others shook their heads. 'It says: "Your petrol must be switched through to the tank with the extended breather. Your engine must be *hot* before wading otherwise it will stall on contact with the water. Engage four-wheel drive and lowest gear. Let your vehicle run down the ramp *slowly* on the handbrake, keeping your engine revving *hard* in gear, clutch depressed. As soon as your radiator disappears under the water let your clutch full in and put your foot *flat* on the accelerator and *keep* it there." And get this.' He shook his head. '"Don't get the wind up – *there is nothing to it*." Cheeky bastards. Some jobsworth with nothing better to do. Probably never driven a truck in his life.' To laughter, he screwed their copy of the paper into a ball and threw it to the ground.

On Thursday 11 May, 50th Division was reviewed by General Eisenhower, Allied Supreme Commander. They listened with rapt attention as he lauded the wonderful traditions of the 50th, how proud he was to have them with him and that they had a very special fighting job in the invasion.

'As if we don't already know,' grunted Neville.

Four days later, they were addressed by General Montgomery, who told them they were the finest fighting division in the British Army. It was going to be their job to go in first and clear the way when the invasion came.

'Did you hear that! *It's a nasty job*. That's some understatement,' spluttered Nick afterwards.

'I wish we could have a bit less of the top-brass bullshit and just get on with it,' grunted Neville. 'Nasty job or not, he knows we'll do it. The sooner the better.'

The waiting game continued. They washed, wrote their wills, checked the vehicles and moved supplies. Then on Friday 26 May the order came through that the camp was to be sealed. No one was allowed in or out. This time, it felt like the real thing. On Monday 29 May, 522 Company were called together and briefed by Lieutenant Carton.

'Well, lads, this is what we've all been waiting for,' he said, standing in front of a large map of France. 'The party's on and boy what a party it will be. So listen and look carefully.' He moved over to the map. 'The naval force which will carry the 50th across to France is codenamed *Force G*. Where we are to land is held, we are told, by the 716th German Infantry Division who occupy a series of strong points along the coast. Between these points will be fences of barbed wire, minefields, stakes, interlocking rows of tank traps called tetrahedras, and booby traps. Other than that they will welcome us with open arms.' There was a ripple of nervous laughter around the room.

'Expect the land to be marshy. The overall plan is to secure lodgement on the continent and the plan is fourfold,' Carton continued. 'First there will be airborne landings during the night, D-Day minus one hour. Second there will be the assault on a five-division front, with three British divisions and two American. Third will be to land two follow-up divisions, one British and one American, later on D-Day. Finally the plan is to build our forces by a minimum one and one third a division per day. The job of 50th Division is to spearhead the assault and smash the enemy between Le Hamel and La Rivière. We will then secure a covering position on Bayeux and the area of Saint Léger.'

He pointed at the map. Neville peered forwards to take in where they were heading. 'The time the first craft hit the beaches is coded as H hour. 552 will go ashore at H plus four hours. The 69th Brigade will attack La Rivière, and that is where we expect to go ashore. The village has high sea walls but the beaches are sandy with low sand dunes. From the beach is a road, here, and behind that a bog, but there are some useable exits through that bog here, here and here.' He pointed to three positions on the map. 'That said, we will be directed by a beachmaster once ashore. Our beach codename is King Red. We will carry composite loads of ammo, fuel and rations. Any questions?'

'When will it be, sir?' a voice shouted out from the back.

'Imminent. I can't be more specific than that.' There was a general murmur of excitement and anticipation.

The next day, they moved camp to C17. Carton called them together once more.

'I have been asked to read to you a message from our commanding officer. It says . . .' He paused and looked up. There was total silence from the assembled soldiers. "'The time is at hand to strike, to break through the Western Wall and into the continent of Europe. To you, officers and men of the 50th (Northumbrian) Division, has been given the great honour of being in the vanguard of this mighty blow for freedom. It is my unshakeable belief that we, together with Force G of the Royal Navy, the special regiments of the Royal Armoured Corps, the Royal Artillery and the Royal Engineers attached to us and with the help of the RAF and the American Air Force, will deliver such an overpowering punch that the enemy will be unable to recover. Thus shall we be well set to carry through to a glorious and successful end all that is now entrusted to us. Much has been asked of you in the past and great have been your achievements, but this will be the greatest adventure of all. It will add yet another fine chapter to your already long and distinguished record – the grandest chapter of all. Very best of luck to every one of you."' Carton folded the paper away slowly. 'You will gather from this we are almost go. Be ready.'

On Friday 2 June 1944 the 38,000 men and vehicles of 50th Division boarded their ships and landing craft at Southampton. The sea was rough. Neville and the others waited anxiously, playing cards, reading books and magazines to pass the time. On Sunday 4 June, the invasion was postponed for twenty-four hours due to inclement weather and sea conditions.

But on Monday 5 June they were briefed again. This was it – the real thing, the green light. The invasion of mainland Europe was set for the following day, Tuesday 6 June. At 0730 hours the great armada sailed out of the West Solent for France. The final chapter of Neville's war was about to begin.

Chapter 14

D-Day and the Battle of Normandy

June 1944 to August 1944

Dawn, when it broke, was cold and grey. A sea mist shielded the armada of ships from the watchful eyes of the enemy waiting behind the Atlantic wall. Sometimes it is said that it is darkest just before morning breaks. But sometimes the darkness lingers, too, a streak of blackness that colours everything that lies ahead. The mist had the effect not just of masking the ships, but dampening their engines too, silencing their sound as they moved towards the French coast, almost like ghost ships.

All through the night, their path had been laid out by the efforts of the minesweepers, sweeping back and forth to clear a path through the mines. On ship, Neville and the others could do little but wait, watching the hands of the clock tick by. Some fortunate souls took the chance to get some sleep. But most were awake, writing letters home they were aware could be their last, others playing cards – pontoon and slippery Sam – anything to take their minds off what lay ahead.

As the blackness of night faded into the grey of morning, so the silence, too, started to disperse. What began as a distant hum became a nearby drone then a deafening roar as wave upon wave of heavy bombers passed overhead. They were barely visible from the ships as they opened their bomb doors, but their explosive ordnance landing on the coastal defences could be heard loud and clear. The warships opened up next, broadsides of heavy guns belching out flame and smoke, thundering shells into the midst of the enemy, landing with precision and devastating effect. Rockets blasted out from their launchers, arcing through the grey sky to pound the enemy still further.

The first wave of infantry clambered down the nets of the nearest ships into the landing craft. Once full, they moved away and circled, bobbing and lurching in the rough sea. The soldiers near the sides of the craft were the fortunate ones, as they vomited into the sea. Those in the centre of the craft had little option but to throw up over one another, the combined effect of seasickness and terror. Prayers were muttered but little else was said as they waited to head for land.

At 0725 hours, H hour for 50th Division, the ramps hit the surf and the infantry fought their way ashore. In some places along its front the troops moved off the beaches and advanced inland rapidly. But in others, it was a killing ground. La Rivière was attacked by the East Yorkshires, where the German 88mm and 50mm guns and machine guns had largely escaped the Allied bombardment. Enemy machine-gunners crouched and waited behind the formidable sea wall or in the houses of the village. The resulting fighting was brutal as the Yorkshiremen breached the sea wall and began clearing the enemy house by house. By 0900 the Germans were either dead or taken prisoner.

Back on the LST, Neville was standing between Alan and Nick watching the picture unfold, trying to make sense from the noise and the flashes exactly what was going on. Behind them, Joe paced up and down, muttering to himself, agitated.

'I think he should have stayed home. He's making me bloody nervous,' muttered Neville. The others nodded.

At 0945 all the drivers were called together. 'La Rivière is secured,' announced Lieutenant Carton. 'We're on our way in.'

This is it, thought Neville. *Here goes nothing.*

'We're heading for the beach just to the south of La Rivière. But I'm afraid there will be no Mulberry,' Carton continued. 'We're having difficulty getting it across because of the rough sea, so it could be a wet landing. If you haven't waterproofed your trucks properly, you're about to go for a swim. When the ramp drops get your vehicle through the water on to the beach and then get off it sharpish. We don't want a traffic jam and an easy target for Jerry. The beachmasters will direct you. Understood?' The Mulberry, a British invention, was a temporary portable harbour designed to help get supplies ashore as quickly as possible.

At 1130 hours on Tuesday 6 June 1944, Neville and 552 Company drove out again on to the European mainland. The doors of the LST swung aside and the ramp crashed into the surf. Neville's wagon lurched into the water up to the air intake. He hit the accelerator hard and rocked and rolled up the beach, enemy shells exploding all around him in eruptions of sand, debris and body parts. He tried not to think about the fact the beach was littered with bodies, the water draining off the wagon tinged with red. Vehicles were everywhere; prisoners were under guard, their hands behind their heads, receiving an occasional kick to remind them they were now under British orders. But there was no sign of the infantry, already advancing inland to establish the bridgehead and with it the first-day objective of Bayeux.

Neville was waved away from the beach and westwards. He

stopped along with the other vehicles at Manvieux to await further orders. Shells continued to whistle overhead: at this early stage the Allied artillery support was still largely coming from the warships, although artillery was being brought ashore rapidly. Neville joined the other drivers, staying under cover of their cabs facing the sea. Sniper bullets pinged off the wagons if any of them so much as showed any sign of moving into the open. The whole area was littered with dead bodies contorted in the agony of death. British and German soldiers seemed to be hugging each other in a deadly embrace as they had died fighting hand to hand.

Sergeant Thompson came running at a crouch along the line of wagons, stopping briefly by each. 'Infantry about four clicks ahead,' he said to Neville. 'The lads are trying to locate and kill that bloody sniper, but, irrespective, get ready to move inland to Sommervieu.'

As they waited for the order to move, crouching behind their cabs in small groups, smoking and debating if everything was going to plan, Neville heard a shout.

'Mon ami! Mon liberateur! Bienvenue en France!'

An elderly French couple was approaching down the narrow country road, hands held aloft in welcome, holding a bottle of wine, joy etched on their faces. Neville looked up in alarm and waved frantically for the couple to take cover. Whether they couldn't hear him or didn't understand, the sound of a single rifle shot cut through the crump of the big guns, followed by a smash as the wine bottle hit the floor. The old man spun through the air on to his back, shot through the head by the sniper. The blood oozing from his temple mingled with the spilt wine staining the dusty road red. The joy of the elderly lady was replaced by wails of despair: the death of her husband right at the moment of freedom. Two drivers crabbed to her quickly and dragged her away to the cover of the wagons. Not far away there was a short burst from a Sten gun.

The only consolation from the episode was that the final shot had given away the position of the sniper.

On the morning of 7 June, the 50th cleared Bayeux. The bridgehead was firmly established, the Germans having failed to stop the Allies on the beaches. They now concentrated their armoured divisions for a decisive counter-attack. The 50th were faced by the Panzer Lehr Division and the 12th SS Panzer Hitler Jugend. Its task was to contain the enemy armour and, by aggressive action, to prevent him from concentrating his armoured forces for a powerful and sustained counter-attack. The key objective was the capture of Villers Bocage, twenty miles south of the beaches and the junction of five important roads.

The battle was relentless for everyone: the infantry, the armour, artillery and 552 Company. To maintain the momentum of the aggressive offensive action, shells and ammunition had to be carried right to the front line, which was shifting all the time. Neville repeatedly ran the gauntlet of strafing by the Luftwaffe and ambush by well-concealed and determined German infantry and armour. And then there was the Normandy countryside for his vehicle to contend with as well – steep hills flanking deep, lush valleys, field after field divided by deep ditches or high, dense hedges with the only transport arteries narrow, twisting lanes. This was ambush and concealment country – a stark contrast to the wide-open space of the desert campaign.

'Lot of the new lads are scared to death,' observed Neville as they loaded for another perilous trip to the Field Artillery.

'Some of the old lads as well, I expect,' nodded Nick.

'Wonder if I was the same four and a half years ago?' *Damned if I can remember*, Neville thought.

'Some nerves are good. Keeps you on edge, no complacency, no silly mistakes,' said Nick. Neville grunted and continued to load the twenty-five-pounder shells, 280 rounds per gun.

He was up with the guns constantly, running on no sleep and with ears ringing from the muzzle blasts. The 50th's salient edged forward to Tilly-sur-Seulles and the infantry pushed on again. On 14 June they attacked Lingèvres and moved south towards Hottot. The enemy here were deeply dug into the ditches and poured a murderous fire into the killing ground. Coming under counter-attack from the Germans, the 50th and the Panzer Lehr shuffled backwards and forwards over the following days in a macabre dance of death. The field regiments laid down barrage upon barrage, but it was the bombs and rockets rained down from the awesome air power wielded by the Allies that made the difference. Slowly but irrevocably the Germans began to wilt in this war of attrition.

It wasn't just men who were being killed. As Neville watched the bulldozers at work in the fields, he saw cattle lying dead everywhere, slaughtered as they stood in the middle of a hail of lead. The stench was overpowering as the bloated carcasses were heaped together and set alight in a giant funeral pyre.

'Not sure who are the lucky ones, them or us,' he grunted.

When he took his next load of shells towards Arency Wood, another gruesome sight awaited him. Bodies of German soldiers were swaying, hanged from the trees. Pinned to one was a paper on which was scrawled, 'Deserteur'.

Wednesday 21 June was Neville's 24th birthday. It was nearly his last. He was one of six wagons heading towards Arency Wood, when he heard a knocking sound that seemed to be coming from underneath the vehicle. He waved out of his side window to indicate to the other drivers that he was stopping. The four wagons in front continued for another 200 yards to avoid clustering and making themselves an easy target for enemy aircraft. Alan, who was following behind, stopped a short distance away.

Neville dismounted from his cab and walked to the side of the wagon, ducking underneath the chassis. He couldn't see a problem so moved round to the other side. He stood for a moment, wondering what the knocking sound could be and decided to take a final check under the chassis on this side. As he dropped to his knees, he was startled by a thud and the canvas rippling above him. Instinct kicked in and he rolled under the wagon as a German sniper put a second bullet just past his head and into the superstructure of the truck. Alan, who had almost reached him, sprinted the last few yards to dive behind the rear wheel. He helped Neville out from underneath and they sat with their backs to the wheel, debating what to do next. Neither man had his weapons with him.

'Think that was Happy Birthday from Jerry,' gasped Alan.

Neville checked his head for any sign of damage. 'Wish I could tell where the bastard is,' he snarled.

'And what?' asked Alan. 'Your rifle's in your cab; and in case you hadn't noticed my wagon is twenty yards away, which makes me feel a bit like a duck in a shooting gallery.'

Neville thought for a moment. 'Okay, here's what we'll do: I'll get back in and reverse my wagon to yours. You stay on this side near the rear and walk back under cover.' Alan nodded agreement and Neville moved rapidly along the side of the wagon and into his cab, crouching low in his seat. He started the engine, engaged reverse and slowly moved back to within a yard of Alan's wagon. Alan leapt past the small gap and got into his cab. He fired the engine and waved out of the side window. They both moved off, accelerator flat to the floor, but there were no more sniper bullets. It was just one more near miss to chalk off.

The next few days were a stalemate, the British holding the

might of the German Panzer Divisions while the Americans cleared the Cherbourg Peninsula. All the while the heavens opened, incessant rain compounding the misery, soaking everyone to the skin.

'I need some sleep but there's a Field Service. I've been lucky so far so I want to keep in His good books,' said Neville, raising his eyes to the heavens as he slicked back his hair with engine oil. 'Coming?' Nick, Alan and Tommy Oates nodded. Joe shook his head sullenly.

The respite was brief. The next big push was in the offing and the guns needed ammunition. 552 was travelling in convoy just south of Tilly as German fighters screamed out of the sky, their machine guns strafing the column mercilessly. Fifty yards ahead of Neville were Joe Franklin and Tommy Jackson. Which meant that he could only watch as the white-hot lead ripped through their wagons erupting into balls of flame. Tommy leapt from his cab, his uniform and hair alight, screaming and rolling. Neville was out of his cab and running towards him to help, but before the flames could be extinguished his blackened, charred body lay motionless, dead. Nothing was found of Joe Franklin. Neville felt winded, as though someone had punched him in the stomach, but there was no time to stop or for reflection. Irrespective of the grief, the war had to go on. The wrecks were pushed into the ditches and the ammunition was delivered.

On 11 July, 552 Company were assigned troop-carrying duties. They transported the 6th and 7th Green Howards into the line towards Hottot, where they faced bitter fighting. They returned via most of the forward positions around Tilly and Lingèvres: every few yards revealed dreadful sights with dead bodies everywhere. The crushed and charred hulks of German Tiger and Panther tanks were all around, their crews burned to death, draped over or beside the remains of their infernal machines. The whole front-line area reeked of death and decay.

On Monday 24 July Neville was soaked to the skin and chilled to the bone once more. He had his rum ration, which he was grateful for, and two letters from Sheila, which he was even happier to receive. The first was general news from home and he smiled to himself, transported briefly from his surroundings as he read through it, folding it and putting it in his breast pocket. As he read the second letter his brow creased into a frown and the colour rose in his cheeks. The letter was telling him that someone had asked for Sheila's hand in marriage, but she had declined the proposal. Anger welled up inside him as he tried to imagine what might have happened.

'Ye gods, if I could get my hands on him,' he muttered. But there was no time to dwell further. The guns needed the shells and he pocketed the letter, resolving to write a curt response at the earliest opportunity. As Neville headed towards his truck he noticed the whine of shells sounded closer than normal. A sudden detonation about fifteen yards away threw him into the air backwards. He lay on his back, gasping for air, relieved that he was only winded. Looking up, he could see how fortunate he had been: the shell had hit an apple tree, sending the blast away from him.

'He'll get me one of these times,' he muttered as he climbed back to his feet.

The 50th moved forward again. On 4 August they entered a deserted Villers Bocage. Two days later they took Mont Pinçon and attacked Condé-sur-Noireau on 9 August. By 13 August the Green Howards had driven the Germans out of St Pierre. As the Americans were sweeping around from the west and the south, the Allies were slowly closing the Falaise Gap, the mouth of a pocket in which a trapped German army had been ordered by Hitler to stand and die.

552 Company advanced in column to one and a half miles north of Villers Bocage. The smell of death was overpowering once more, not just men but horses by the hundreds, bloated and infested with flies. This was an anomaly of the German Army – supposedly highly mechanised yet still dependent on horse-drawn transport. The area had been heavily mined, and on one dark day twenty-one members of 552 were injured and three killed. Before he moved off again, Neville jammed sandbags under his clutch, brake and accelerator pedals to give his legs what protection he could from the blast of an exploding mine.

As he continued to drive around the devastated countryside, he was appalled by the destruction. Villers Bocage, Hottot, Arency: all were smashed to pieces, just rubble remaining. And yet they were still greeted as heroes by the French, men and women who picked their way through what had once been home to salvage what little they could. What had been salvaged was their freedom and self-respect, for which they were pitifully grateful.

The fighting continued without pause, for the noose around the German 7th Army and 5th Panzer Army in the Falaise Pocket was tightening. Such was the demand for ammunition that Neville went five nights without sleep. His eyes were puffed up and felt like raw meat. He was constantly in the front line, sometimes no more than 200 yards from the retreating Germans. The smell of death made him feel physically sick and he winced as he felt the wagon running over bodies in the dark. He wondered, *Are they ours or theirs, dead or alive?*

By 13 August the gap between Falaise and Argenta was less than twenty miles. Neville alone had carried some 2,000 rounds of shells to the guns, some of which were now discarded, their barrels burned out. The gap was closed fully on 19 August and the final destruction of the trapped German 7th Army began. The Allies divided the Falaise Pocket into zones, one for air power, one for artillery, one for armour and so on. The zones became known as the 'killing grounds', as shells, bombs, rockets and machine guns devastated the enemy jammed in a bottleneck from which there was no escape. They began to surrender in their tens of thousands, trudging to captivity, emaciated, haunted, beaten.

The battle for Normandy was over.

As the 50th paused, their job for D-Day and beyond completed, Neville listened silently to the words of Lieutenant General B. G. Horrocks, Commander of XXX Corps, read to the Company by their Commanding Officer: 'I would like all ranks of 50 (N) Division to realise how much their efforts of the last few days have contributed to the general plan for the encirclement and destruction of the German Army.

'The road Vire-Conde and to the east has been one of the main German supply routes and recently the enemy has done his best to use it for the withdrawal of the large forces west of our present area. It was vital that this escape route should be closed and the task was given initially to 50 (N) Division.

'During the last week the Division has been fighting down towards Condé from Mount Pinçon. Although the country was suited for defence, and although the enemy was fighting stubbornly, all the attacks launched by 50 (N) Division have been successful and many prisoners have been taken.

'Owing to the scarcity of roads, deployment was difficult, yet the Division never faltered and we can now say that the escape route through Conde is closed to the Germans.

'I cannot give you higher praise than by saying that the most experienced battle-fighting Division in the British Army has once more lived up to its high reputation.

'Well done, 50 Div.'

Such was the horror and devastation that Neville had seen that, for all their achievements, this didn't feel like a moment for celebration. The opportunity for self-congratulation would come some time in the future. This battle might have been won, but there remained more to be fought, and a war that needed bringing to its conclusion.

Chapter 15

Back to Where it All Began

August 1944 to December 1944

——————————

The windscreen wipers juddered against the flow of water, making little discernible impression against the rain lashing down. Neville blinked rapidly, trying to keep his focus as he peered through the deluge, driving by instinct and good fortune. He was tired, fatigued after a relentless push forwards across France and towards Belgium. There was no pause for anyone – the Allies had the Germans on the run, and like Neville in his wagon, with his foot pressed to the floor, they were pushing forwards and pushing the advantage home.

A few days earlier the Free French had liberated Paris to scenes of wild rejoicing. The rapturous reception the 50th Division had been greeted with as they crossed the Seine at Vernon, north-west of Paris, would linger long in Neville's memory. Joyous crowds had mobbed the soldiers, tanks and trucks. Thankful arms had passed bread, cheese and bottles of wine through the cab window into Neville's grateful hands. By the end of it, the tarpaulin of Neville's wagon had looked like a wildflower garden. As he drove through

Vernon, he did so to a chorus of gunshots – mostly in Gallic celebration, but some were the execution of known collaborators.

For 552 Company the celebrations had been brief. They were tasked with travelling back and forth the 180 miles from bridgehead to front line, bringing ammunition forward so the momentum of the advance could be maintained. Neville and the other drivers grumbled as they went three or four nights without sleep, but the tiredness dropped away each time they passed through a liberated French town. The communities in every town greeted the British ecstatically, filling their cabs with fruit. At times it was also pitiful to drive through the rubble, poverty and desolation of what had once been a town and to see the emaciated civilians waving wearily and offering what little they had left. One of the nicer moments for Neville was stopping to hand out chocolate and sweets to the children who congregated.

'Makes it all worthwhile,' he said to Nick.

'I gather the SS has been round here so it must have been one damned rough time for them,' Nick replied. On 29 August, XXX Corps began the advance north-north-east to Amiens. Neville stayed behind the wheel, moving up to Gisors and Crèvecoeur. The Division took Amiens on 31 August, including two bridges over the Somme, wired for demolition by the Germans but captured before they could be blown.

As the rain lashed down, Neville had been following the infantry and armour. Prisoners by this point were coming in by the thousand, creating their own problems. Out of nowhere, two bedraggled figures stumbled into the road ahead of him. Neville hit the brake hard, only just in time to avoid them. Letting the engine idle, he grabbed his rifle and jumped from his cab.

'Hands in the air!' he shouted, gesturing with his weapon. The two German soldiers looked at him through sunken eyes, terrified. In truth, they looked little more than boys.

'*Schiesse nicht, wir geben auf. Bitte essen und wasser.*' Don't shoot, we surrender. Please food and water.

'In the wagon.' Neville pointed, shepherding the Germans to the rear of his truck. They climbed in, sodden to the skin. They looked so young that Neville felt moved to give them a water bottle and a bar of chocolate. 'More than you bloody deserve,' he grunted. He drove to Arras, which the Guards Armoured Division had captured as part of the drive towards Brussels. Neville dropped off his prisoners there, and as he moved away, they bowed and waved at him.

Neville glared back. *Cheeky bastards*, he thought.

By this point, Neville had gone thirty-two hours without sleep. But 552 Company were ordered to move again and follow the Guards towards the Belgian capital. Neville drove towards Lens in what felt like a drunken stupor. He pinched his legs and slapped his own face, sang songs, anything to keep his eyes open. Not every driver was able to do so. Even though the road ahead was relatively straight, he watched, almost in disbelief, as one wagon veered across the road and the one following, despite being the regulation fifty yards behind, ploughed into the side of it. Snapping out of his exhaustion, Neville leapt from the cab and ran to the pile-up. The two drivers had been extracted from their cabs: both alive but badly hurt.

'I'm sorry, Jim,' he heard one of them cry out. 'I fell asleep. I didn't see you, I'm so sorry.'

'You'll both be fine, lad.' Sergeant Thompson was also on the scene, already taking charge. 'Get these two in your wagon, Roberts, and get back to Arras. The rest of you, get the ammo out of these two wrecks and get them off the road. Quickly, before Jerry sees a line of sitting ducks.'

On Monday 4 September they pulled up through Lens and parked for the night. The drivers staggered around like drunks as they hastily brewed tea and ate meagre rations before flopping down exhausted. Some fell asleep on the ground; some were propped against a wheel; some, like Neville, slept in their cabs.

After a welcome few hours' rest, 552 Company left Lens and headed for the Belgian border. The Guards Armoured Division were ahead, having entered Brussels at 2000 hours the day before. Thirty miles from the border Neville's convoy was passing a thick copse off to the left of the road when the woodland suddenly erupted with machine-gun and shell fire. Neville followed the other wagons, turning quickly to the right, off the road and down a small incline. They were no longer side-on to the enemy fire, making them a more difficult target, and also clearing the road for armoured support.

Neville jumped down from his cab with his rifle, took cover and fired at the flashes in the woodland. He could hear the squeal of tank tracks above the cacophony of battle as three Cromwell Cruiser Tanks, part of the convoy tank escort, rumbled forward. Their turrets swivelled ninety degrees and poured six-pounder shells and withering machine-gun fire into the dense trees. The barrage was followed by a loud silence, then a white flag appeared as German survivors emerged from the burning woodland, their hands in the air. Neville watched the prisoners being shepherded away as he hurried back to his wagon. Alan joined him and they stared at the smoking copse.

'Yet another close shave,' sighed Alan.

'You know, it seems odd to me sometimes,' Neville said. 'A few minutes ago they were trying to blast me to kingdom come. Now they've waved a flag and they can just troop off, just like that.'

'Think it's called playing the game by the rules,' said Alan.

'Not sure they do,' muttered Neville.

⋆   ⋆   ⋆

Neville entered Brussels on Thursday 7 September to scenes he would never forget. The whole convoy ground to a halt as the welcoming crowds surrounded them. Neville could only watch as people climbed on his wagon. He found himself pulled from his cab, hugged and kissed more times than he could remember. It was overwhelming, moving and in some ways embarrassing. It was almost with relief that the convoy managed to edge through the city to Zemst, just to the north-east. Later that evening, as they enjoyed the first respite for weeks, Sergeant Thompson came around, handing out small booklets.

'Major's orders, everyone to have a copy,' he said, handing out the booklet headed *Brussels Leave*. It had a map of the city and information on what could be found where. 'The Major wants to draw your attention to the back page and what you can and cannot do. You in particular, Timber.' Neville grinned as they all turned the booklet over and began reading the back page.

'Okay,' said Nick, scanning its contents. 'Always carry your pass. Out the cafés by 2300. Curfew midnight to 0500. Hey, Tommy, seen this one? All brothels are out of bounds to service personnel.' Tommy coloured while Nick carried on. 'Dress has to be battledress, web belt, boots or polished shoes. No weapons and we've got to salute as per regulations. Does that include you, Sarge?'

'Particularly me, Jones,' smiled Thompson.

'Does that mean we're getting some leave, Sarge?' asked Neville.

'Your guess is as good as mine.' Thompson shrugged. 'But if you do . . .' He waved the booklet in the air.

Neville's opportunity to test the regulations would be limited. The 50th Division was warned that it should prepare itself for an assault on the Albert Canal at the crossing to Geel. All the battalions were moved to concentrate in the area of Herselt, less than ten miles from the canal.

'Well, did you all enjoy Brussels?' asked Neville sarcastically as the boxes of twenty-five-pounder shells were loaded on to his wagon.

'It's not a holiday, Timber,' Alan reproached him.

'No, but a couple of days at least would have been nice.'

Neville ferried ammunition forward continuously to Westmeerbeek, where his wagons ran the gauntlet of concentrated enemy artillery fire. The assault went in at 0130 on 8 September, quickly at first as the infantry crossed the canal in boat relays. But then as the Germans woke to the threat, all hell broke loose. The artillery thundered in support as 552 continued to transport twenty-five-pounders in great quantities. Over the next four days, the battle raged: infantry and tanks slugging it out mercilessly. It got to the point that civilians had to intervene on one occasion, telling the British that the Germans wished to surrender but they couldn't as, every time they made a move to come out, they were shot at. Not everyone was keen to wave the white flag: one fanatical German tank commander urged his tanks forward from his turret, screaming, '*Ich will fuer Hitler sterben*' (I want to die for Hitler). His wish was promptly granted.

By 12 September, the Germans had retreated over the Escaut Canal. The 50th were relieved by the 15th Scottish Division and Neville and the rest of the Division moved to Diest. Here they were briefed immediately on what lay ahead – *Operation Market Garden*.

Market Garden was conceived as a thrust to the north to the shores of the Zuyder Zee, splitting Holland and trapping significant German forces to the west of the line of attack. *Market* referred to the airborne forces who were tasked with seizing bridges over three major rivers – the Maas, the Waal and the Lower Rhine. *Garden* referred to the British XXX Corps, which would drive over the captured bridges, relieving the lightly armed paratroopers. The ultimate objective was the bridge over the Lower Rhine at Arnhem. The thrust would then continue into the heart of Germany, neutralising the industrial heartland of the Ruhr.

The airborne attack had three main components. The US 101st was tasked with seizing the canal and stream crossings in the area of Eindhoven, Zon and Veghel. The US 82nd was to seize the bridges over the Maas at Grave and the Waal at Nijmegen. Thirdly, the 1st British Airborne would take and hold the furthest bridge over the Lower Rhine at Arnhem. XXX Corps would be led by the Guards Armoured Division, supported by the 43rd Division, followed by the 50th Division, whose main objectives were Corps reserve and to secure a crossing over the River Ijssel at Duisburg, about twelve miles north-east of Arnhem. It was set to begin at 1330 hours on Sunday 17 September.

'Final blow into Germany,' Neville said to Alan after the briefing. 'Just what I wanted to hear. Going to be dangerous with all these pockets of Jerry units around but as far as I'm concerned let's get cracking and wipe him up.'

The following day Neville was completing the final maintenance checks to his wagon when a low droning noise rapidly intensified into a deafening roar. He craned his neck skywards to watch an awe-inspiring sight. It felt as if he was watching a huge swarm of angry bees, with wave upon wave of bombers and fighters, followed by the gliders, heading to the drop zones, now just a few miles away.

'Smashing job!' Neville slapped the bonnet of his wagon. 'Payback time for all those poor buggers in France and Belgium.'

The subsequent battle, however, went less well. There were delays due to formidable enemy defences and the XXX Corps route clogged with vehicles, slowing the advance to a crawl. To intensify their attack on the British in Arnhem, the Germans cut the road between Ugen and Veghel, preventing XXX Corps providing much-needed support. This was the main area of action for the 50th

Division. On 23 September the Division moved north and west of Eindhoven and despite continued fierce German resistance the road was secured and defended. But despite this success, the Arnhem bridgehead was a failure. Aside from patrol activity, the 50th played no further part in the action.

'A lively day!' exclaimed Neville as he dived for cover.

'If you mean bombed, strafed, shelled, mortared and bombed again, then *lively* is one hell of an understatement,' gasped Nick. 552 Company were moved up to an area around Nijmegen where the Germans were preparing for an aggressive counter-offensive.

'Some of the wagons have copped it and quite a lot of lads got hurt,' commented Neville.

'I must say, I have a sneaking admiration for Jerry. He doesn't give up easily,' said Nick. Another German plane flew over and its bomb doors opened to spray out what looked like confetti. It caught the wind and scattered widely, drifting to earth.

'What the dickens . . . ?' Neville stood up from cover in the temporary respite and picked up one of the nearest pieces of paper.

'What is it?' asked Nick. 'Is it in English?'

'Of course it's in bloody English,' snorted Neville. 'I'm not likely to be able to read it otherwise. It says, "Why die for Stalin?"' His brow creased into a frown as he began to read:

> In dying for Stalin your soldiers are not dying for democracy or the preservation of the democratic form of government – they are dying for the establishment of Communism and a form of Stalinist tyranny throughout the world. Furthermore, they are not dying for the preservation of the integrity of small nations (England's old war cry) but are dying so that Poland shall be a Soviet state: so that the Baltic States shall be incorporated in the

Soviet Union and so that Soviet influence shall extend from the Baltic to the Balkans.

Every British soldier who lays down his life in this war is not only a loss to his own country; he is a loss to the common cause of European civilisation. Germany's and England's quarrel is a form of traditional rivalry. It is more in the nature of a private quarrel which Germany did not seek. The Soviet Union's quarrel, however, is a quarrel with the world. It is a quarrel with our common heritage and with all those values – moral, spiritual, cultural and material which we have, all of us – Englishman and German alike – recognised, cherished and striven to maintain. To die for the destruction of these values is to die in vain.

Stalin, with all the diabolical power of Communism behind him, is seeking to profit from Britain's and Germany's preoccupation. The amount of influence which Britain can exercise on Stalin can be measured by the latter's undisputed claims to the sovereign territories of other nations. The only controlling influence left on Stalin is the strength and tenacity of the German Wehrmacht and of the European volunteers who support Germany in her fight for the survival of Europe, and its position as the cradle of our common civilisation.

Every British soldier who dies for Stalin is another nail in the coffin of Britain's hopes of maintaining a 'Balance of Power' in Europe.

Should the 'Equilibrium' pass to Stalin then the equilibrium of the world is at an end.

Those who are about to die – think it over.

Neville folded the sheet and put it in his breast pocket. He looked at Nick and they burst out laughing. 'He must be getting desperate if he's trying that rubbish.'

The German attack on Nijmegen was ferocious. The Green Howards hung on grimly until relieved by the East Yorkshires. Neville and 552 Company brought up the shells to the supporting artillery who, in the two days of action on 1 and 2 October, fired 95,500 rounds, an onslaught that eventually crushed the resolve of the enemy.

'I've been ordered down to Leopoldsburg. One hundred and forty bloomin' miles, to pick up a highly dangerous load,' said Neville.

'Highly dangerous? What's that?' asked Alan.

'Bread!' snorted Neville with disgust.

Alan laughed. 'Ah well, not all bad, Timber. Should allow you to put on some weight. I'll check with Thomo if Nick and I can come with you for some company.'

Permission was granted and they travelled south on Saturday 7 October. It turned out to be a lucky commission. When they returned to the camp later that day, they were greeted with a sight of devastation. The camp had been attacked with anti-personnel bombs and thirty men had been killed. The mood was grim as Neville helped to move stretchers, collect personal effects and cover the dead. He stood near a corpse, just the muddy boots protruding from the blanket. He turned over a dog tag in his hand. Nick came over and stood beside him.

'Eighteen, Nick; been here less than a month. Hell, what do you say to his folks, his girlfriend? And the damned Boche are up to their tricks again. Wires across the road. Nearly decapitated Tom. Not heard from Sheila for four days, either, so I wonder if she's all right.' Neville stared into the distance.

'Could be any number of reasons,' Nick murmured.

'And here we are stuck in this mud. Water everywhere. Hell, I'm fed up with this life beyond words. Roll on death.' Neville's voice was full of anguish and bitterness.

Nick looked across at him sharply. 'Enough of that talk, Nev, and be careful what you wish for. That poor young lad there would much sooner be here with us still,' he snapped, pointing at the corpse.

Neville nodded slightly and turned away. He barely noticed as wave upon wave of British bombers droned overhead, flying to disgorge vengeance.

The Company was moved again, about six miles north, to what became known as 'The Island', or as Neville grumbled: 'This blasted place, absolute swamp.' The low-lying fields were criss-crossed by dykes and, at times, it gave the impression of being surrounded by water. The only link with terra firma was the bridge at Nijmegen, where a smoke screen was maintained. At night, searchlights swept the river in case the enemy were intent on planting explosives to blow the bridge.

Neville was moved to billets in Weurt just outside Nijmegen. He stayed with Nicolas and Maxime Smits and their large family. They had four sons, Victor, Thomas, Oscar and Alexander, and three daughters, Dora, Anna and Henia, all of whom made a fuss of their guest. It piqued Neville's interest only a little as he was more concerned by the fact that Sheila's letters were becoming increasingly sporadic. There was no respite from war, though, as shells continued to rain down, including into the Smits' back garden, blowing the glass out of all the windows of the house.

Ammunition and infantry still had to be moved. On one occasion, Neville was delivering a wagon of high explosives to the forward ammunition dumps, when he was strafed. The German plane missed and aside from ageing him ten years he was unscathed. He carried American infantry to the north of Elst and as he crossed Nijmegen Bridge on the return two wagons were hit, with several killed and wounded. He arrived back at Weurt still unscathed. Dora came to meet him and saw his ashen face.

'How are you?' she asked in accented English.

'Just makes me wonder,' Neville smiled. Dora looked puzzled but said nothing. That evening he was in the back garden, looking to the north-east and watching what looked like shooting stars streaking across the night sky. He thought of home as he pictured the V2 rockets in his mind, hurtling across the North Sea to wreak havoc on an English city. He couldn't help but worry for Sheila, his family and friends, imagining the rockets plummeting to earth to deliver their destructive force on homes and families.

On Thursday 29 November, Neville told the Smitses it was time for him to go. Dora burst into tears and left the front room in a hurry. The time had been short but the bond between the family and Neville had grown strong. Two days later, 50th Division moved to Roeselare in the Flemish province of West Flanders, seventy miles east of Brussels. Neville moved into billets once more, this time he and Alan were put with the Claerbout-Delforge family at 48 Henri Horriestraat. They were immediately made to feel welcome by the hospitality of Maurice and Jeanette, their eldest daughter Paula and the three younger children. They treated Neville and Alan like members of the family: a home from home as the war raged on.

Neville hadn't been long in the billet when Nick and some of the other lads came to see him. Neville knew Nick well enough by now to know when something wasn't right, but even he couldn't have expected the news that Nick was about to tell him.

'The 50th Division,' Nick said simply. 'I've heard it's about to be split up.'

'Is this some kind of sick joke?' Rumour and counter-rumour were part and parcel of war, but there was something in Nick's demeanour that suggested this was more than just gossip. 'How do you know?' Neville asked.

'I bumped into Charlie, picking up the CO.' Nick sighed. 'Told me it's about to be announced.'

'I can't believe it. We're the best Division in the British Army. What the hell have we done wrong?' Neville spoke for all of them but got no answer, each man looking away, head down. After everything they'd been through, and everything they'd fought for, this felt like a huge kick in the teeth. The 50th was their identity, an identity which had been built on blood, guts, sacrifice and shared endeavours.

On 8 December, the whispers were confirmed as General Montgomery arrived to address the 552 Company parade. The fighting career of the 50th was over, he told them. Urgent reinforcements were needed and the 21st Army Group had to be reduced by one Division. To preserve the identity of a fine command it would now become a Training Division in Yorkshire to train the next generation of infantrymen. For 552 Company, he assured, the war was not over. The general praised their fine record and informed them they were to remain with 21st Army Group as a General Transport Company.

'Bullshit!' snapped Neville.

No matter how it was framed it was the end of an era and it felt lousy.

Chapter 16

The Final Push to Victory

December 1944 to May 1945

In Roeselare, the relationship between Neville and the Claerbout-Delforge's eldest daughter, Paula, began to flourish. They started going out dancing together almost daily and Neville began looking forward to a surrogate family Christmas. It was not quite to be as he was assigned Yuletide troop-carrying details, bringing the 6th Airborne Division from a smashed-up Calais to Cambrai and Tournai. It was cold, dark and miserable, made worse by knowing what he was missing out in his billet.

'They're paratroopers, for goodness' sake,' he grumbled. 'Couldn't they have just jumped into France?'

He returned to Roeselare on Boxing Day, enjoying a great night dancing at the house and a belated Christmas dinner.

'Are you and Paula getting serious?' asked Alan later that evening.

'I don't know what you mean.' Neville looked to the floor.

Alan laughed. 'You do get yourself in some scrapes, mate.'

But the relationship continued. New Year's Eve was duty free, allowing Neville to see in the New Year in style. It was a great party: at midnight, he held Paula tightly as the chimes faded away. As Paula put him to bed, somewhat inebriated, at 5.30 in the morning on New Year's Day, Neville knew that heartache was inevitable.

Over the next few days, most of Neville's platoon were assigned a seven-day detail. Neville was fortunate to remain as the rear party. He and Paula continued to dance, went to the pictures, had supper together and revelled in each other's company – until, that is, his next orders came through on Sunday 7 January.

'We leave tomorrow at 1100,' he broke the news to Paula.

She nestled her head against his chest and squeezed him hard. He could feel her shoulders moving as she sobbed quietly. The following day as he prepared to leave, having said a fond farewell to Maurice and Jeanette, Paula appeared. She came towards him, stood on tiptoe and kissed him on the lips, placing her finger there immediately with a 'Ssshhh'. She took his hand, placed a picture in it, smiled a tearful smile and left the room. Neville looked at the picture of Paula and turned it over. The writing on the back said simply: *Mon cher Nev. Je vous attend, je ne vous oublie jamais. Paula.* My dear Nev. I wait for you, I never forget you. Paula.

Neville's next posting was one marked by inaction, rather than action. Lommel was his base now, lodged in the local convent, where he was tasked with transporting Bailey Bridge materials for the engineers to prepare for crossing the Rhine. After everything that had gone on before, and also what he had left behind in Roeselare, it felt mundane and frustrating. For the first time in a while, Neville had time to think. He found himself drawn to Lommel's church of St Pietersbanden. The interior was a sight to behold, the light streaming in through its many stained-glass windows. The wall paintings were faded or damaged but the magnificent Clerinx organ had survived the ravages of war and soared above the entrance to the nave. Neville appreciated the church's peacefulness, and sat in a front pew to take it in. The church was all but empty: in front of him, an elderly lady scurried back and forth arranging flowers. Neville sighed and looked down forlornly at his hands clasped in his lap. Then a gentle rustle caused him to look up and he saw a nun genuflecting and crossing herself. She glanced across at Neville's woeful face and smiled kindly.

'You have sought peace with God?' she asked in slightly accented English.

Neville, who'd been deep in his own thoughts, smiled back, but said nothing.

'I don't wish to intrude but may I sit with you a moment?' asked the nun.

Neville shrugged and shuffled across the pew to make space.

'I am Sister Margaret,' the nun introduced herself, 'and I saw you arrive at the convent yesterday. I thought then you looked troubled. I listen well if you would like to share your troubles with me.'

Despite the urge to ask to be left in peace, there was something about the kindly face of the Sister, full of compassion and warmth, that gave him pause. Her blue eyes seemed to bore into his soul. They remained locked with his for what felt like several minutes, before Neville looked down and spoke.

'I, I just feel there's something wrong with me. I've lost touch with things that once meant a lot and it's no good.'

'Tell me why,' encouraged Sister Margaret.

Neville's mind and memories seemed to race in rapid retrospection. Once he started talking, he couldn't stop. He talked of his time in the army, where he had been and what he had seen. The emotions ran high as he told her of the people he had met, and lost, the family at home and the lovely Belgian family he had stayed with in Roeselare.

'And then we get moved again and for what?' he asked. 'The Division, the best one in the British Army, has been sent home, the war goes on, never seems to end, and I'm kicking my heels for a month around Brussels. Now it's backwards and forwards to Lommel with Bailey Bridge stuff. And what's going to happen when it's all over?' He stared up at one of the stained-glass windows, barely noticing as Sister Margaret took his hand.

'Let us pray together,' she said quietly. Neville continued to stare at the windows as the nun bowed her head in prayer. He felt his hand being released and snapped back to reality. He looked at the nun beside him.

'I'm sorry,' he said. 'You people have suffered enough under the Nazis. I shouldn't have burdened you, but thank you anyway.'

'We are all burdened in many different ways. Bless you, Neville Wood.' Sister Margaret smiled, placing her hand on Neville's shoulder. She got up and moved slowly towards the altar. Neville watched her before he got up and quietly left the church. It was a moment he would remember for a long time.

As the tedium and relative inactivity continued throughout February, the one bright spot for Neville was being told that he would be granted leave of one week at home from 15 March.

'Me too,' said Alan, as Neville joined him and Tommy Oates for tea in Lommel. 'And I've got a favour to ask of you. When we're home Sarah and I are getting married and I'd like you to be my best man.'

Neville's face broke into a beaming smile. 'That's wonderful news, Alan.' He shook his hand warmly. 'And yes, of course, I will be thrilled.'

Deciding it was time for a celebration, the tea was drunk quickly and the three of them went in search of something stronger. They found local beer and French wine in surprising abundance. Several drinks later, they headed back to lodgings at the convent with arms round their shoulders to help them stay upright. As they staggered along past a field with a working windmill on a slight rise, Tommy pulled away from the other two, fell over a gate into the field and staggered towards the windmill.

'What's he up to?' asked Alan, gazing after Tommy.

'Best follow,' grunted Neville.

They navigated the gate into the field slightly more elegantly than Tommy and were staggering through the grass, when Neville stopped suddenly, looking ahead.

'Oh no, stop, you silly bugger!' he shouted.

In front of them, Tommy had reached the windmill. As one of the four blades came round to the vertical he jumped up, taking hold of the stock. The sails jerked but whizzed him into the air. As the sail reached the perpendicular, he lost his grip and plummeted to the ground, hitting it with a sickening thud, then lying motionless in a crumpled heap.

'Tommy, are you all right?' gasped Alan, he and Neville arriving beside the moaning form under the swishing sails.

'Of course he's not all right,' said Neville. 'Can you move your arms and legs?' He knelt beside Tommy and began to untangle him none too gently. 'It hurts then,' he commented as Tommy yelled and moaned each time he was moved. *Serves you damned well right*, he thought.

'I'll go for help.' Alan headed back down the field. Army traffic was regular and within minutes a jeep bounced up the field.

'Oh great!' muttered Neville. 'He had to find two damned MPs.' Fortunately the Military Policemen were not officious. They helped Tommy into the back of the jeep and despite driving back out of the field with some care, Neville and Alan could still hear the groans and yells from the back seat.

★   ★   ★

On Saturday 3 March, 552 Company were briefed that they were
going back into action. 'At last doing something useful again,'
Neville said to Nick as a letter from Field Marshall Montgomery
was read out to them:

> The operations of the Allies on all fronts have now brought the
> German war to its final stage. There was a time, some years
> ago, when it did not seem possible that we could win this war;
> the present situation is that we cannot lose it; in fact the terrific
> successes of our Russian allies on the eastern front have brought
> victory in sight.
>
> In 21 Army Group we stand ready for the last round. There are
> many of us who have fought through the previous rounds; we
> have won every round on points; we now come to the last and
> final round, and we want, and will go for, the knock-out blow.
>
> The rules of the last round will be that we continue fighting
> till the final count; there is no time limit. We know our enemy
> well; we must expect him to fight hard to stave off defeat, possibly
> in the vain hope that we may crack before he does. But we shall
> not crack; we shall see this thing through to the end. The last
> round may be long and difficult, and the fighting hard; but we
> now fight on German soil; we have got our opponent where we
> want him; and he is going to receive the knock-out blow, a
> somewhat unusual one delivered from more than one direction.
>
> You remember a poem written by a soldier of the Eighth Army
> in Africa before going into battle, in one verse of which he
> described what he considered we were fighting for: 'Peace for the
> kids, our brothers freed, a kinder world, a cleaner breed.' Let us
> see to it that we achieve this object, so well expressed by a
> fighting man of the British Empire.

And so we embark on the final round, in close cooperation with our American allies on our right and with the complete confidence in the successful outcome of the onslaught being delivered by our Russian allies on the other side of the ring. Somewhat curious rules you may say. But the whole match has been most curious; the Germans began this all-out contest and they must not complain when in the last round they are hit from several directions at the same time.

Into the ring, then, let us go. And do not relax till the knock-out blow has been delivered.

Good luck to you all – and God bless you.

'Officer bullshit,' whispered Nick.

'Well, he's got us this far, and he cares about his men,' countered Neville.

Nick tutted and raised his eyes. 'Contrary!'

552 Company moved up to Helmond, transporting bridging materials for a major crossing of the northern River Rhine into Germany. The crossing of the Rhine was code-named *Operation Plunder*, and the massive airborne operation was called *Operation Varsity*. Returning to hard work and positive action improved Neville's state of mind significantly.

In spite of the impending Rhine assault, those soldiers selected for leave were still allowed to travel home. In mid-March, Neville, Alan and about thirty others from 552 Company headed back to Calais to the transit camp, where they received their pink tickets for haversack rations, supper, cigarettes and tea. Neville read through his 'Leave without tears – North' leaflet, which provided instructions on the journey and the requirements for the return, on time, to Dover.

On Saturday 17 March the train pulled into Paragon Station in Hull. The morning was cold, damp and grey, but Neville easily

spotted the angular figure of his father in the gloom. He was
thrilled to see him, and the greeting between father and son was a
warm one. Even so, Neville knew his father well enough to know
that there was something on his mind. They were on the drive back
home to Holderness Road when Fred turned to him.

'No good time to tell you, Nev, but Mother has to have an
operation.'

'I thought you were keeping something from me,' said Neville.
'For what exactly?'

'Cancer of the spine,' his father said, staring out of the
windscreen.

Neville was acutely aware that his father had lost his first wife,
Neville's mother, just twelve years before. 'I can't believe it. I'm so
sorry, Dad,' he said.

Despite the sombre news, the week that followed was a joy. On
Monday 19 March, Neville stood proudly beside Alan at his
wedding, dreaming of the day when it would be his turn and he
would be waiting for Sheila to walk down the aisle. He saw Sheila
every day during his visit. The subject of their own engagement
was broached but they decided to wait a little longer, mainly due
to reticence on Sheila's part, but also because the war was coming
to a conclusion.

It felt as though they had only just arrived when the tears of
farewell flowed again as Neville and Alan caught the train to
Doncaster and from there headed back to Dover. They arrived at
their unit on Monday 26 March, and were pleased to find a fit-again
Tommy there to greet them.

By this point, *Plunder* and *Varsity* were already under way, and
Neville and Alan were called in for a briefing, along with the rest of
the leave returners. In the NAAFI, Carton gave them an update on
what was happening.

'Okay, sit down,' he ordered as they stood to attention and saluted. 'I've a fair bit to get through. We will be helping with bridge-building over the Rhine at a place called Rees, about fifty miles north-east and thirty-five miles from Arnhem. From there we will be crossing into Germany and even deeper into enemy territory until Jerry's decided he's had enough. I have a letter from Monty for you on non-fraternisation and some things you really need to bear in mind. Listen carefully; many of you have come a long way on this journey and we don't want any slip-ups near its end.

'First of all we have completed a leaflet drop over key concentrations of the German Army. This is it.' He held up a green piece of paper headed *Safe Conduct*. 'It says, "The German soldier who carries this safe conduct is using it as a sign of his genuine wish to give himself up. He is to be disarmed, to be well looked after, to receive food and medical attention as required, and is to be removed from the danger zone as soon as possible."' Carton paused, turning the paper over in his hands. 'Frankly I don't trust the bastards,' he added, 'so always cover each other, look for tricks and, at the first sign of trouble, shoot.' There was a ripple of laughter, which died away quickly as they saw he was serious.

'You will read the orders on non-fraternisation. In a nutshell the Germans are masters at organising sympathy and the Nazis are fanatics. They will organise resistance and they will give instructions to, and I quote: "Give the impression of submitting. Say you never liked the Nazis, they were the people responsible for the war. Argue that Germany has never had a fair chance. Get the soldiers arguing; they are not trained for it and you are. Use old folks, girls and children and play up every case of devastation or poverty. Ask the troops to your homes, sabotage or steal equipment, petrol or rations. Get troops to sell you these things if you can. Spread stories about Americans or Russians in the British zone and about the

British to other allies."' He put the small booklet down and paused, scanning the faces watching him intently. 'In other words, you steer clear of the bastards, is that understood?' He glared at all the nodding heads. 'You'll remember that these are the same Germans who a short while ago were drunk with victory, who were boasting what they, as the Master Race, would do to you as their slaves. So no cosying up; arm's length, right? If they play up, give the bastards a good kicking.' The letter was handed out.

As Neville took his copy and started to skim through, Carton said, 'Leave that, read it later, I'm not finished yet. We know the Krauts are innovative and tricky bastards. We've all come across their booby traps. The information you will be given when dismissed has been put together with the help of the Dutch and Belgian resistance who came across all the tricks in the book. The overriding principle is: don't believe there are any good Germans in Germany. A German is, by nature, a liar. We have seen this in areas we already occupy. Twice at night, Germans have strung wires across the main road at Aachen to tear off the head of some jeep driver. Don't open fountain pens, cigarette cases, spectacle cases or any other container. It may be a small grenade. Step back and make the bastards open it themselves. If he attempts to throw it at you, shoot him.

'Guard duty,' Carton continued, 'will always, I repeat always, be double sentries. Two of them may work together, one to distract you, the other to stick his knife in your back. As for German women, remember they have been trained to seduce you. They will knife you or take you for a quiet stroll, on a promise, to where the killers are waiting.' He paused, scanning the faces.

Neville was sure he wasn't the only one thinking, *Is he looking at me?*

'And don't get soft on the kids. Yell *"achtung"* at them and see them jump to attention like trained monkeys. They can shoot you just like an adult. No going out alone at night and always let others know where you are going and when you will be back. Watch out for concealed weapons, either at the chest, lower part of the trousers, on the abdomen or in the sleeve. Watch for weapons in walking sticks and wooden legs, seriously.' He sighed and waved the paper. 'There are a few more tricks you need to be aware of so read it carefully. Any offence by any German in whatever circumstances, you come down on them hard. They operate by brute force and, if necessary, we'll deal with them the same way. Clear?' There were silent nods all round and Lieutenant Carton dismissed the men.

'Blimey. Welcome to Germany,' muttered Neville.

The crossing of the Rhine for the first time was a poignant moment. As the construction of the Tyne and Tees bridges, as they were known, continued, Neville drove to Rees on the German side on Thursday 29 March, and it felt momentous, significant. It felt slightly less significant with each trip, as he continued to cross it repeatedly, 552 Company bringing forward the bridging materials from Holland for the Royal Engineers to complete the construction work. It was striking how different the mood was on either side of the river. The civilians on the German side of the mighty river tried to be friendly and many could not understand why the British were aloof. This was in stark contrast to the journey back to Holland where soldiers and civilians co-existed in warm friendship.

Maintaining the discipline of non-fraternisation with the German population became far easier when word reached 552 Company of an appalling discovery. Neville and Nick were heading to the NAAFI and were waved over by Alan.

'You lads need to hear this,' he said grimly, as Neville and Nick joined him at the radio. 'It's Richard Dimbleby.' The date was 15 April and the British and Canadians had just liberated

Bergen-Belsen concentration camp. The sombre voice from the radio conveyed the sickening scene to those listening:

'Here over an acre of ground lay dead and dying people. You could not see which was which. The living lay with their heads against the corpses and around them moved the awful, ghostly procession of emaciated, aimless people, with nothing to do and with no hope of life, unable to move out of your way, unable to look at the terrible sights around them. Babies had been born here, tiny wizened things that could not live. A mother, driven mad, screamed at a British sentry to give her milk for her child, and thrust the tiny mite into his arms, then ran off, crying terribly. He opened the bundle and found the baby had been dead for days. This day at Belsen was the most horrible of my life.'

Three days later, Neville met soldiers of the 11th Armoured Division heading to Holland on relief. Their faces bore the ashen, haunted look of the soldiers who had first relieved the concentration camp. A crowd gathered round a small group of soldiers who were describing the horrors they had witnessed.

'You can't comprehend it,' one corporal was saying, shaking his head in disbelief. 'There were sixty thousand poor souls in there, I can't call them people, and there must have been upwards of thirteen thousand corpses. Piled high they were and you know what, you'd move some thinking they were dead and the eyes would open. And there they were piled with so many bodies in various states of decomposition. Yet, it was so quiet. No noise, no birds, no talking, just ... just ...' His voice trailed away as he bowed his head and wiped his eyes.

'I've been all over with the Division,' said another. 'I've seen some horrible sights, but nothing, absolutely nothing, could prepare me for that. I hope to God I never see anything like it again!'

The shock and horror was palpable, nothing Neville could say in response felt enough.

With dark thoughts of the discovery hanging over them, 552 Company resumed their bridging duties. On Sunday 6 May, Neville joined Nick, Alan and other members of C Platoon. He had just finished a conversation with Sergeant Thompson and had some news he'd been instructed to report back.

'What's up, Timber?' asked Nick, looking at the frown on Neville's forehead.

'Well, that's just about it,' began Neville. He looked at the quizzical expressions, unsure where to start. 'Surrender of all German troops in north-west Germany.' They all looked at Neville and at each other. Their mood seemed the same as Neville's: there was no rejoicing, just something akin to bewilderment.

'So it's all over then, done with?' asked Nick.

'Well, that's good then, I guess,' commented Alan.

'Yes, I suppose it is,' agreed Nick.

'Gave me a funny feeling when I heard,' said Neville. His head was fizzing with questions about the future. 'What happens now? And what about all of you lads?'

'Japan?' suggested Nick.

They looked at each other, appalled at the thought.

On Monday 7 May 1945 the unconditional surrender of Germany was signed by General Jodl at Reims in north-eastern France. The war in Europe was over.

Chapter 17

A New Enemy

May 1945 to April 1946

The task which we set ourselves is finished, and the time has come for me to relinquish Combined Command.

In the name of the United States and the British Commonwealth, from whom my authority is derived, I should like to convey to you the gratitude and admiration of our two nations for the manner in which you have responded to every demand that has been made of you. At times, conditions have been hard and the tasks to be performed arduous. No praise is too high for the manner in which you have surmounted every obstacle.

I should like, also, to add my own personal word of thanks to each one of you for the part you have played, and the contribution you have made to our joint victory.

Now that you are about to pass to other spheres of activity, I say Goodbye to you and wish you Good Luck and God-Speed.

Dwight D. Eisenhower.

Nick, Tommy, Alan and Neville were crowded round the notice-board outside the NAAFI where the letter was pinned.

'Job done and the brass bugger off,' snorted Tommy.

'To some kind of hero's welcome, I bet,' concurred Alan.

'Didn't take him long, did it?' commented Neville. 'Day after Germany surrenders and it's, "Thanks, lads, great job, I'm off."' He grunted and turned away. 'Meanwhile, for those of us poor buggers left, there's work to do.'

The work to do for C Platoon of 552 Company was driving American tank transports, moving the armour from the western European battlefield to the American-occupied zone of Germany based around Frankfurt. Neville didn't mind the assignment so much – the Americans were generous with their hospitality and provisions, particularly cigarettes and beer.

On Monday 4 June, Neville was back in the British sector based around Bad Oeynhausen, north-east of Dortmund. He had mail from home and he opened it to see his father's writing. It wasn't often he heard from his father so he read the letter quickly, knowing it must be important.

'Poor Gran,' he muttered, on reading that his maternal Grandmother, Grandma Clayton, who had been poorly for some time, had died suddenly. He put the letter in his breast pocket and began to open four letters from Sheila. 'What a girl,' he said, smiling to himself.

The Company were moved again in the middle of June, this time to Schmalforden, a pretty little town in Lower Saxony. Eggs and milk were plentiful and kept them nourished as they were tasked with building a Romney hut. The work was completed to coincide with Neville's twenty-fifth birthday, Thursday 21 June 1945, which they all celebrated with a well-earned drink.

The week that followed required a number of jobs to be

completed. Neville was working on pontoons and panels as infrastructure, particularly over rivers, was constructed, albeit temporarily in some cases. Shortly after the surrender of Germany the Canadians began withdrawing their troops from Europe. Neville then travelled the eighty-two miles north to Wilhelmshaven to move the Canadian hospital to the area around Bad Oeynhausen.

In mid-July, having just relocated east to Hodenhagen, Neville was given an urgent detail. On Wednesday 18 July, he was ordered to report to General Officer Commanding XXX Corps at Eystrup. He was to take three days' kit and rations and take orders as NCO in charge from a Lieutenant Cole. There were two wagons, Neville in one with Nick, and Alan in the other with Tommy. Pairing up was unusual so they knew it must be an important or difficult job.

Setting out in bright summer sunshine, they parked up in front of the church at Eystrup as instructed, and waited for orders. First, Lieutenant Cole emerged from the church and gave Neville his instructions. Then a few minutes later, the doors of the church opened and two Military Policemen emerged, followed by thirty men, dressed in civilian clothes, haggard, but watchful and grim-faced. Two more MPs followed and fifteen of the prisoners were loaded into each of the wagons. Two of the four MPs climbed into each and the tailgates were raised and bolted.

'Not quite what I expected of a group of Nazis,' said Nick.

'What did you expect?' asked Neville. 'Horns and a trident?'

'And a tail – forked, of course,' laughed Alan.

The journey was 250 miles to Braunschweig via Blankenburg and Hanover. They arrived late in the afternoon and the Nazis were ordered off the wagon and into the Dankwarderode Castle.

'Deepest dungeon,' said Alan as he lit a cigarette.

'And throw away the key,' grunted Neville.

Told they were no longer required, the four of them returned to

Hodenhagen the following day. Here, they discovered that a new directive had been issued on non-fraternisation. Neville and the others scanned the small booklet they had been given.

'Well, we can now speak and play with little children and engage in conversation with adult Germans in the street and public places. No entering homes, though,' said Nick, summarising.

'Can't say I feel inclined to do either.' Neville finished his booklet. 'We've been fighting them for six years and I'm not one for letting bygones be bygones in this case. That bloke telling us about the concentration camp sticks in my mind. I look at every German now and think, *You must have known.*'

Neville's opinion hardened still further when, on Thursday 2 August, he drove on a detail seventeen miles east to Bergen-Belsen. He was delivering food supplies, although the amount the army could spare was limited. Once the wagon was unloaded and readied for his return journey, he decided to take some time to look around. Part of him just wanted to leave, but he felt that he would be in denial to do so, and he was driven on by a morbid fascination.

Bergen-Belsen was now a camp for Displaced Persons, housing 25,000 women of many nationalities and ages. Most of the original huts had been burned due to the appalling stench, hygiene and risk of disease. Some new huts had been erected, but not enough, which meant the living space for those remaining was limited. Signage had been erected marking the mass graves, and despite the fact that most corpses had now been removed, the place still reeked of death. Neville stood beside one huge mound and recalled the words of the soldiers of 11th Armoured, picturing the piles of decomposing bodies, now buried beneath the grey, bare earth. It had the same eerie quiet as it had when first relieved, and he stood, head bowed, and wept.

Neville wasn't sure how long he had stood there. He felt a light touch on his arm and jumped: three women had approached, quietly, and were standing watching him. He turned away quickly and wiped his eyes and blew his nose. He shuddered as he looked into their lifeless eyes and shook his head as they held out emaciated arms and hands. 'I'm sorry,' he said, 'I have nothing I can give you.' The women dropped their arms to their sides and turned away, shuffling to wherever they were able to go in this godforsaken place. Neville had seen enough. He marched back to his wagon, looking round one final time before pulling himself up into his cab. Then he started the engine and drove through the gates, leaving hell on earth behind.

When he returned to camp Alan greeted him glumly.

'What's up with you?' grunted Neville, in no mood to sympathise.

'Leave's been stopped: rail strike in Blighty,' replied Alan morosely.

'Oh, smashing effort,' snarled Neville sarcastically and he stalked away to wash.

On 9 August, 552 Company received news of the atomic bomb being dropped on Hiroshima, little knowing that a second had been dropped on Nagasaki that day.

'Hopefully we won't need to be shipped over there now,' observed Neville with some relief. 'Looks like the war there is nearly over too.' It was, and Japan surrendered on Wednesday 15 August.

The war was now over but the dangers still persisted. Neville and three other soldiers were ordered to a remote farmhouse in the countryside occupied by a young German family. The family had complained to the British authorities about roaming bands of Polish and Russian soldiers determined to loot, rape and destroy.

'It's a funny old world. We're guarding the buggers now,' grumbled Neville, but without conviction. He saw the fear in the eyes of the two young children and shuddered at what would happen if drunken Russian soldiers found them.

Guard duty was rewarded with a rest day at XXX Corps rest camp in the Harz Mountains at Bad Harzburg. Things were looking up even more when Neville was told he would be granted immediate leave. He was in fine spirits when he boarded the train to Ostend on Sunday 19 August. His good mood and enthusiasm was tempered somewhat by the hard wooden seats, particularly after hours on the train. But he still arrived home tired but happy on the Wednesday, looking forward to seeing Sheila the following day. Perhaps with the war over it was time to discuss an engagement, he mused to himself.

But when Neville met Sheila in Hornsea the following evening, he could tell immediately all was not well. Her greeting was cool and reserved, Neville's heart sinking as he tried to maintain an outward appearance of calm. The signals he had read in some of Sheila's letters now began to make sense. Free French Forces had been in the Hornsea area and it transpired that Sheila had begun a relationship with a French soldier. That soldier, now a civilian, had invited Sheila to Paris, and she had accepted. Neville closed his eyes and breathed evenly. He got up and left without saying a word.

With their relationship over, the next few days' leave seemed to drag like an anchor, to the point that Neville was pleased to head back to Germany and his mates. His misery was soon forgotten when he was assigned to what turned out to be his final, terrifying detail: to take charge of a convoy of seven wagons into the British sector of West Berlin. This meant travelling through a swathe of Russian-held Germany.

Lieutenant Carton was deadly serious with his instructions, which he repeated for certainty: 'You will not stop; you will not sleep in Russian territory. You will not raise your rifle if threatened and if a wagon breaks down you get the driver out and leave it. No matter what you feel about what you see, your sole purpose is to get those supplies into our sector of Berlin. Is that absolutely clear?'

'Yes, sir.' Neville saluted.

The route took him 190 miles from Hodenhagen through Hanover, Brunswick, Magdeburg and Brandenburg: four to five hours riding the gauntlet of Russian suspicion, hostility and brutality. The convoy moved quickly through the countryside between the centres of population. As they came to the towns and cities they were forced to slow. The stares from the Russian troops lining the routes through the urban areas were hostile, silent, menacing. Occasionally, some brave, or foolhardy, Germans made a run for the British wagons. Before they could scramble aboard they would be clubbed by rifle butts, knocked to the ground, kicked senseless, beaten and in some cases shot. Neville and the rest of the small convoy had no choice but to keep moving, which they did in close order now the war and the threat from the skies was no more. Neville focused on the road ahead, trying to ignore what was happening in his peripheral vision. When they finally arrived in West Berlin, the drivers gathered together to smoke, weary and relieved to have made it.

'Dim view of that,' said Neville with a sigh. 'The war might be over but I can honestly say I've never been as frightened as that.'

For the remainder of his active service Neville worked with the Control Commission, which was set up to support the Military Government that was to be gradually phased out. His final run to Berlin ended on 19 October 1945.

The plan to demobilise British forces was designed by the Minister of Labour and National Service, Ernest Bevin. Service men and women were to be released from the armed forces according to their age and service number.

On 2 February 1946 Neville was summoned to Headquarters, British Army, on the Rhine and was presented with his notice of impending release. He had been allocated to Group 27 and would return home in April, although he would remain on the reserve list.

'Congratulations,' said the officer, a captain, handing him his papers. 'Your military conduct has been classified as exemplary.'

As Neville left the office, he looked down at the testimonial: *A good NCO and a very good driver with an excellent record and character. He is most conscientious and willing and has a good mechanical knowledge. Intelligent, capable and trustworthy, he has initiative and tact and is a good type of man.*

Of his close comrades only Alan was with him as Group 27 partied in the camp canteen. The schnapps flowed freely and in the competition to see who could maintain equilibrium down a straight line, Neville came last. The following day he was in charge of the extensive sick parade. Indeed, he was the first in the queue.

The adventure that had absorbed nearly seven years of his young life ended on 13 April 1946 at York. Neville was presented with his felt hat, double-breasted pinstripe three-piece suit, two shirts with matching collar studs, a tie, shoes and a raincoat. Scant reward, it seemed, for seven years' service. But it was time to return to Civvy Street, to normality, whatever normality was now.

It was time to go home.

Epilogue

The train pulled into Paragon Station, Hull, at 5.45 p.m. The engine came to a halt in an exhalation of steam, almost like an expression of relief. The two young couples in the compartment collected their belongings and hurried for the exit doors. Neville and Bob, the other former soldier he'd shared his journey with, moved more slowly. On the journey, they'd quickly established a camaraderie and shared experiences only people like them could understand. In many ways sharing their experiences, so closely interlinked within one division, had exorcised some of the ghosts both could sense within the other.

Arriving back at Hull, uncertainty lingered as to what their future might hold. Neville and Bob collected their meagre belongings from the luggage rack and disembarked on to the platform. They stood facing each other, neither wishing to break the immediate bond of friendship the train journey had established.

'Well,' said Bob, 'what now, Nev?'

Neville thought for a moment, then pulling his shoulders back, he fixed Bob with a determined look.

'You know what,' he said, 'we'll do what we've always done. When you think what we've been through over seven years, I'm sure we can deal with anything Civvy Street can throw at us. We'll just damned well get on with it, all guns blazing!'

The two former soldiers shook hands and smiled at each other. Then they turned together and marched with pride and purpose down the platform to the station exit.

What awaited Neville at the other side of the station barrier? He went back to work immediately, in his father's butcher shop. Not long after returning home, he was delivering meat to a shop in East Hull where he met Peggy Taylor. They married in Hull, on 3 July 1948 and had three sons, Stephen, David and Michael.

His army life did not end entirely. Neville was called up for Reservists training which took place in Durham, where it had all begun in 1939. He worked for the Ministry of Agriculture, Fisheries and Food for a short spell before joining Fatstock Marketing Corporation (FMC), a wholesale butcher. He progressed to Area Manager, responsible for a number of abattoirs in Yorkshire, and this prompted a move of home to facilitate work travel. In 1969, the family moved from Hull to the market town of Beverley and there Peggy and Neville would remain for the rest of their lives.

In September 2001, they were driving to Scarborough for their usual Friday fish and chips. A car, coming the other way, veered towards them as the driver suffered heart failure and hit Neville's car head-on. They both survived, although the ravages of old age accelerated. Peggy developed vascular dementia, a tragic disease; and even though he was in his late eighties, Neville cared for her until it was no longer feasible. That incredible sense of duty, and what he felt was right, was rarely more prevalent, and he often displayed that stubborn, bloody-mindedness evident from his story. Peggy passed away in 2012.

Neville found it progressively difficult to care for himself. He spent his final days in the same care home where Peggy had been. Early in the morning of Friday 20 February 2015 he passed away at the age of ninety-four.

What of his friends from 522? Sadly it's not a conversation I had with my dad. I cannot recall meeting or hearing of any of the main characters in this book. In 1969 when the family moved to Beverley our new home was a few doors away from a 50th veteran, Alf Moss. Another lifelong friend from the division was John Mundell, but neither of these veterans appeared in his diaries. It was at Dad's funeral, in 2015, that I spoke to retired Chief Inspector Jack Naylor, our neighbour in Hull for many years. He told me that after the war Charlie Spandler became a policeman, and by all accounts he never lost those cheeky character traits. Let's be thankful for that and for all those men who fought for us in that dreadful conflict.

Acknowledgements

This is the first book I have attempted to write and it has been a learning journey. There have been difficult times, particularly picking up the threads again following Dad's death. The love and support of my wife, Anita, was instrumental in getting me focused again on the task in hand.

The help I have had along the way from Mark Johnson and Ruth Canham who have been my 'critical friends' has been immense. All of their encouragement and positive feedback has kept me going when I lost impetus or became bogged down. Fleur Bradnock did an excellent job proofreading the manuscript and proving to me that, no matter how many times you read something, you see what you expect to see rather than what is written.

I was fortunate to discover a book that went out of print in the 1950s, *The Path of the 50th* by Major Ewart Clay MBE. This was critical to allow me to visualise where Dad was, what he was doing and why. For some of the military detail I am indebted to *Companion to the British Army* by George Forty. It was also fascinating to read some of the stories in *Forgotten Voices of the Second World War* by Max Arthur. Let us hope those voices are never forgotten. They were a remarkable generation.

I have used a number of 'briefings' in the book and in many instances these are taken word for word from original documents which Dad had saved from the war years. For example, copies of the letters to the troops issued by General Montgomery, General Eisenhower's farewell note, the Stalin propaganda leaflet and German trickery to name but a few.

But above all, thank you, Dad. Without your diaries and the many wonderful hours we spent reflecting and recalling as we worked through them together, there would be no story. My only regret is that you are not here to enjoy your book, but I've no doubt you are reminiscing avidly with all your old mates in that big 50th Division reunion up above. Smashing job!

Index